Henry James

EVOLUTION AND MORAL VALUE
OF A FICTIVE CHARACTER

SISTER M. CORONA SHARP, O.S.U.

UNIVERSITY OF NOTRE DAME PRESS · 1963

Copyright © 1963 by the
University of Notre Dame Press
Notre Dame, Indiana

Library of Congress Catalog
Card Number 63-19326

Manufactured in the United States of America

FOR *Carola*
WITH GRATITUDE
FOR HER
CONFIDENTIAL FRIENDSHIP

The pleasure which I have found in pursuing the study of Henry James and his confidantes was due in part to the scholarship, discernment, and enthusiasm of my former professors at the University of Notre Dame. My first expression of gratitude is to Professor Joseph X. Brennan for suggesting the topic, and giving valuable criticism. To Professor John Edward Hardy I owe a special debt for indicating the wider moral scope in the role of the Jamesian confidante. I greatly appreciate the encouragement and professional friendship of Professor John T. Frederick, formerly of Notre Dame, and Professors Ernest E. Sandeen and Joseph M. Duffy. I especially wish to thank my religious superiors, Very Reverend Mother M. St. David, Superior General of the Ursulines of Chatham, and Reverend Mother M. Victoria, for enabling me to see this research through to publication, and the Canada Council, whose two-year grant made this work possible.

Acknowledgments for permission to quote are hereby made to the following publishers: To Charles Scribner's Sons, for excerpts reprinted with their permission from *The Art of the Novel* by Henry James, with an Introduction by Richard P. Blackmur. Copyright 1934 Charles Scribner's Sons; renewal copyright © 1962; excerpts reprinted with the permission of Charles Scribner's Sons from *The Wings of the Dove* by Henry James (1902); from The New York Edition of *Roderick Hudson, The American, The Princess Casamassima, The Aspern Papers,* and "The

Acknowledgment

Jolly Corner," by Henry James; from *The Letters of Henry James,* edited by Percy Lubbock; and from *The Writing of Fiction* by Edith Wharton.

Also, to Paul R. Reynolds and Son, representative of the Henry James estate, for permission to quote in the British Commonwealth (excluding Canada) from *Roderick Hudson, The American, The Princess Casamassima, The Aspern Papers* and "The Jolly Corner" (all in The New York Edition); from *The Wings of the Dove* (1902); and from *The Letters of Henry James,* ed. Percy Lubbock.

Also for permission to quote from *What Maisie Knew* by Henry James (Anchor Books) Doubleday and Company, Inc.; from *The American Essays* by Henry James, ed. Leon Edel, Vintage Books; and *The Turn of the Screw* in *A Casebook on the Turn of the Screw,* ed. Gerald Willen, Thomas Y. Crowell Company; to Oxford University Press, publishers of *The Notebooks of Henry James,* ed. F. O. Matthiessen and Kenneth B. Murdock, Copyright 1947 by Oxford University Press, New York, Inc.

Also, to Grove Press, Inc., publishers of *The Golden Bowl* by Henry James (1904 edition); to Chatto and Windus Ltd., publishers of *The Complex Fate* by Marius Bewley; to William Morrow and Company, Inc., publishers of *Henry James* by F. W. Dupee, Copyright, 1951, by William Sloane Associates, Inc.

ACKNOWLEDGMENTS   vi

INTRODUCTION   xi

Part 1 THE MINOR CONFIDANTES

CHAPTER 1. MINOR CONFIDANTES OF THE EARLY
     AND MIDDLE PERIODS   3

 1. The Early Period: *Roderick Hudson, The American,*
  and "Daisy Miller"   4

 2. The Middle Period: *The Princess Casamassima,*
  "The Aspern Papers," and "A London Life" 14

CHAPTER 2. MINOR CONFIDANTES OF THE LATER PERIOD 28

 1. The Lighter Stories: "Nona Vincent," "The Death of the
  Lion," and "Flickerbridge"   29

 2. The Ghostly Tales: "The Turn of the Screw," "The Altar of
  the Dead," "The Beast in the Jungle," and "The Jolly Corner" 40

 3. The Last Representatives: "Crapy Cornelia" and *The Outcry* 60

Contents

Part 2   THE MAJOR CONFIDANTES

CHAPTER 3. THE PORTRAIT OF A LADY   67

CHAPTER 4. THE SPOILS OF POYNTON   97

CHAPTER 5. WHAT MAISIE KNEW   127

CHAPTER 6. THE AMBASSADORS   150

CHAPTER 7. THE WINGS OF THE DOVE   181

CHAPTER 8. THE GOLDEN BOWL   214

CONCLUSION   247

NOTES   284

INDEX   295

Introduction

One of the greatest themes in fiction is that of friendship—comradeship between persons of the same sex, or the highly refined friendship of respect and confidence between persons of opposite sex. It is the most natural thing for a hero of fiction to confide his troubles or ambitions to a close and sympathetic listener. Sometimes this listener is a faithful servant, sometimes an equal in class or profession; or again, though less frequently, a tenderhearted woman. In cases of a heroine confiding in a friend, the latter is usually another woman. In most instances, the role of the confidant is subordinate to that of the hero.

For two centuries, the relation of such friends was a pleasant feature in many English novels; but as long as the author wrote from the omniscient point of view, he could readily dispense with the confidant when this character ceased to attract interest. Heroes could cease confiding, because their intimate conversations were not the only means of exposing their thoughts to the reader's scrutiny. Omniscient authors could invade the minds of their heroes at will. Generally speaking, there was no attempt to restrict the point of view in the novels before James; and consequently, the deepest resources of the confidential relation remained untapped.

The only exception to this common practice in the English

novel is Emily Brontë's *Wuthering Heights.* Here the use of the confidante, Nelly Dean, is intricately bound up with a difficult and involved method of narration, and their interdependence is so great that they are inseparable. Mrs. Dean's narration to Mr. Lockwood, who is himself the first narrator, consists of facts seen and heard by herself—many of which were received through confidential talks with Heathcliff and Catherine Earnshaw. For both persons, she is the only confidante available, and their revelations are of a confessional character. The role of this confidante differs from that of the Jamesian *ficelle,* because Mr. Lockwood, who receives the information, is scarcely a confider himself, although his relation with Nelly Dean serves the purpose of eliciting exposition. Notwithstanding these differences, *Wuthering Heights* is the closest antecedent in the novel tradition to James's use of the confidante.

In the tradition of the drama there is a difference. The Greek chorus formed the corporate confidant and adviser of the hero; and one of its uses was to dramatize exposition. In Aeschylus, for example, an individual friend of the hero, such as Pylades, was scarcely noticed. But Euripides made much of this confidant of Orestes, and so did Goethe, in his neoclassical imitation, *Iphigenie auf Tauris.* Shakespeare made extensive use of the confidant as technical device: Horatio, Bassanio, Iago, the Nurse, and Nerissa are only some of the characters put to this use.[1] Jonson, Tourneur, and other Renaissance dramatists did the same. The hero confides his background, his problem, or his plan to his friend; or in turn gains information from him, which otherwise was not accessible.

From childhood on, James was interested in the theater. His later study and practice of the drama did much to influence the techniques in his fiction, and the majority of his confidantes appear in works written during or after his dramatic years, 1890-1895. The early ones, however, created in the 1870's and 1880's, already bear the distinguishing features of the later ones.

The evolution of the confidante in James's work can be attributed to the influence of the author's personal life and social background, as well as to his method of narration. These factors show the confidante as a feature peculiar to James's fiction. The type was perfected by him to meet a fictive need which was not generally felt before his time, and which was to be met by other devices, such as the stream of consciousness, by his followers.

When James was born (1843), American women already enjoyed considerable freedom in matters of inheritance, marriage, self-support, and travel. In his own family James was used to a matriarchal system. "Father and his ideas" were a constant source of amusement, whereas the mother was the heart of family unity. The father leaned on her like a child; and her death left him with simply nothing to live for. The mother's powerful influence on the entire family and on Henry in particular is related in Leon Edel's biography.[2] It was a tense control, masked by loving devotion, which in the biographer's eyes preferred the second son to the first and was responsible for the eventual breakdown of the younger children. The power-seeking mothers of James's fiction are the unconscious re-creations of his mother's concealed force; for consciously James could only idealize her.

The attachments which the young James formed to his sister Alice and his cousin Minny Temple are irrelevant here. Our concern is rather with the friendships of a confidential nature with women older than himself in which he found an extension of the original filial relationship. Both James's life and his work provide vivid examples of the mother-child absorption, which is one of nature's most possessive drives. Often characterized by ruthless use on either side, this primal, double force is mitigated only by acquired selflessness. In cases of unequal polarity, destruction or abandonment ensues. James's numerous maternal friends form a long line of usable mothers for his childish egotism. Each filled a particular need—some as simple listeners, others as dispensers of admiration and affection, and all as intelligent, sometimes brilliant, entertainers. James had no use for the ugly, awkward or stupid female; and he fled from her society much as a child would from anything distasteful, with grimaces, transmuted, in his case, into caustic literary remarks.[3] From his earliest tales to his latest work, the intelligent woman predominates. One outstanding exception is the woman in "The Madonna of the Future," a distinctly maternal type, but in whom the narrator quickly loses interest because "this *bourgeoise* Egeria, if I viewed her right, betrayed a rather vulgar stagnation of mind."[4]

The mother-type that James repeatedly found in life and projected into his writing is first exemplified by Grace Norton, his senior by ten years.

A member of a Cambridge family distinguished for fostering art and literature, Grace Norton was herself the author of several books on Montaigne, and a scholar of no mean stature. After traveling in Europe she spent a quiet life in Cambridge. James's correspondence with her lasted over forty years. Perhaps some of his most self-revelatory letters were addressed to Grace Norton. There was a mutual sympathy and trust between them in which he could as gaily joke about his London women friends as compose the following beautiful tribute to her share in human suffering:

Before the sufferings of others I am always utterly powerless, and your letter reveals such depths of suffering that I hardly know what to say to you. This indeed is not my last word—but it must be my first. You are not isolated, verily, in such states of feeling as this— that is, in the sense that you appear to make all the misery of all mankind your own; only I have a terrible sense that you give all and receive nothing—that there is no reciprocity in your sympathy—that you have all the afflictions of it and none of the returns. . . . You are right in your consciousness that we are all echoes and reverberations of the *same* [universe], and you are noble when your interest and pity as to everything that surrounds you, appears to have a sustaining and harmonizing power. Only don't, I beseech you, *generalize* too much in these sympathies and tendernesses—remember that every life is a special problem which is not yours but another's, and content your-

self with the terrible algebra of your own. Don't melt too much into
the universe, but be as solid and dense and fixed as you can. We all
live together, and those of us who love and know, live so most. We
help each other—even unconsciously, each in our own effort, we
lighten the effort of others, we contribute to the sum of success, make
it possible for others to live. . . . Everything will pass, and serenity
and *accepted* mysteries and disillusionments, and the tenderness of a
few good people, and new opportunities and ever so much of life, in
a word, will remain. You will do all sorts of things yet, and I will
help you.[5]

A deep spiritual affinity must have underlain this intimate
letter. As his correspondence with Grace Norton progressed,
James dwelt chiefly on the sights and impressions of his sojourns
in England and intermittent travels on the Continent; but between the lines there recur the personal touch and the kindness
which he felt for her from the beginning. Once, upon reflecting
on Mrs. Kemble's utterly whole personality, he gave Grace this
brotherly advice: "Let us be flexible, dear Grace; let us be flexible! And even if we don't reach the sun we shall at least have
been up in a balloon."[6] Later, his reflections on literature and
famous persons (such as the occasion of Daudet's death), as
well as his own literary undertakings, are the subjects of his confidences. He notes "the comfort and charm it is to be talking with
you even by this horrid machinery [his secretary's typewriter],
and to squeeze the little round golden orange of your note dry
of every testimony to your honoured tranquillity that I can gouge
out of it. My metaphors are mixed, but my fidelity is pure."[7]

Perhaps the most detailed reference to his acknowledgment
of her influence is given in the following passage:

Great, every way, dear Grace, and all-exemplary, I thought the dignity and coherency and benignity of your life—long after beholding
it as it has taken me . . . to make you this declaration. I at any rate
have the greatest satisfaction in the thought—the fireside vision—
of your still and always nobly leading it. I don't know, and how
should I? much about you in detail—but I think I have a kind of
instinct of how the sidebrush of the things that I do get in a general

way a reverberation of touches and affects you, and as in one way or another there seems to have been plenty of the stress and strain and pain of life on the circumference (and even some of it at the centre, as it were) of your circle, I've not been without feeling (and responding to,) I boldly say, *some* of your vibrations. I hope at least the most acute of them have proceeded from causes presenting for you—well, what shall I say?—an *interest!!* Even the most worrying businesses often have one—but there are sides of them that we could discover in talk over the fire but that I don't appeal to you lucidly to portray to me. Besides, I can imagine them exquisitely—as well as where they fail of that beguilement, and believe me, therefore, I am living with you, as I write, quite as much as if I made out—as I used to—by your pharos-looking lamplight through your ample and lucid window-pane, that you were sitting "in," as they say here, and were thereupon planning an immediate invasion.[8]

The fireside scene evoked in this letter reminds one of the typical Jamesian hero—Strether, for instance—sharing the warmth of his confidante's fire.

Grace Norton received most of James's confidences by letter. But on the Italian and London scenes closer friendships were maturing for the young man. In Italy, there were American ladies of distincton, especially Mrs. Sarah Butler Wister; later Mrs. Isabella Gardner and Mrs. Katherine Bronson qualified eminently as mature friends. In London, Mrs. Anne Benson Procter and Mrs. Duncan Stewart—both very old—seconded the famous Mrs. Fanny Kemble as James's maternal friends. Mrs. Humphrey Ward soon joined their ranks; and there were others. Two of these ladies, Mrs. Bronson and Mrs. Stewart, appear in the fiction as the confidantes Mrs. Prest ("The Aspern Papers"), and Lady Davenant ("A London Life"). James's attraction to the brilliant Mrs. Kemble was paralleled in later life by his admiration for Mrs. Edith Wharton.

To Grace Norton he described Mrs. Kemble as "a great friend of mine and to my sense one of the most interesting and delightful of women. . . . She is to my mind the first woman in London, and is moreover one of the consolations of my life."[9] This lady was older than James's mother. After her death, in 1893, he published a long tribute to this "extraordinary woman," who "had abundantly lived and, in more than one meaning of the word, acted—felt, observed, imagined, reflected, reasoned, gathered in her passage the abiding impression, the sense and suggestion of things."[10]

Although younger than James, Mrs. Wharton filled the role of mature friend with vitality and glamor. He calls her "indeed my ideal of the dashing woman," in whose company he yearns to have traversed Germany: "Vivid and charming and sympathetic *au possible* your image and echo of it all; only making me gnash my teeth that I wasn't with you. . . ."[11] Repeatedly he lavishes superlatives on this friend: "I am in receipt of endless bounties from you and dazzling revelations about you . . . your exquisite appeal . . . your gentle 'holograph' letter. . . ."[12] In this American woman of the world James admired mastery of travel and description: ". . . before your great heroic rushes and revolutions I can only gape and sigh and sink back. . . . Great will be the glory and the joy, and the rushing to and fro, when the wide wings are able, marvellously, to show us symptoms of spreading again. . . ."[13] To James, Edith Wharton was a stimulus and a delight. His letters express mostly his admiration for her personality; but we know from her own reminiscences that he loved outings in her motor car as well. The elderly James had lost none of the child's admiration and dependence which are so appealing to motherly women.

The entertaining conversations to which Mrs. Kemble, Mrs. Procter, Mrs. Stewart, and Mrs. Wharton treated James filled his need for information about society in the past and present. They also offered his soul the sustaining firmness which had so characterized his mother. James was very much the "poor sensitive gentleman" described in the Preface to "The Altar of the Dead." A certain hardness stiffened the characters of these clever women and attracted the shy, introspective man. They filled his deeper need for sympathy as well as strength, since even in minor crises Henry James is known to have succumbed emotionally. His utter helplessness on such occasions as a heat wave is humorously described by Mrs. Wharton in *A Backward Glance*. As Mr. Dupee remarks, James no doubt "enjoyed playing the captive" when visiting his maternal friends, so they could lavish on him their solicitude.[14]

But beyond this petty dependence, James showed a deeper failure to measure up emotionally to demands made on himself. Mr. Edel points out James's fear of the marriage tie. "The Lesson of the Master" states the surface reason as the artist's need for freedom; the union, however, with his mother and her surrogates gives evidence of a deeper reason. It indicates a crippling in the boy's development toward emotional maturity. Mr. Edel speculates, "that if Henry had married, he would have sought a young woman who outwardly seemed in full possession of herself and in full conformity with the laws of her sex, but who beneath the surface belonged to the order of the all-demanding and governing matriarchs."[15]

It is significant that James did not marry. And the Jamesian male confider usually remains unattached to his confidante. The only exceptions are the young man in "The Death of the Lion" and Lord Theign in *The Outcry;* for the brides of Allan Wayworth ("Nona Vincent"), of Owen Gereth (*The Spoils of Poynton*), and Prince Amerigo (*The Golden Bowl*) are not their confidantes. Furthermore, very few of the male protagonists choose celibacy for professional reasons. The most outstanding confiders who reject their confidantes and potential lovers are Lambert Strether (*The Ambassadors*), John Marcher ("The Beast in the Jungle"), and Spencer Brydon ("The Jolly Corner"); and these characters reflect their author's personality most clearly. Their rejections are due to a failure in self-commitment.

James was probably incapable of giving in marriage the love that even a domineering wife would have wanted. From childhood on, he had been conditioned to the child's role of asking and receiving. As a man he ever tried to shield himself emotionally, giving only to his invalid sister what her demands made imperative. Even in her case he was obliged to let Miss Loring provide the emotional shock absorber and be a kind of sacred fount. Between himself and other women there existed an effective barrier of reticence. As Mr. Edel has recently discovered, James greatly failed his devoted friend, Miss Woolson. She seems to have desired more from him; but he succeeded in keeping her in the relatively distant position of confidante, treating her as a woman as old as Mrs. Kemble, although she was his senior only by three years.

Although in his personal life James was probably crippled by immature egotism, as an author he clearly perceived and recorded with pathetic accuracy the anguish of the unrequited woman's love. This aspect of the confidante's portrait is identified with the author's moral sense regarding friendship. It is perhaps an indication that his own selfish withdrawal was due rather to insurmountable circumstances in his childhood, than to coldhearted deliberation in adulthood.

Aside from these personal friendships, James met many society women whom he could observe at ease. The London society which accepted and lionized the author was dominated by brilliant hostesses surrounded by all the trappings of wealth. The women of this class lived in leisure, devoting their time to the arts of conversation, music, and reading. The theater and opera, as well as foreign travel and the collecting of art treasures, supplemented their sphere in the drawing room. The mistress of a large house was like a queen in her castle. She presided over the rituals of the formal dinner table and the drawing room. Exempt from the irritations of practical problems by a hierarchy of perfectly-trained servants, she could spend her life entertaining and being entertained. Superficially, at least, this life flowed smoothly for the women in its sheltered groove. It was a life wholly fashioned by forms and conventions. James himself liked the protection of social traditions. William observed of his brother in 1889:

Harry is as nice and simple and amiable as he can be. He has covered himself, like some marine crustacean, with all sorts of material growths, rich sea-weeds and rigid barnacles and things, and lives hidden in the midst of his strange heavy alien manners and customs; but these are all but "protective resemblances," under which the same dear old, good, innocent and at bottom very powerless-feeling Harry remains, caring for little but his writing, and full of dutifulness and affection for all gentle things.[16]

James always admired the aristocratic life with its wealth and culture. Refinement was the essence of his own code as well as that of his leading fictive characters. It was the ideal of a life centered around the lady, in whose presence only courtly manners were tolerated, and whose tastes did much to determine the tenor of literature. Although James is known to have objected to these female restrictions on the scope of the English and American novel, still the refinement of an Englishwoman's taste was closer to his own discreet preferences than was the naturalism of some French authors. The taste of women readers in both England and America facilitated the rise of the female writers of sentimental fiction, who received the recognition of James, the book reviewer, and whom he immortalized in Susan Stringham (*The Wings of the Dove*). In his essay on Mrs. Humphrey Ward (1891) James comments on this rise of women authors:

In England to-day, and in the United States, no one thinks of asking whether or no a book be by a woman, so completely, to the Anglo-American sense, has the tradition of the difference of dignity between the sorts been lost. . . . the position achieved by the sex formerly overshadowed has been a well-fought battle, in which that sex has again and again returned to the charge. In other words, if women take up (in fiction for instance) an equal room in the public eye, it is because they have been remarkably clever. They have carried the defences line by line, and they may justly pretend that they have at last made the English novel speak their language.[17]

As a literary critic, from the very early review of Louisa May Alcott's *Moods* to the latest critical remarks made to Mrs. Wharton and recorded by her, James was gentlemanly, and generous with praise, even when barely justified.[18] In his essay on Miss Woolson, for example, he singles out her "tenderness of feeling," her "compassionate sense," and her "sympathy altogether feminine."[19]

The cultural background of James's women friends was a great attraction for him. In his appraisal of them he was often witty, sometimes amazed, but always kind. His appreciation of their kindness was sincere, and one feels that he enjoyed their company whenever he found it. His accurate knowledge of the woman's heart and behavior came from years of friendship and keen, comprehensive observation. To him, the woman's place, whether in emancipated America, or in high English society, seemed equally natural. He found it delightful that custom prescribed a lone woman to take on a female traveling companion, and he made the most of this prescription in *The Portrait of a Lady*, *The Princess Casamassima*, and *The Wings of the Dove*. He enjoyed his British hostesses, to the extent of dining out one hundred and forty times during the season of 1878-1879. The art of conversation, as he found it practised at dinners and in drawing rooms, was transferred to his fiction; for not only do his confidantes function in the way of talk, but all his major characters of the middle and later periods are exceptional conversationalists. The kindness of his motherly friends James portrays in such characters as Henrietta Stackpole *(The Portrait of a Lady)* and Mrs. Grose ("The Turn of the Screw"). He also relished the comedy of some women around him, and reflects it in Henrietta, Madame Grandoni *(The Princess Casamassima)*, and Mrs. Wix *(What Maisie Knew)*. The feminine flair for romance is concretized in such characters as Susan Stringham *(The Wings of the Dove)* and Fanny Assingham *(The Golden Bowl)*. The rejected woman is idealized in Miss Tina Bordereau ("The Aspern Papers"), in May Bartram ("The Beast in the Jungle"), and in Alice Staverton ("The Jolly Corner"). And the experienced woman of the world is represented by Madame Merle *(The Portrait of a Lady)* and Maria Gostrey *(The Ambassadors)*. In many ways, therefore, James's personal friendships and social background influenced the creation and evolution of his fictive confidantes.

In addition to these influences, James sought to meet the demands made by his method of narration. As he approximated the dramatic method in general, moving away from expository to dramatic narrative, he devised and perfected the limited point of view. A survey of his fiction written from the limited point of view (first or third person), will show that most of the central intelligences are male observers. They fall into three classes. First, the peripheral observers, as in "The Author of Beltraffio" (1885), "Pandora" (1885), " 'Europe' " (1900), and "The Tree of Knowledge" (1900), who are not directly involved in the plot, but discover what is to be revealed about the central characters; and in their discovery lies the telling of the story. In these stories the author is most inclined to use the first person narrator.

Second, those observers who are more closely involved in the complexities of the story, as in *Roderick Hudson* (1875), "Louisa Pallant" (1888), and "The Patagonia" (1889), participate in the action directly by their influence, without being the protagonists. And finally, the observers who are intimately involved as the protagonists are, from *The American* to *The Golden Bowl*, best represented in the novels, although there are a few in the short stories. In this last group, the third person narration is nearly always used, and never the omniscient author.

The male observer is, therefore, indispensable to James's fiction. Usually he is like James himself—a cultured, humane, and inquiring bachelor. Women are his particular subject for ob-

servation—the scintillating and clever, or the patient and griev-
ing. Very often he accepts one of them in a friendship.

Our present concern is with the observer as protagonist.
While developing this type of character, James saw the technical
advantage of converting the friendship with a mature woman
into a confidential relation. It would meet his need for a device
to supplement the limited point of view. This device, the confidante, he called a *ficelle*. A *ficelle* is any device (literally,
"string," and by extension, "stage trick") used by James to
obviate a difficulty in the method of narration, or presentation
of character. The confidante as a *ficelle* is primarily a device to
obtain greater lucidity.[20] The protagonist and center of consciousness needs another character from whom he can elicit
facts and interpretations unknown to himself. Secondly, the
ficelle is designed to elicit data, impressions, and feelings from
the "center," for the benefit of the reader.[21] To this double end,
a relation of a confidential nature proves to be the most promising. In order to facilitate this exchange of perceptions, both
"center" and confidante require exceptional intelligence. Furthermore, James's increasing urge to "dramatise, dramatise" his
fiction demanded the conversion of lengthy narrative into
dramatized scenes. The closer the minds of persons in dialogue
coincide, the more fluent will that dialogue be. And so the con-
fidante-"center" relation offered a source of dramatization. As
a comparison of the traditions of novel and drama will show,
the confidante in this sense is a dramatic, not a narrative device.
James's own works illustrate the point.

Already in stories of 1873 and 1874 James was sending his
male observers to older women for information and advice
about the object of their interest. The basic pattern of the con-
fidante-"center" relation was already emerging from the author's
subconscious. For James, it became more and more natural to
direct the male inquirer to a mature woman for interest and
guidance. But in stories and novels where the omniscient point
of view prevails, as in *Washington Square* (1880), or where the

male observer holds only a peripheral position, as in "The Private Life" (1893), the mature woman friend is not a real confidante. She is only a lesser device, used by the author solely for exposition or ancillary purposes. The observer must be the protagonist—must be totally immersed in the experience at hand—before he needs the guidance of a real confidante. With the exception of only three novels—*Roderick Hudson,* the first, *The Outcry,* the last, and *The Spoils of Poynton,* an anomaly— the confiders discussed in the present work are all observing protagonists.

Furthermore, the basis of close friendship is requisite to the confidante-"center" relation. In this respect *The Sacred Fount* (1901) is deficient. A confidential friendship presupposes personal confidences made by the confider. Most Jamesian protagonists are isolated and lonely. They need and desire a friendship to help them unfold, expand, and make their way. In order to achieve this, the confidante must be sympathetic, must have a keen intelligence to keep up with the divinations of the "center," and is better off if endowed with a vivid imagination. Confidence presupposes not only kindred souls but also equally gifted minds. Thus the scenes between confider and confidante can proceed by quick insights and profound analyses. When James introduces a dull character, such as Bob Assingham or Owen Gereth, it is for the purpose of broader analysis and clarification of obscure points. But his confidantes are never of this lower intelligence. Sometimes their role is compared to the function of a sibyl or an oracle. The more James became absorbed in exposing consciousness, the more he welcomed a character-type wholly fashioned for its exposure.

Another aspect of the confidante's role is to guide the "center" and protagonist through presumably perilous undertakings. She may speak only in warning, as do Henrietta Stackpole and Madame Grandoni; or she may actively lead her confider into the realm where she already moves and where he is to meet his destiny, as is done by Maria Gostrey and Fanny Assingham.

As a type, the confidante is usually middle-aged, sometimes

battered-looking, often plain. She is accessible to her friend in holding equal or nearly equal social rank with him, and being frequently unmarried, widowed, or past the marriageable age. The two husbands of confidantes who appear, Tom Tristram *(The American)* and Bob Assingham, are pressed into service in ways tributary to their wives' activities, often for comic effect.

James preferred women to men in the role. There are two early attempts at using male confidants—the narrator H––in "The Madonna of the Future" (first published in 1873) and the narrator in "Eugene Pickering" (first published in 1874), both of whom receive the confidences of the male protagonist, in the former instance without previous acquaintance. In both stories, the confidences are the principal means of exposition. Valentin, in *The American* (1877), represents a bolder attempt on the author's part to sustain a man in the role, but he is relegated, before very long, to the oblivion of death. Much later, James begins with a man as confidant in mind, as the second *Notebook* entry on *The Wings of the Dove* testifies, but he ends by converting him into a woman in the novel itself. The *homme d'affaires* of the dying girl, who was to be the confidant of the hero, was metamorphosed into Susan Stringham, the confidante of the heroine.[22] The question, why a woman rather than a man? is therefore legitimate.

One notices that of the twenty-one works under present discussion sixteen of the "centers" are occupied by men. Although two of these, Densher and Prince Amerigo, share their posts with women, the male observers are in the majority. A further restriction on the role of the female observer is that three of the women "centers"—Fleda Vetch, Susan Stringham, and Fanny Assingham—are also confidantes. The obvious natural attraction between the sexes is doubtless a factor, especially since most of these male "centers" are troubled and bewildered in one way or another, and find the sympathy of a tender woman's heart more in accordance with their needs. But there are other reasons as well.

Socially, the type that interested James was the independent woman of the world, the well-read, far-travelled, aesthetically inclined lady whose freedom of movement arose either from her being an American or from her professional or social position in England. Only one confidante, Madame Grandoni, is neither American nor English; but her independence is secured by her age and separation from her husband. Most of James's women characters, whether they be confidante or center of consciousness, or both, fit this description. Since he preferred the intelligent, resourceful woman, James was more apt to place her, rather than a man, in the role of guide and oracle. Nor did the general social dependence of women in nineteenth-century England interfere with the activities of the Jamesian confidantes. James's concern with social problems is chiefly limited to *The Bostonians* and *The Princess Casamassima*. The dependence of the English widow causes the conflict in *The Spoils of Poynton,* but it involves principally the confider, not the confidante. Fleda Vetch is fairly independent in being thrown by her father upon her own resources. Her having studied painting alone in Paris was her preparation for this independence. Mrs. Wix, who is an employee, compensates for her social inferiority by asserting the independence of a woman above her station. May Bartram, the most submissive of all, is financially independent.

Usually, in the Jamesian universe, the women influence the men, and this relationship exists likewise between the confidantes and their male confiders. From Christopher Newman *(The American)* to Prince Amerigo, the men are very susceptible to the influence of their confidantes, although, ironically, many reject them in the end. These women have what Mr. Edel calls "the unlived life of passion."[23] Although financially independent, they are seldom emotionally so. Love is still the greatest object in their lives; and in the case of those confidantes of a woman "center"—Henrietta Stackpole and Madame Merle— they seek the fulfillment of love elsewhere. Still, most of the confidantes who seek love from their male confiders are frustrated; and this fact is one of James's pathetic ironies, which in several cases he emphasizes with tragic overtones. The need for love combines with the female receptiveness to make excellent confidantes.

For these technical reasons, as well as from his personal experience, James preferred women to men for this important role; and though he varied the combination of male "center" and female confidante to a combination of two women, as in *The Portrait of a Lady* and "The Turn of the Screw," he avoided—with only one important exception—the combination of a woman confider and a male confidant.[24] His last attempt at combining two men did not have much success, either. According to his *Project* for *The Ambassadors,* Waymarsh was to have had a bigger part; but as the novel now stands, he drops out of Strether's confidence already in Book Third, after Maria joins them in Paris. It is obvious that James could not perpetuate the Renaissance dramatic device of trusted comrade-at-arms or devoted manservant as confidant; for in the society of the drawing room in which he moved, such friendships were nonexistent. It was therefore inevitable that James should prefer women to men in the confidential role.

The evolution of the generic type of confidante is traceable not only in the fiction itself, but also in the *Notebooks* and Prefaces. This evolution shows variations in the character and in the function of the confidante. In character she changes from the mere adviser (Mrs. Costello in "Daisy Miller") to the intimate guide (Madame Merle) and the lover (Maria Gostrey and May Bartram). In function she grows from the simple undisguised *ficelle* used to elicit and give information (Cecilia in *Roderick Hudson*) to the "friend of the reader" and most perfect *ficelle* (Maria Gostrey), and the active agent in the plot (Fanny Assingham). But in spite of the definite evolution, James retained his freedom in later years to reach back and use the simple *ficelle* when it suited him. Nevertheless, in all these variations in character and function, one element remains constant: the confidante is a friend who receives confidences over a considerable period of time, and in this feature one recognizes James's personal experiences in friendship, which no one could duplicate.

Before *The Portrait of a Lady* (1881), James made uncertain experiments with the technique and character of the confidante. But in this novel he firmly seizes the *ficelle* and exploits her dramatic possibilities to the fullest. From now on his method and management of the confidante are unerring, and the direction of her evolution is clear. Dramatic importance and subtle psychological analysis assure for her the position of a prominent secondary character in James's fiction.

What was it that made James abandon so decisively the older novelistic technique of the omniscient author, thus creating for himself the necessity of developing the confidante's role? It may be that the author's personal need for maternal friends and his literary need for technical confidantes had a co-genesis. As James consciously attempted to prove, experience is the foundation of fiction; and it seems quite probable that his ideas on limited point of view and attendant techniques arose from his personal position *vis-à-vis* the world. James was his own "center." From childhood he cultivated the art of observation. Like his fictive centers of consciousness he moved cautiously into experience, savored it, analyzed it, discussed it with his friends, recorded it in his letters, journal, and *Notebooks*. For him, the analysis of states of mind was the object of fiction. "The story in it" was not a record of events, but a vital unfolding of consciousness. While his own consciousness was expanding, he was making his fictive characters pass through the same evolution; and while he was cultivating confidantes, his fictive counterparts entered into similar relations. For both author and protagonists, the expansion of consciousness was aided by friendly dialogue. In real life, the intelligence of his women friends increased the relish in conversation, much as it accelerates the process of discovery in his fiction. The period of the late 1870's through the 1880's abounded in newly-found confidential friendships for the author; in his fiction it was likewise the maturing-time of the confidante-"center" relation.

With the progression of time, consequently, there was for

James a diminution in the usability of the omniscient point of view. By the time he reached his later period, the identification of himself and his mature women friends with the fictive counterparts was practically complete. The "sensitive gentlemen," Stransom, Strether, Marcher, Brydon, are imaginative portraits of their author—as he *might have been*. Similarly, the confidantes of these men solemnly reflect some features of the women he had known, used and—rejected in his life. As the double likeness grew more pronounced, so the elderly James endowed it with a deepening appreciation of the abandoned woman's plight; and his reverence for feminine selflessness as shown in these confidantes is exceeded only in the portrait of Milly Theale. A thorough egotist himself, James was observant enough to appreciate genuine altruism in others. Growing more and more lonely in his old age, he must have yearned for what *might have been;* for from 1879 when he published "The Diary of a Man of Fifty," to 1903, the date of "The Beast in the Jungle," he had not forgotten the theme of what a man may have missed by rejecting a woman's love in marriage.

Having practically invented the role of the confidante as a fictive aid in the expression of his innermost experiences, and having placed her historically in his own period and society, James bequeathed the *ficelle* to posterity mainly as an object of interest. Very few successors exist in the post-Jamesian novel. Edith Wharton, who for a time was influenced by the master, uses a confidante in *The Children* (1928); but Rose Sellars, the friend of Martin Boyne, plays only a minor technical role. Conrad's use of the confidant serves to emphasize the differences from, rather than the similarities to, the Jamesian confidante. The evidence points to the fact that after James's death, with the social upheaval accelerated by World War I, the old order he had known passed, and with it passed certain types of women whom he had concretized in his confidantes; the wealthy American expatriate, the Edwardian society woman, the governess, the companion, and the quiet, demure little writer of sentimental fiction. James's method of narration was also modified by his successors, so that the *ficelle* as confidante was no longer needed. Indeed, it would seem that the master himself had exhausted the possibilities of further development of this device, for the last attempt, Lady Sandgate in *The Outcry* (1911), represents a regression to the older type of simple *ficelle*.

In Chapters I and II I shall discuss the minor confidantes and the variations observable in them. The term "minor" is used in two senses: first, denoting the appearance of the confidante as a minor figure in any work; and second, her part in a short story as equal to the "center" in dramatic importance. As James's fiction falls into three main periods, so my groupings of these minor confidantes indicate a development parallel to the larger growth in the roles of the major characters. The remaining chapters discuss these major confidantes.

In each case, the type, the character, and the technical function is investigated, and parallels and contrasts are noted. Since the function of the confidante is normally a subordinate one, an anomaly is found in her use as center of consciousness in three of the later novels. Each confidante contributes to the total picture, and all are integrally related to the narrative method of the author.

In the Conclusion I shall endeavor to place the Jamesian confidantes in a wider perspective, in order to make an assessment of the implications of James's fondness for this technique in relation to his total moral sense.

Part 1

THE

MINOR

CONFIDANTES

Chapter 1

MINOR CONFIDANTES

OF THE EARLY AND MIDDLE PERIODS

*I*N DEVELOPING THE ROLE of the confidante, James began with several simple *ficelles,* whose appearance is justified only by their technical use to elicit or give information. He was to expand the role, even in the case of the minor confidantes, into a character of considerable dramatic importance. The culmination of the development is to be found in the stories of the later period, "The Altar of the Dead," "The Beast in the Jungle," and "The Jolly Corner." In these stories the confidante not only serves the original and fundamental, technical purpose, but is also a character whose presence forms an integral part of the story.

The confidantes of the early period, Cecilia, Mrs. Tristram, and Mrs. Costello, all bear the distinctive marks of the undisguised *ficelle.* Their function is to step in and give the center of consciousness the necessary exposition at the required moment. Only in a limited way do they receive the confidences of the "center." Limited confidence is due either to the use of other means of exposition, such as narration, in *Roderick Hudson* and *The American,* or the presence of certain reservations in the relationship, as in "Daisy Miller."

But in the three early confidantes, there are already traces of

3

later development, namely an interest in the welfare of the confider, and a measure of self-interest as well. Of these three
women, interest and self-interest are most obvious in Mrs.
Tristram and most concealed in Mrs. Costello. Their position
of monitor is another feature to be found in later confidantes.
And finally, friendship, the most important factor of all, exists
in two of these three relations. As a group, the first three confidantes are similar in their characteristics, yet sufficiently diversified to show the versatility of the young author.

1. The Early Period:

Roderick Hudson, The American, and "Daisy Miller"

Early forerunners of the confidante are the two *ficelles*, Mrs.
Coventry in "The Madonna of the Future" (1873), and Mrs.
Draper in "Madame de Mauves" (serialized in 1874). But their
function of giving information is practically the only one common to the genuine confidantes, of whom Cecilia in *Roderick
Hudson* (1875) is the first. A widowed cousin and friend of
Rowland Mallet, Cecilia as *ficelle* is more of a dramatized character than her predecessors. Rowland, who is the center of consciousness and the first Jamesian observer in a novel, turns to
Cecilia in the opening chapter. Already James has felt the
usefulness of a confidante to elicit exposition from the "center"
and to supplement that information with her own.

Although Rowland is at first reserved in confiding in Cecilia,
fearing her irony, he still expatiates on his need

"to care for something or for somebody. And I want to care, don't
you see? with a certain intensity; even, if you can believe it, with a
certain passion . . . Do you know I sometimes think that I'm a man
of genius half-finished? The genius has been left out, the faculty of
expression is wanting; but the need for expression remains, and I
spend my days groping for the latch of a closed door."[1]

Cecilia at once interprets this as meaning he wants to be in love, which he does not deny.

Near the center of the novel Rowland again turns to his confidante. This time he unburdens himself in a lengthy letter from Rome, disclosing his anxieties over Roderick's involvement with Christina Light. The letter is useful for the commentary on Roderick's character, and for its display of Rowland's own feelings. He acknowledges the value of Cecilia's previous warning that Roderick would be difficult to handle; and he declares her to be his favorite confidante: " 'You know I like discussion in a quiet way, and there's no one with whom I can have it as quietly as with you, most abysmal of cousins' " (p. 298). The letter brings the reader up to date on the events of the past month, and is a welcome interval in the narrative, of which James uses a good deal in this early novel. But there is no successive account of Cecilia's relation with Rowland until the very end, where it is briefly noted that Rowland still gives her an occasional account of Roderick's history.

As the recipient of these two confidences, Cecilia's role is rather meager; but her other technical pupose of introducing Roderick to Rowland is perhaps more important. This clever, proud, and independent woman, with her inclination to sarcasm, is herself hopelessly attracted to Rowland, and in her frustration she resembles other confidantes in their unrequited love. Added to this, through Rowland she loses Roderick, who has provided her only amusement in a dull New England town. It is in Cecilia's parlor that Rowland sees Roderick's statuette, and upon questioning his cousin, learns the details of Roderick's background, family, and temperament. After the first encounter on Cecilia's verandah, Rowland is quite impressed by the charming artistic youth. He determines to give him a future by taking him to Europe to study sculpture.

The slight use made of this type of *ficelle*, the confidante, in *Roderick Hudson*, is scarcely a forecast of the great things to come. However, it is a beginning, and the next novel, *The American,* shows a considerable advance in the technique.

Only two years elapsed between *Roderick Hudson* and *The American,* but in that time James's concept of the confidante developed rapidly. Mrs. Tristram, the American expatriate living with her husband in Paris, has some marks of a full-fledged confidante. At once attracted to Christopher Newman, she takes a personal interest in his search for a wife. It is through her instrumentality that Newman meets Claire de Cintré, her old schoolmate, with whom he falls in love.

Mrs. Tristram, like the other confidantes, is a clever woman, but her cleverness has been so oppressed by an unhappy marriage that "circumstances had done much to cultivate in [her] . . . the need for any little intellectual luxury she could pick up by the way."[2] Newman's quest provides her with some of that luxury. As the novel progresses, her personal interest in the young man becomes unmistakably clear, and overrides all doubts as to the success of her efforts.

James gives much space to authorial exposition of this woman's character. He is obviously interested in the type. Her frustration, her imagination, her zeal in offering guidance and unasked advice, are the features he singles out for elaboration. In these, as well as in her plain face, and cosmopolitan experience, she is the forerunner of Maria Gostrey. In imagination and in possessiveness she parallels Mrs. Wix, and like that poor woman, she is "full—both for good and for ill—of beginnings that came to nothing; but she had nevertheless, morally, a spark of the sacred fire" (p. 38). Like other confidantes, she quickly analyzes the protagonist's character, and concludes that he is "a child of nature."

The conversations between the young man and his confidante serve expository purposes—they reveal his background, financial success, and determination to enjoy life. A note of envy comes through her provoking comments. On the subject of a wife she draws him out effectively, finally concluding that she has the very type he wants, "the best article in the market" (p. 49), the "finest creature in the world" (p. 52). She also describes the young woman's family in picturesque language: " 'They're terrible people—her *monde;* all mounted upon stilts a mile high and with pedigrees long in proportion' " (pp. 53-54).

To balance the romantic picture of Claire de Cintré drawn by Mrs. Tristram, James uses the plain realism of her husband, who calls the lady "as plain as a copy of a copy-book" (p. 54), and who foresees only trouble in the proposed match. In Mrs. Tristram James created an officious busybody, who keeps pushing her man as soon as he shows signs of slackening.[3] Her urgent appeal to his sense of justice is to rescue Madame de Cintré from her terrible family. Picking up her husband's ironic image of the American spread eagle, she says seriously: "Pounce down, seize her in your talons and carry her off. Marry her yourself' " (p. 112). As the difficulties mount, Newman certainly needs explicit encouragement, and this he gets aplenty from his confidante.

After the proposal Newman returns to brief Mrs. Tristram. She now appears to take a critical attitude toward Claire—the sense of rivalry is too strong not to assert itself, and she blames Newman for neglecting herself and her husband.

The inconsistent little lady . . . had an insuperable need of intellectual movement, of critical, or ironic exercise. She had a lively imagination, and was capable at times of holding views, of entertaining beliefs, directly opposed to her most cherished opinions and convictions. . . . In the midst of her mysterious perversities she had admirable flashes of justice (p. 178).

Later, when Newman is telling her his impressions of the Bellegardes, Mrs. Tristram takes their side and finds him sardonic. The effect of these scenes of recapitulation is repetitious. James was later to perfect the technique of exposition through the confidante-"center" dialogue so that for the most part it gives only new light to the reader. In *The American,* however, these later scenes give little new information, occurring as they do right after the respective original encounter. Mrs. Tristram's interpretations of the events are new, but so little diversified that they turn quickly stale. Chapter X is a case in point.

Although Mrs. Tristram continues to receive Newman's confidences and to console him after his rejection, the fact of her being outside the social circle he is trying to penetrate limits her function considerably. Experience had not yet taught James to place the confidante within the social sphere which his hero or heroine is to enter. But Newman needs someone on the inside who can continue to guide, advise, and listen to him. To obviate the difficulty James created Valentin, Claire's younger brother, and Mrs. Bread, the faithful old English waiting-woman in the Bellegarde household. Taking a fancy to Newman, Valentin encourages him in his suit, and on his deathbed intimates to Newman the existence of some family scandal, a secret which, if he can discover it, Newman may use as a weapon against the mother and older brother. Newman is shocked by this apparently "illicit way of arriving at information" (p. 401). Valentin, however, presses the information upon him, declaring his suspicion of a crime committed by his mother and brother. He directs Newman to apply to Mrs. Bread for the details. If Newman cannot blackmail the Bellegardes into releasing Claire to him, the knowledge of their crime if published will at least repay them.

The melodrama of this scene holds sway to the novel's end. Mrs. Bread, who provides the information, is really more of an agent of disclosure than a confidante. Newman needs to confide nothing of his personal troubles to her, as she knows them already. Her inferior social position makes her knowledge of the facts possible; but it further incapacitates her as Newman's confidante, though he does admit to the motive of revenge in soliciting the facts from her. So conscious is she, as an Englishwoman, of her place, that she hesitates even to shake hands with the democratic American. But with the promise of describing her dear Valentin's death, he lures her into giving the details of the Bellegarde crime.

Mrs. Bread, on her side, becomes quite enamored of Newman, especially after he engages her as his housekeeper, and she gives him the information as to the location of Claire's convent. The use to which James puts Mrs. Bread was not again repeated. It is too contrived, and is only a further indication of the inadequacy of Mrs. Tristram's role as confidante.

That lady reappears at the end in an effort to console her friend. The marriage would probably have failed, she states; admitting that her motive had partly been curiosity. It is a different tune to her previously taking the blame for his rejection. " 'I wanted very much to see, first, if such a union could actually come through; second, what would happen afterwards. . . . it was the highest flight ever taken by a tolerably rich imagination!' " (pp. 512-513). She seems to accept Newman's accusation of cynicism.[4] Regretting that he does not confide to her the secret of the Bellegardes—it would have been pleasant to share in his revenge—Mrs. Tristram tries to console him with the assurance that she likes him as he is.

The confidante-"center" relation in *The American* is still quite superficial. At best, Mrs. Tristram is only a poorly disguised *ficelle,* hampered by certain technical limitations. The clumsy use of two auxiliary confidants aggravates the deficiencies of this novel. But James tries to compensate for the technical shortcomings by touching up Mrs. Tristram's character. Her curiosity, personal interest, and critical attitude make her a credible female character; and her frustration relates her to her sister-confidantes in subsequent works.

Of the three early confidantes, Mrs. Costello in "Daisy Miller" (1879), has the most clearly etched character: her impregnable moral code, her withering scorn, and her consummate snobbery, are effectively matched by her social position and her refined appearance. In this woman one feels the demand to raise one's eyes and lower one's voice. As a figure of sheer imposing dignity she is one of James's most successful older women. The first strokes with which the young author depicts her show the keenness with which her entire portrait is drawn: "Mrs. Costello was a widow of fortune, a person of much distinction and who frequently intimated that if she hadn't been so dreadfully liable to sick-headaches she would probably have left a deeper impress on her time."[5] The authority with which she speaks denotes a domineering personality which has never tolerated contradiction. Her appearance is as distinguished as her character: "She had a long pale face, a high nose and a great deal of very striking white hair, which she wore in large puffs and over the top of her head" (p. 16).

This august aunt, whom Winterbourne calls on for the first time in years, proceeds to initiate "him into many of the secrets of that social sway which, as he could see she would like him to think, she exerted from her stronghold" in New York (p. 16). Cast in this manner in the role of monitor, Mrs. Costello shows a purportedly unselfish interest in her nephew's affairs. But it is quite different from Mrs. Tristram's open interest, prompted by curiosity. Mrs. Costello's concern is fed by a deep-seated haughtiness and class pride, which soon spark resentment at her nephew's independence of judgment; and she proceeds to undermine his opinion of Daisy Miller as thoroughly as possible.

Winterbourne has already been impressed by the Genevan insistence on the observance of forms. So when his aunt delivers her first blow against the Millers, " 'Oh yes, I've noticed them. Seen them, heard them and kept out of their way' " (p. 16), it strikes Winterbourne in the spot already softened by European conventions. The narrator adds, "He at once recognised from her tone that Miss Daisy Miller's place in the social scale was low" (p. 17). This social scale is a fabrication of Mrs. Costello, oppressively combining New York hierarchical social standards with European mores.

The information about the Millers which she deigns to give

her nephew serves the author's purpose of exposition, but it also further illumines the character of the speaker. The young man listens with interest to the details about the Millers' intimacy with their courier, but insists on Daisy's innocence. The persistence with which his aunt counters his statements indicates her self-interest; at all costs she must be proved correct, and if Winterbourne is to continue the acquaintance, it will be at his own risk: " 'You've lived too long out of the country. You'll be sure to make some great mistake. You're too innocent' " (p. 19). This warning comes true, but, ironically, not in the way it was intended. For although it is true that Winterbourne has lived a long time away from home, still he has a correct sense of what American girls do there: " 'But don't they all do these things—the little American girls at home?' " (p. 19). The query forces the aunt to beg the question: " 'I should like to see my granddaughters do them!' she then grimly returned" (p. 19). The question of whether American girls go out unchaperoned is simply dropped. Accepting the standards of his cousins as applicable to Daisy, Winterbourne begins to weaken.

In this, as well as the subsequent scenes with her nephew, Mrs. Costello appears to use the force of argument. But her reasoning, especially when faulty, is reinforced with the vehemence of prejudice. Winterbourne cannot help being swayed by the power of his aunt's feelings which color her every utterance. The more she sees her nephew vacillate, the more she disclaims involvement; but the more also her interest increases in scaring him off. His continued association with Daisy is in some oblique way a compromise of Mrs. Costello's norms, which she would like her nephew to observe. " 'Of course, [she taunts, somewhat later] you're not squeamish—a man may know everyone. Men are welcome to the privilege!' " (p. 35).

The struggle that ensues for Winterbourne is mainly one of head versus heart. On the one hand there are the accusations of vulgarity and the insinuations of immorality with which Mrs. Costello asperses Daisy; on the other hand there is the girl's simplicity and natural charm. Winterbourne is irritated "that he shouldn't by instinct appreciate her justly" (p. 20). His dilemma cannot be resolved by instinct alone, and he weighs his aunt's assertions tormentedly against the evidence of his eyes: " 'Common' she might be, as Mrs. Costello had pronounced her; yet what provision was made by that epithet for her queer little native grace?" (p. 23). And when conversing with his aunt, he finds himself defending the Millers: " 'Depend on it they're not 'bad.' " But this redoubtable lady opposes: " 'They're hopelessly vulgar. . . . Whether or no being hopelessly vulgar is being "bad" is a question for the metaphysicians' " (p. 36). In this remark there is a degree of cynicism not found in any other confidante, except Madame Merle, who tries to conceal it. Winterbourne's difficulty arises mainly from his own lack of American "moral spontaneity." He is too stiff, as Daisy herself remarks (p. 56), but not as rigid as his aunt and the expatriates in Rome. He is somewhat softened by a masculine attraction for Daisy, whereas the women feel the added animosity for one of their own sex. Still, the stiffness in him prevents his recognizing Daisy's innate moral sense which makes her blush at the insinuations against her (p. 57). Vainly he tries to mediate between two points of view: the manners and sense of propriety of sophisticated European society, and the natural freedom of the girl from an American small town.

The four scenes with Mrs. Costello are spaced at the beginning, the middle, and the end of the story. The first two occur after the initial scenes between Winterbourne and Daisy. They present the hostility of the old lady toward the girl. The third one, laid in St. Peter's, serves as a kind of climax in Mrs. Costello's attempts to influence her nephew's judgment. Probing into his preoccupation with the girl, her slightly mocking tone soon turns derisive: Giovanelli indeed is handsome, she concedes, but "the courier probably . . . introduced him" (p. 60). But Winterbourne still defends Giovanelli's respectability.

The attitude of Mrs. Costello is supported by the rejection of Daisy Miller on all sides by the American colony in Rome. Mrs. Walker's contribution of censure reinforces Mrs. Costello's position, although it is less cruel. Winterbourne himself "felt very sorry for her—not exactly that he believed she had completely lost her wits, but because it was painful to see so much that was pretty and undefended and natural sink so low in human estimation" (p. 62). It is this weight of public opinion that finally crushes his resistance. When he meets the girl in the Colosseum he is willing to believe the worst. Wearied of "chopping logic and vexed at his poor fallibility, his want of instinctive certitude as to how far her extravagance was generic and national and how far it was crudely personal" (p. 64), he gives up the struggle in her defense. It is not until after her funeral that he changes his mind in her favor. The evidence which his logic sought has come in the testimony of Giovanelli, the only one who has understood Daisy. But it comes too late. His only compensation is to approach his aunt with self-recrimination— "it was on his conscience he had done her an injustice" (p. 74). Mrs. Costello, reduced by the death of her bête-noir to cautious questioning, raises no more objections. For her the zest has gone from condemnation, and her interests do not extend beyond the grave. She listens to her nephew's confession without comment. At all events she has preserved herself uncontaminated; and whatever feelings of guilt may plague her nephew, they leave her untouched. The hardness and cynicism of her former accusations never bother the conscience of this self-righteous woman. She is one of the best portraits of a woman masking cynicism with morality.

From the technical point of view, Mrs. Costello's role is necessary in order to prejudice Winterbourne and sustain the conflict in his mind over Daisy's reputation. Once that conflict is resolved, her function ceases. Furthermore, in her character of snob she represents a formidable sector of James's social background. Although the center of consciousness confides but little in her, she fulfills the other duties of confidante, namely, of supplying information and predicting the future.

As between Cecilia and Mrs. Tristram, so between Mrs. Tristram and Mrs. Costello there is a marked development in the author's grasp of the technique of his *ficelle*. There is likewise a commensurate growth in character portrayal—the strokes are firmer, the color more vivid. In two more years James would give the reading public his two major confidantes in *The Portrait of a Lady*. These are so outstanding that they crowd out all but four minor ones in the 1880's: Madame Grandoni in *The Princess Casamassima,* Mrs. Prest and Miss Tina Bordereau in "The Aspern Papers," and Lady Davenant in "A London Life."

2. The Middle Period:

The Princess Casamassima, "The Aspern Papers," and "A London Life"

The three minor confidantes of James's middle period are unequal in function and characterization. Madame Grandoni, the ugly old companion in *The Princess Casamassima* (1886), plays only a minor role in the life of the protagonist, Hyacinth Robinson. But her characterization is both colorful and amusing. Mrs. Prest, the undisguised *ficelle* in "The Aspern Papers" (1888), claims attention mainly on functionary grounds. Both in characterization and in function she finally yields to Miss Tina Bordereau, who is an interesting type, resurrected from a tomb-like existence by a forward young man. Not only does she become the protagonist's confidante, but she falls hopelessly in love with him, and the final issue of the story is made to turn upon the demands of this love. Of the three, Miss Tina is undoubtedly the most important. Chronologically, she stands midway between the early and the later confidantes.

But her middle position is also recognizable in the features of her character. In her love for the protagonist, she harks back to Mrs. Tristram, and even faintly, to Cecilia; she also anticipates the loves of several later characters, especially Maria Gostrey. Nevertheless, in her advantage over the protagonist she is peculiar—none of the other confidantes is capable of inflicting retribution. Also, Tina's wraith-like manner and appearance and strangely secluded life relate her to the ladies in the ghostly tales of the next decade. James's use of two confidantes in "The Aspern Papers" draws attention, by way of contrast, to the larger juxtaposition of the two major confidantes in *The Portrait of a Lady.* By this time the author has mastered his device so well that when his first confidante is no longer useful, he can substitute another one, of entirely different cast, who is more closely connected with the protagonist than the first one. This mastery of the technique accounts for the obvious improvement in "The Aspern Papers" over *The American,* with its awkward triangle of confidants.

It is well to remember that *The Princess Casamassima* is a continuation of the adventures of Christina Light, the glamorous heroine of *Roderick Hudson.* In tracing her further exploits, James allows her former companion, Madame Grandoni, to continue in the wake of this gorgeous creature. As companion, Madame Grandoni's obvious role is the comic foil. She is ugly; she wears a wig and frumpy clothes; and as this novel progresses, she grows increasingly depressed and at odds with her patroness. Even in her alarm over the latter's questionable undertakings, she retains her comic quality.

But this ridiculous exterior conceals a kindly heart. In *Roderick Hudson* she lends an ear and some advice to Rowland Mallet; and in the sequel she plays the part of a double confidante. Hyacinth Robinson gives her only a small share of confidence, for which she rewards him with a large share of admonition. Her role in Hyacinth's regard is to warn him of the dangers attendant on his attachment to the Princess. Go and see her once or twice, she advises him in the theater box. Then she counsels him not to give himself up to Christina, not to get involved in revolutionary ventures. She knows her patroness only too well, and now she penetrates the young man's infatuation. Later, at Medley, she urges him to leave the place early.

When Hyacinth finds her in the little house at Madeira Crescent she expresses her displeasure at the way the Princess is living, gives him an expository account of her life since he left Medley, and hints darkly at her revolutionary connections. Her moral stand regarding the liberties taken by her patroness is a useful key to the involvement confronting Hyacinth. That he should ignore her warnings is required by his character and fate. It is these which prevent the young man from making Madame Grandoni a confidante in the full sense. Hyacinth does not want a confidante as Strether does; for the young man is comparatively uncommunicative; nor is he looking for a motherly friend, having already had enough mothering from Miss Pynsent. The barrier usually found between a Jamesian "center" and his confidante is, in Hyacinth's case, this inability to confide and take advice. In Strether's case, on the other hand, it is the reluctance of the confidante to give any warning. In both instances the result is negative: the loss of confidence.

As the point of view in this novel shifts, so Madame Grandoni's function shifts from advising Hyacinth to listening to the Prince. In three scenes the Prince pours out to her his misery over his wife's separation from himself; and he urgently solicits her aid in bringing them together again. She pities the poor man, but her advice in his case too is ineffectual. She urges him to patience, to forebearance. Their two big scenes, one in Christina's residence in South Street, Mayfair (Chapter XVI), the other at Madeira Crescent (Chapter XL), both serve as exposition, for the reader as well as for the Prince. In the first scene, Madame Grandoni utters the warning that she will leave the Princess if the latter should do "certain things." In the second scene, she indicates her impending departure. The contrasted emotions of these two intimates of Christina help to illuminate her character.

Although the Prince receives more attention from Madame Grandoni than Hyacinth does, it is the little bookbinder who feels more deeply for her:

"And Madame Grandoni then?" he asked, all loth to turn away. He felt pretty sure he should never knock at that door again, and the desire was strong in him to see once more, for the last time, the ancient afflicted titular "companion" of the Princess, whom he had always liked. She had struck him as ever in the slightly ridiculous position of a confidant of tragedy in whom the heroine, stricken with reserves unfavourable to the dramatic progression, should have ceased to confide.[6]

This sensitive summary of the old lady's role indicates clearly the ancillary character of her part as undisguised *ficelle,* in spite of which, however, she serves as a kind of barometer for the observers of the Princess, including the reader.

From the *ficelle,* Madame Grandoni, to the *ficelle,* Mrs. Prest, it was only a step for James. But this lady, the friend of the protagonist in "The Aspern Papers," is more fully integrated into the story by being more indispensable. Were it not for her, the young man would simply not have got near his goal. Writing the story as his personal reminiscence, the protagonist launches right into the relation with his first confidante:

I had taken Mrs. Prest into my confidence; without her in truth I should have made but little advance, for the fruitful idea in the whole business dropped from her friendly lips. It was she who found the short cut and loosed the Gordian knot. It is not supposed easy for women to rise to the large free view of anything, anything to be done; but they sometimes throw off a bold conception—such as a man wouldn't have risen to—with singular serenity. "Simply make them take you in on the footing of a lodger"—I don't think that unaided I should have risen to that.[7]

The young editor's problem is to have access to the famous Aspern love-letters; and James's problem is to get him inside the house where it is believed they lie concealed. In solving these problems the confidante as *ficelle* is an obvious device, and she receives only confidences sufficient to act as effectively as necessary.

Mechanical as this relation is, the maturer James was able to inject more of a clash of character into it than he had achieved in Madame Grandoni's friendships. The editor acknowledges that Mrs. Prest is an exception, because she could throw off a bold conception, and he is duly grateful to her. But he soon discovers her fickleness. With her cleverness, she envisages failure soon enough to elude personal responsibility. From the very start she takes a pessimistic view. She pretends to make light of Aspern's genius, and derides Miss Bordereau for having fallen in love with the poet. Her contradictory attitude furnishes James with the requisite conflict to get his exposition told in the most effective manner possible. Endeavoring to explain Mrs. Prest's indifference to the fame of Aspern, the narrator notes that she does not have the "nerves of an editor."

Although deficient in this respect, Mrs. Prest compensates by charitably taking the protagonist to see the old palace of Miss Bordereau. Further discussion ensues when he raises an objection: perhaps Miss Bodereau is in no need of a lodger? But his confidante straightens him out in that respect. To live in an old Venetian palace is no indication of wealth. In fact, one could reside there in direst poverty. Besides, how could there be a question of letting rooms if she did not have a large house? Finally, his friend's practical knowledge of the situation helps him to arrive at a decision; but her skepticism makes him very uncomfortable. " 'The aunt will refuse,' " she tells him later, " 'she'll think the whole proceeding very *louche*!' . . . She had put the idea into my head and now—so little are women to be counted on—she appeared to take a despondent view of it" (p. 308).

The editor is very glad when his confidante departs from Venice. Her taunts, he feels, are provoked by her disappointment in having missed an interesting and amusing drama enacted between the narrator and the Misses Bordereau. Formidably, she predicts his utter failure: " 'They'll lead you on to your ruin. . . . They'll get all your money without showing you a scrap' " (p. 320). In uttering this prediction Mrs. Prest functions as other confidantes who prognosticate for their confiders. The ironical twist in the fulfillment of the forecast adds to the depth of the story.

By eliminating Mrs. Prest the author clears the stage for Miss Tina Bordereau, the second confidante in this short story. As James had already demonstrated in *The Portrait of a Lady,* it is impossible to play two confidantes against each other in full view. Any contrast must be merely implied. The difference between Mrs. Prest and Miss Tina is in the importance of their roles; the first is definitely minor, the second is major to the degree of becoming the antagonist.

As it unfolds before the editor's eyes, the character of Miss Tina is one of a strange lady, subdued by tyranny and "ages" of cloistered seclusion, yet heightened by naïve reminiscences of her rather uneventful past. James avails himself of a broader scope in portraying this confidante than he does for her kindred spirits in the ghostly tales to follow. One sees an artlessness bordering on witlessness, in spite of which the feminine instinct asserts itself quite unpredictably. James's success in blending surface qualities with deep-seated instinctual drives is evident in the convincing way in which Miss Tina guides the relation with the editor by working unwittingly on his conscience.

From Chapter V onward, the relationship of these two disparate characters constitutes the whole story. But it is not a friendship. Rather, it is a study in the psychology of self-deception. The woman deceives herself in believing that the man is interested in her; and the man deceives himself by thinking at first that he is not creating a false impression. This double self-deception is rare in a Jamesian confidante-"center" relation. Somehow, both parties hold each other at their mercy, and the quiet struggle between them, which originally concerns possession of the Aspern papers, eventually involves the deeper issue of personal freedom. The editor's belief that he has the advantage over Miss Tina's artlessness and limpidity founders when her simple-minded self-interest begins to thwart his plan. His conscience gives him the first warning.

For the editor *does* have a conscience, subject though he is to self-deception and an unhealthy obsession with Aspern's private life.[8] After his flippant remark to Mrs. Prest that he might make love to the niece, acquaintance with Miss Tina does make him soberly reconsider: ". . . I had no wish to have it on my conscience that I might pass for having made love to her" (p. 338). During the same interview he honestly confesses his intention of getting at the aunt's papers, for conscience prevents him from denying it to Tina. Sometime later he perceives that "She was of a yielding nature and capable of doing almost anything to please a person markedly kind to her; but the greatest kindness of all would be not to presume too much on this" (p. 354).

These observations of the editor's stand as extenuating evidence in favor of his moral character. It is indeed his admiration for Miss Tina's guileless trust that carries him further than he intended, involving him finally in the mortifying predicament of receiving from her a marriage proposal. Nonetheless, his basic honesty, which responds to her goodness, is what attracts Tina herself. Although driven by an unseemly passion to pry into Aspern's life, the editor retains some decency throughout the crisis. Having estimated her as "a perfectly artless and a considerably witless woman" (p. 339), he remains blind to her deeper subtlety and feminine desires, and consequently unaware of her growing attachment. The proposal, therefore, comes as a shock.

But from Tina's point of view, the development of events moves naturally toward her taking the initiative. From the start, she had indeed noticed his attentions to herself. The flowers, once he admits they were for her, give her new pleasure. She also guards his secret jealously from her aunt. As a woman, it is most natural for her to think in terms of personalities. In her estimation, the Aspern papers could hardly be so important as to exact the sacrifices and attention which the editor is willing to give. Urged on by her malicious, matchmaking aunt, poor Tina willingly believes the gentleman is attracted to herself. To help him get the papers becomes a cherished confidential relation; no regard for prized biographical discoveries ever bothers this almost unlettered woman; and no concept of his eagerness to be such a discoverer ever enters her head. The editor's most reprehensible act is to disallow for this narrow view of Tina's. He simply takes her devotion for granted with the calmness of excessive conceit. In concentrating only on his own advantage, the editor resembles other Jamesian confiders; but Miss Tina proves to be exceptional among the confidantes. For beneath her unselfishness, the feminine instinct is less inhibited than it is in Maria Gostrey or May Bartram. As the editor notices, "From the moment you were kind to her she depended on you absolutely; her self-consciousness dropped and she took the greatest intimacy, the innocent intimacy that was all she could conceive, for granted" (pp. 349-350).

Conscience, that saving feature in the "publishing scoundrel," reacts perceptibly to the helpless appeal of this child-like woman; but it does not hinder him from exploiting her by eliciting still further information. Miss Tina is the very antithesis of the woman of the world. It is significant that in order to create such a woman, James had to immure her for many years. In the society of his acquaintance there simply were no such innocents, except the gaping American type who comes abroad to be initiated. But James's analysis of this woman's soul is kindly, though keen. Despite her naïveté, he preserves her dignity. Tina's place is not among the caricatures of women occasionally found in James's fiction.[9] Her trusting disclosures and her growing confidence are both touching and true. From the nocturnal visit on, when the confidential basis is established, Tina leans more and more on her confider. The relation is a reversal of the normal order. Having received his initial confidence, she makes revelations which exceed it both in their number and in her simplicity. On his part, the narrator feels drawn by her apparent and unusual selflessness: ". . . the look and tone which accompanied these words betrayed so the absence of the habit of thinking of herself that I almost thought her charming" (p. 357).

Her charm changes, first into pathos during the crisis of her proposal, then into transcending moral beauty after his rejection. For the editor, the acute embarrassment of these scenes is an object lesson in humility. He is made the unwilling—and perhaps unworthy—witness of a good woman's self-abasement. To expose her emotional need to a relative stranger costs poor Tina all the courage which her desperate position can summon. Faced by terrible loneliness after the aunt's death, she clutches at the one hope of her withered life—the hope that this man may, after all, be willing to fill her deepest need for love. With a cunning not precluded by her naïveté, Tina makes the possession of the papers contingent upon her proposal: " 'Anything that's mine would be yours, and you could do what you like' " (p. 396). The aunt's possible disapproval of the arrangement is also anticipated: " 'I'd give you everything, and she'd understand, where she is—she'd forgive me!' " (p. 397).

After his abrupt rejection, Miss Tina appears briefly transfigured: "She stood in the middle of the room with a face of mildness bent upon me, and her look of forgiveness, of absolution, made her angelic. It beautified her; she was younger; she was not the ridiculous old woman. This trick of her expression, this magic of her spirit, transfigured her. . . . now she had the force of soul—Miss Tina with force of soul was a new conception—to smile at me in her abjection" (pp. 402-403). Admitting that his preoccupation had prevented him from noticing this before, the editor does not suspect that when the news of the holocaust casts him into gloom, he sees the same on her face by transference: ". . . the transfiguration was over and she had changed back to a plain dingy elderly person" (p. 403).

Throughout the story, this problem of the narrator's questionable objectivity and consequent reliability remains central to the reader's comprehension. One can, at best, make only an approximate estimate of Tina's character as it is reflected in the shifting view of the editor. Somehow, however, the lines form themselves into a basic pattern which impresses the man with its moral worth and pitiable fate. It is hard to agree with the assumption that the editor fails to profit by Tina's forgiveness. For at the conclusion, describing the last look she gave him, he adds, "I have never forgotten it and I sometimes still suffer from it, though it was not resentful" (p. 404). The admission of suffering, even in subsequent years, signifies that, in spite of all his rationalizing, the editor's conscience remains restless. And so his mental progress through the story is seen as a development from an obsession, through the agency of an unquiet conscience, to the partial awareness, at least, of a guilt in his dealings with Miss Tina Bordereau.[10]

The irony which pervades the confidante-"center" relation in this story is particularly evident in the editor's view of women in general. Early in the narrative he expresses a condescending opinion of women's lack of speculative intellect. For a man equipped with this conventional view he is, before the end of the story, singularly punished by the experimental, opportunistic, and self-interested practical intellect of Juliana, and the simple-mindedness of her niece. The two Bordereau ladies may indeed lack speculative intellect; but their complementary qualities baffle the man seeking to outwit them.

The women's world presented in "The Aspern Papers" foreshadows a similar one in *The Wings of the Dove*. Besides, this short story is outstanding for the use of two confidantes, the first one a mere *ficelle,* the second one a major character. The dramatic importance of Miss Tina's role links "The Aspern Papers" with the major works, and forms the transition from the middle to the later period. The appearance of "A London Life" a year later does not relegate "The Aspern Papers" from

its transitional position, for in the latter story the role of the confidante is less important and of a different nature.

Another reason for the transitional position of "The Aspern
Papers" is the depth to which the author explores the theme of
betrayal in the confidante-"center" relation. None of the confidantes preceding Miss Tina is so victimized by her confider.
Among the later ones, few even are trifled with to the same degree. She also fills the singular role of being both a dupe and
an avenger, whose forgiving glance haunts the "publishing
scoundrel" throughout his life. In this manner she is a harbinger
of the fate and posthumous power of May Bartram. The story
is consequently outstanding for its meaning as well as for its
irony and artistic finish.

"A London Life" (1889) is set in the *fin de siècle* London society, with its garish moral decadence. The Jamesian observer,
Laura Wing, an American girl armed with the strict moral code
of her ancestors, finds herself surrounded in her married sister's
home by shocking conditions. As center of consciousness, Laura
perceives all that she needs to know by merely relying on the
evidence of her senses, and can easily dispense with the revelations of an initiated confidante. That James should introduce
such a character is, however, no superfluous trick; for in Lady
Davenant he has created another distinctive female type, as well
as a friend to whom the tormented heroine can unburden herself.

As a type, the old English lady is as fully drawn as Mrs. Costello. Cold by nature, though without the asperity of the latter,
Lady Davenant has ideas that strike her young friend as "very
sharp and hard," for she is not a comforting person. But Laura
confides in her to assuage a prim desire in her own heart—the
desire to be taught fortitude. The two women complement each
other in this ascetical attitude toward life. By her advanced age
and refined English heritage, the confidante provides a social extension to Laura's native moral preconceptions. Her lack of
sentiment, consequently, does not act as a deterrent to the girl's

righteous revolt; but at the same time it balances the impact of
Laura's reaction on the reader. Lady Davenant's cool disdain
and calculating assessment of character and situation represent
the mature judgment of the old world, while Laura's attitude
stands for the new. "Genial, clever, worldly, old-fashioned, half
comforting, half shocking old lady," as James describes her in
his *Notebooks,* Lady Davenant, the realist, offsets Laura, the
impetuous idealist.[11] Acting thus as foil, the old lady represents
a criterion by which to judge the actions of Laura, Selina, and
Wendover. Vainly she tries to convert Laura to a realistic view
of the impending scandal. In seeking to influence both the girl
and the young man she acts as a mother toward children, while
both esteem her intelligence and virtue.

But the girl presently awakens to her friend's matchmaking
propensities, which strike a jarring note:

There was nothing, in general, that the girl liked less than being
spoken of, off-hand, as a marriageable article—being planned and
arranged for in this particular. It made too light of her independence,
and though in general such inventions passed for benevolence they
had always seemed to her to contain at bottom an impertinence—as
if people could be moved about like a game of chequers. There was
a liberty in the way Lady Davenant's imagination disposed of her
(with such an insouciance of her own preferences), but she for-
gave that, because after all this old friend was not obliged to think
of her at all.[12]

The dramatized scene that follows upon this passage discloses more of the old lady's refined hardness. She laughs "dis-
respectfully" at Laura's attempts to reform her sister. Her kindness and solicitude for Laura's future betray an undercurrent of
disturbing irony. Laura squirms under her penetrating inquiries,
which are aimed chiefly in the direction of Mr. Wendover's attentions. James makes Lady Davenant's presence as confidante
and meddler plausible because his heroine is "a nature needing
help and support and unable to stand alone."[13] But Laura is also
endowed with the stubbornness of the weak. At first resenting

her friend's interference, she grows alienated from her and finally severs the connection completely.

Not only is the old lady's interference a stumbling block to Laura, it also culminates in a technical flaw in the narrative. As James himself confessed later in the Preface to *The Spoils of Poynton,* the scene between Lady Davenant and Wendover forms the structural failure in the nouvelle. Aside from being composed outside of the "prime intention" of the work, it shows up the *ficelle* in her most arbitrary use as matchmaker. Shifting her role from sympathetic listener to meddler, Lady Davenant loses in dignity and dramatic stature. As James demonstrates in *The American,* for a confidante to meddle successfully she must have a sufficient hold on her confider's trust. Christopher Newman's child-like trust in Mrs. Tristram prevents him from making incriminations after the failure of her plan. Prince Amerigo has no cause for complaint since he profits in an unexpected way from Fanny's dispositions; but Sir Claude does object to the attempted interference of Mrs. Wix. Laura Wing in like manner resents the pursuit of Wendover, which is encouraged by her erstwhile confidante. Lady Davenant's allusions to marrying her off are probably a contributing factor in the rejection of her suitor. To appear to be in need of his pity is repulsive to her pride.

James originally planned to have the confidante advise Laura to broach the topic of marriage herself. In the nouvelle, however, this plan is changed, and Laura jumps to her own rash conclusion about Wendover's intentions. The change is both a loss and a gain: a loss for the role of the meddling confidante, but a gain for the probability of Laura's distraught impulsiveness. The chief loss is connected with the private interview between the old lady and the young man. If she had previously suggested to Laura that he is attached to her, her own direct appeal to him on behalf of the girl would be better prepared for; and the scene would be less awkward from the dramatic, if not from the narrative point of view.

James placed "A London Life" with *The Spoils of Poynton* in the New York Edition, noting in the preface that Laura Wing's character and predicament closely resemble those of Fleda Vetch:

They are each . . . 'stories about women,' very young women, who, affected with a certain high lucidity, thereby become characters; in consequence of which their doings, their sufferings or whatever, take on, I assume, an importance. Laura Wing . . . has, like Fleda Vetch, acuteness and intensity, reflexion and passion, has above all a contributive and participant view of her situation. . . .[14]

The similarity of their characters does not preclude a contrast of confidante-"center" relations; for Laura needs consolation, whereas Fleda dispenses it to others. In the latter character James shows a marked development in "high lucidity" and "acuteness." Chronologically, Laura's character is a preliminary attempt at what James later achieved in Fleda.

The confidante in "A London Life," on the other hand, marks a regression in dramatic importance when compared to Miss Tina Bordereau before her, and Mrs. Grose after her. As a striking personality Lady Davenant can claim most attention; and in this aspect she joins hands with Mrs. Costello and Madame Merle, and foreshadows Mrs. Gereth and Mrs. Assingham. In the middle period of his creativity, James completed two masterpieces: the frustrated friendships in *The Portrait of a Lady,* and the mistaken friendship in "The Aspern Papers." The lesser achievement in confidential relations in *The Princess Casamassima* and "A London Life" contribute their share of comedy and irony to the Jamesian concept of the confidante at this time. In the 1880's this concept emerges from the bareness of the simple *ficelle* into the fuller portraits of personal friendship—both deluded and betrayed. In the following fifteen years the confidante matures both as a technical device and a fictive character.

Chapter 2

MINOR CONFIDANTES
OF THE LATER PERIOD

*T*HE LATER SHORT STORIES featuring a confidante fall into two groups, the lighter stories and the ghostly tales. Among the last works of the ageing author there are also some survivals, and these may be grouped separately as the final representatives of the type.

In the first three stories certain elements of comedy are evident—marriage, the stock "happy ending" being the most obvious one in both "Nona Vincent" and "The Death of the Lion." There are also a lighter tone and an affirmation of friendship in these stories which distinguish them from the gloomier tales to follow. The latter are already well known as "ghostly," and death, both physical and spiritual, is common to all four of them.

The final representatives of the confidante as type are found in works of decline. Cornelia Rasch and Lady Sandgate bear only outward resemblances to their great and varied predecessors.

1. The Lighter Stories:

"Nona Vincent," "The Death of the Lion," and "Flickerbridge"

These three stories express a mixed view of life and of the confidante-friend relation. Certain comic elements blend with serious undertones. In "Nona Vincent" and "The Death of the Lion" a happy marriage concludes the action, thereby raising the tone to the level of comedy. On the other hand, a peculiar apparition places the former story among the ghostly tales in Mr. Edel's collection; and the death of Neil Paraday casts a shade upon the latter story. In "Flickerbridge" James deals once more with the problems and choices facing the artist, and the conclusion involves renunciation as much as possession.

The constant factor in all three stories is the consolation derived from the confidante-"center" relation. All three protagonists are charmed by the beauty, grace, and kindliness of their female friend, finding in her the assurance of trust and the inspiration for better things. In both "Nona Vincent" and "Flickerbridge" this inspiration is specifically an insight into the mysteries of artistic creation. Both stories are an affirmation of the life of the spirit.

Mrs. Alsager, the confidante in "Nona Vincent" (1893), in many ways heralds the greater figure of Maria Gostrey. The atmosphere of her home is "simply a sort of distillation of herself, so soothing, so beguiling. . . ."[1] Here Allan Wayworth finds solace and oblivion from the loneliness and worries of his life. The essence of his consolation is of course Mrs. Alsager's complete understanding of his literary ambitions. But more than that, she embodies "the principle of giving." Not able to write professionally herself, she gives fecundity to him by the deep understanding of her attention and the breadth of her vision. Generous and artistic, she is poised nymph-like in "the rising tide" of happy thoughts before him.

One of the youngest among the Jamesian confiders (he is only twenty-eight), Wayworth basks in the glow of this woman's personality which pervades her golden drawing room. Here is the unmistakable touch of autobiography. Peace, security, loving admiration, what more did the author himself desire from his confidential friendships? Mrs. Alsager not only listens to the young man's ambitions, she shares also his enthusiasm for the perfection of artistic form. Above all, she abounds in esteem for his originality. When he finally stumbles upon the dramatic form, Mrs. Alsager, a discerning theatergoer, is full of appreciation. Together they move forward in the writing of his play, and upon its completion her enthusiasm is perfectly sincere.

From the start, Nona Vincent, the heroine in the play, is a living person for both of them. A close identification between the confidante and the dramatic heroine becomes apparent in Mrs. Alsager's fondness for her. The young author himself confesses to the likeness, and from the exchange which follows, one guesses the attachment of the married woman to her young friend. Still, Mrs. Alsager refuses to admit to the similarity. Nona Vincent tells her love, she declares, but " 'I should never do that' " (p. 142). Unequally matched with her own rich and vulgar husband, this woman of refined sensibilities allows only one little glimpse into her heart. Wayworth, on his part, pushes the point still further, but without eliciting any confession from his friend.

The likeness, however, is real, as James clearly shows when Violet Grey, cast in the role, discovers it to her own amazement. No amount of coaching from the author can make Miss Grey capture the meaning of her role. The first night she is a flop, and only a visit from Mrs. Alsager herself saves her and the part from dismal failure.

The visit is made on the older woman's initiative, and is a tacit admission of her awareness of the similarity between Nona and herself. The confidante does not go unprepared. Having listened to Wayworth's hopes and fears for his play, she has also studied Miss Grey in her previous role at another theater.

While the two women meet, Wayworth—quite unaware—spends a dreary afternoon in his lodging. It is then that Nona Vincent appears to him—"ineffably beautiful and consoling. . . . quiet as an affectionate sister. . . . She struck him, in the strangest way, both as his creation and as his inspirer, and she gave him the happiest consciousness of success. . . . From time to time she smiled and said: 'I live—I live—I live' " (pp. 172-173). Wayworth rises from this vision filled with "the joy of the artist—in the thought of how right he had been, how exactly like herself he had made her" (p. 173).

That night Violet Grey's rendition of Nona Vincent is perfect. Her explanation to the author afterwards is the account of Mrs. Alsager's visit. For Violet, it was the same thing as if Nona herself had come. She is just like Nona, declares the inspired actress. She did not try to coach Violet, she merely

said she would be so glad if it would help me to see her. And I felt it did help me. I don't know what took place—she only sat there, and she held my hand and smiled at me, and she had tact and grace, and she had goodness and beauty, and she soothed my nerves and lighted up my imagination. . . . she was a revelation (p. 177).

Mrs. Alsager has done her utmost to help her confider. In meeting each other, both women have guessed that each is in love with Wayworth, and both disclose the fact to the young man. Having given her confider his inspiration in creating Nona Vincent, Mrs. Alsager has now helped the other woman to draw from herself the insight to render that part perfectly. Nothing remains for her to do, so she discreetly withdraws from the scene. The beauty of her character, which entered into Nona Vincent, encompasses a pure unselfishness—the strength to stand back and admire a relation from which she herself is necessarily excluded. ". . . The next time he saw her his play had run two hundred nights and he had married Violet Grey" (p. 178).

"Nona Vincent" is a simple little story which James did not include in the New York Edition. Composed in 1892, when James himself was writing for the theater, it reflects the author's hopes and dreams of success. The only significant thing about it is the presence of the benign confidante who mothers the first-born dramatic efforts of the hero. Resorting to a "ghostly" trick, James increases the stature of the confidante by relating her ambiguously with the apparition of Nona Vincent. Did she wear the same garments as my vision? the young man wonders. But the question is never answered.

Somehow, the air of unreality—or preternatural reality—which imbues the story, also colors the confidante-"center" relation. It seems so ideal, so perfect—too rarefied to be essayed in the longer works by James. It is, however, a lovely picture of an ideal friendship, with sufficient realism in the portrait of the confidante who must bear the burden of sacrifice.

In like manner, Wayworth possesses the essential traits of a confider: he draws from his confidante spiritual sustenance and offers very little in return. Like a child, he expects and receives goodness in exceeding measure from his spiritual mother; and he transfers his affections without a qualm to a substitute as soon as she appears. Once he is married, one gathers that the confidante is no longer the sole object of his veneration.

Fanny Hurter, the youthful confidante in "The Death of the Lion" (1895), is in a different position from Mrs. Alsager. Although she too consoles a distressed writer, she is not in a position to inspire his artistic endeavors. Appearing only in the latter half of the story, she seems to be just another fan pursuing the great author, Neil Paraday. It is the narrator's self-appointed task to fend off Paraday's intruders. With this intention uppermost, the young journalist meets the pretty little American. Although categorically she is another intruder, personally she affects the young man quite differently. He finds her charming and at once an interest is struck up between them. The narrator, an Englishman, is particularly impressed by her free American ways. Her willingness to wait all day for the great man strikes him as a romantic trick—

a part of the general romance of her freedom, her errand, her innocence. The confidence of young Americans was notorious, and I speedily arrived at a conviction that no impulse could have been more generous than the impulse that had operated here. I foresaw at that moment that it would make her my peculiar charge, just as circumstances had made Neil Paraday. She would be another person to look after, so that one's honor would be concerned in guiding her straight.[2]

The narrator believes to have gauged her correctly, when she sweetly disconcerts him by putting away the autograph album (which belongs only to a friend) and states that she really came to look straight into the author's face: " 'Because I just love him!' " (p. 31). The journalist senses immediately that he is attracted to this girl and that she in turn can be attracted to a sacrifice for the object of her literary admiration. With no further ado he therefore recommends that she should sacrifice seeing the harassed author: " 'Give up this crude purpose of seeing him. Go away without it. That will be far better' " (p. 32).

To explain such a course of action the young man confides to her tender heart the tormented state of their literary idol: " 'He's badgered, bothered, overwhelmed, on the pretext of being applauded,' " by people who would not give five shillings for one of his books (p. 33). So the greatest consideration she can offer is to avoid him, never to see him at all.

But the shock of this advice is mitigated by the young man's advice for her to read Paraday's books instead, and she gathers at once that her adviser is interested in herself.

Fundamentally, there is a comic vein running through this story, and the infatuation of the young man is part of it. Unconsciously, he aims to keep Miss Hurter away from Paraday, so that he may enjoy her company by himself: " 'Oh, I express it badly; but I should be delighted if you would let me come to see you—to explain it better' " (p. 34). He calls on her the next day, and the alliance to spare Neil Paraday grows—among other feelings—steadily stronger.

The confidence bestowed on Miss Hurter rouses her to

a generous rapture. She positively desired to do something sublime for him, though indeed I could see that, as this particular flight was difficult, she appreciated the fact that my visits kept her up. I had it on my conscience to keep her up; I neglected nothing that would contribute to it. . . . We read him together when I could find time, and the generous creature's sacrifice was fed by our conversation. There were twenty selfish women, about whom I told her, who stirred her with a beautiful rage (pp. 36–37).

Little Miss Hurter does not realize what is happening to her —that she is being "led" into another devotion, and that the confidences of the young journalist are really a means of drawing her to himself. The ingenuousness with which he describes his method provides part of the comic effect. Her technical purpose becomes clearer when her admirer leaves with Paraday to visit Mrs. Wimbush, his worst tormentor, at her estate, Prestidge. It becomes clear that James introduced a confidante merely to fill the gap left by Neil Paraday himself. As the great man wanes, so the role of the young lady increases. A new life of romance begins to burgeon out of another person's decline.

From Prestidge, that abode of abysmal ignorance and presumption, the aggrieved journalist confides in his friend by mail, informing her of the horrid lionizing, of the impossible posers who pretend to literary merit, and of the physical decline of their mutual idol. The last two chapters consist of these letters and a loose diary, kept for her, both rendered in direct and indirect quotation. They offer pleasant variety to the narrative method used in the rest of the story, for they suppose a reading by the sympathetic confidante. The writer's criticism becomes more acrid; his pessimism over Paraday's poor health deepens. The use of the present tense, made possible by the epistolary form, brings the whole scene closer to the reader, and the disgusting menagerie of dilettantes is scourged by the author James, who must have endured many similar inquisitions.

The distressed narrator tries to console himself by turning to his confidante:

"I can't tell you how much more and more *your* attitude to him, in the midst of all this, shines out by contrast. I never willingly talk to these people about him, but see what a comfort I find it to scribble to you! I appreciate it—it keeps me warm; there are no fires in the house" (p. 47).

The news he has to relay grows even more discouraging. The only copy of Paraday's last work has been misplaced by bungling fans. But this news is soon superseded by worse: Neil Paraday is gravely ill; Neil Paraday has died. The narrator concludes the story by indicating how his confidante is still helping him in his efforts to recover the lost manuscript; and there is a hint that by now the young people are married.

In "The Death of the Lion," James has created a role for the confidante like Cecilia's, in that the confidences bestowed do not concern the confider directly, but another person, in whom both he and his confidante are deeply interested. Also, the protagonist uses his confidante directly to the advantage of their mutual friend, and only indirectly for his own benefit; although this ulterior motive proves to be stronger. Furthermore, being a younger and inexperienced girl, Miss Hurter does not assume the initiative as Mrs. Costello or Mrs. Prest do. She is entirely pliable in the gentleman's hands. If the majority of the confidantes are married women, even the minority are predominantly mature in judgment and years. Miss Hurter seems to be the youngest of all, with Fleda Vetch as close competitor. But the latter by far exceeds the former in maturity. Yet Miss Hurter's youthful innocence is not a mark of victimhood. James plays with her, but it is the light and pleasant game of comedy; and for her, as for Henrietta Stackpole, all's well that ends well.

Like Miss Hurter, Frank Granger, the protagonist in "Flickerbridge" (1903), is an American who, stepping into an English setting, resembles a stranger in fairyland. His encounter with Miss Wenham brings him to Flickerbridge, a perfect haven of beauty, where age is charmed into timelessness and is endowed with incomparable simplicity, freshness, and beauty. Coming from the modern world of bustling activity and greedy exploitation, the young man lends himself with delight to the exquisiteness of the "still backwater—a deep and quiet pool in which objects were sharply mirrored."[3]

Occupying the center of this charmed existence is the quaint, elderly mistress of the ancient English mansion, Miss Wenham, whose almost fantastic features and dress both delight and enthuse the young man. With protruding eyes, receding chin and a nose that "carried on in conversation a queer little independent motion," she wears "on top of her head an upright circular cap that [makes] her resemble a caryatid disburdened, and on other parts of her person strange combinations of colours, stuffs, shapes, of metal, mineral and plant" (p. 111). Both shy and friendly, she rushes at topics with either "the indirectness of terror or with the violence of despair." Full of "refinements of oddity and intensities of custom," Miss Wenham is undoubtedly a comic type (p. 112). She might even take her place in a gnome-like retinue of Susan Stringham, the fairy godmother with peaked hat and buckle shoes.

For Granger, and for the reader, the novelty of this meeting makes a lasting impression. One is pleased by the inestimable value found behind personal idiosyncrasies. And the charm of Miss Wenham's merging with a sacred past of "holy calm" fills the young man with delicious peace. Inevitably, a confidential friendship ensues. In length of duration it is very limited; but the intensity of the man's devotion makes it rank among the outstanding friendships described by James. Here the author concentrates his sense of the past, his moral sense, and his sense of beauty—all of which have achieved the fullness of his literary achievement—into a few pages. Granger is an artist—more perhaps in appreciation than in actual productivity—and his soul vibrates in response to the perfection before him: " 'You're *all* type,' " he tells his wistful hostess, " 'It has taken long, delicious years of security and monotony to produce you' " (p. 115). The precious, mellow beauty of herself and her environment would crumble, he feels, at the least touch from the outside world.

Unwittingly, Miss Wenham symbolizes the past. Quintessentially united with it, her little personal insecurity and timidity form a humorous contrast to the time-softened frame around her. Mystified by the adulation of the young aesthete, she can only wonder at his fear of breaking her exquisite spellbound slumber in the past. Much as he confides his appreciation of her picturesqueness, as well as his own personal problems, she never quite grasps his meaning. Still less can she conceive of the hectic, chattering world that pollutes as it raves about newly-discovered rarities. An affinity of puzzlement unites Miss Wenham to Miss Tina Bordereau, as a similarity of seclusion segregates them from the world. In Miss Wenham's simplicity Granger finds added cause for joy. It is "so wonderful that *she* should be so simple and yet so little of a bore" (p. 116). Their relationship consists of their moving together in the "silver haze" of an April *aquarelle*, "with all communication blurred" (p. 116).

One of the most remarkable things about this little tale is its distinctive type of confidante-"center" relation. A communion there is, certainly, but it is a union without intellection. It is wholly a contemplative movement which attracts these two people. Granger observes and worships the beauty before him. Miss Wenham sees and marvels at the "delightfully droll" young man. In womanly fashion, she stresses his convalescent need for leisure, never once following him in his deeper experience of aesthetic luxury.

Imbibing with keenest relish the bliss of his experience, Granger resolves on keeping it solely for himself. No alien eyes are to intrude; no curious questioner is to rob him of his exquisite possession. Miss Wenham is not to allow the young lady, his supposed fiancée, and her relation, to visit them. Being one of the crude modern minds, she would inevitably ruin Miss Wenham by publicizing her. In this unique way, James introduces the inevitable selfishness of the male confider. Miss Wenham, confidante, symbol of ancient beauty and style, and unconscious source of endless, esoteric pleasure, is to be kept as the treasure for himself. "That was the art of life—what the real artist would consistently do. He would close the door on his impression, treat it as a private museum," a private source of inspiration, and a secret refuge to paint "in a key he had never thought of before" (p. 117). The confidante has turned into the supreme fount of inspiration, more so by her simple, unaware existence than by her serviceable ministrations. "Flickerbridge" is consequently a distinctive variation on the old theme. Its uniqueness includes the mellow shades and warm, hazy glow which pervade and irradiate *The Ambassadors,* to which time so closely linked its composition.[4]

Writing of "Flickerbridge" in his Preface to the New York Edition, James calls it a "highly-finished little anecdote," and its perfection is already latent in the first conception recorded in the *Notebooks.* With all his mature skill James achieved in this narrative the perfection equal to a perfect experience. So closely can the reader identify himself with the fatigued and harassed young man of the world, that the revelation of the serenity of Flickerbridge and the refined singularity of its mistress can only soothe and delight. And one cannot blame the young man for determining to preserve his friend for his own private delectation, since her exposure would only mean her dissipation among the gaping, vulgar crowd.[5] The story's ending in Granger's flight before the inevitable is in itself an artistic touch, preserving unsullied the fine pleasure of his—and our—delight. To introduce the chattering journalistic Addie would have disrupted the story's essential perfection before one's very eyes.

The confidante has perfectly served her confider with the fruits of "the lonely little decencies and modest dignities of her life, the fine grain of its conservatism, the innocence of its ignorance, all its monotony of stupidity and salubrity, its cold dulness and dim brightness . . ." (p. 116). She is indeed set aside, not only from the train of the later Jamesian confidantes, those battered women of the world, or conscious aesthetes, who predominate in the novels; she is also separated from the victimized confidantes of the later short stories. As a matter of fact, her present immunity is part of Miss Wenham's charm. It would seem that in her the author was paying a tribute to the serenity and perfection of idealized old age, glimmers of which the author's eye could distinguish even in worldly women, but still more so in the priceless works of art and rural scenes noted and loved by him for many years. What especially stands out besides her eccentricities is the attraction of Miss Wenham's moral beauty—her sweetness, her modesty, her amenity; and what the author visibly most delights in is the singular combination he has created of human character with appropriate setting. Frank Granger is the rare Jamesian confider who finds his fulfillment in contemplating his friend without exploiting her. Rather, his sole aim is to leave undesecrated the sublime tranquillity of her little life. By way of contrast, Strether at last finds Maria Gostrey insufficient, and Prince Amerigo callously debases Fanny Assingham. But Granger's sensibilities are so refined that he is not even tempted to improve on the object of his admiration. Through Granger, James let himself go in unrestrained and generous contemplation of a woman blended with artistic and natural beauty: "Her opinions were like dried roseleaves; her attitudes like British sculpture; her voice was what he imagined of the possible tone of the old gilded, silver-strained harp in one of the corners of the drawing-room" (p. 116). Quite unconsciously, the elderly lady renders her friend the greatest service:

she deepens his insight into beauty. James's admiration for his little masterpiece doubtless includes an appreciation for this rare example of friendly giving.

Mrs. Alsager, Miss Hurter, and Miss Wenham complement each other in offering their confiders joy and tranquillity. The two older women add the sublime gift of artistic inspiration and deeper penetration of beauty. Their relation with their young men is spiritualized and rarefied through their own maturity and selflessness. They represent James's ideal of woman and art. Miss Hurter, on the other hand, is a concession to popular taste. Young, pretty, naïve, and successful in capturing the hero, she still sports a few Jamesian touches in her heroic (and exaggerated) self-denial regarding Paraday. A certain passivity characterizes all three women; their wealth lies chiefly in the fullness of their being.

> 2. *The Ghostly Tales:*
>
> > *"The Turn of the Screw," "The Altar of the Dead," "The Beast in the Jungle," and "The Jolly Corner"*

The technical importance of Miss Wenham's role is indicative of the trend followed by the other confidantes in the later stories. The ghostly tales of this period utilize the confidante as sole listener to the fullest. Mrs. Grose, the least prominent of all, has a big role as the only friend of the protagonist. More important, the lady in "The Altar of the Dead" is the only other character present, and like Miss Tina turns out to be the antagonist. Finally, the confidantes in the last two stories function as the "second consciousness," and represent the acme of the minor confidante's dramatic value.

Another feature common to these four ghostly tales is the atmosphere of tragic loss. It distinguishes the role of the confidante from her part in the other stories of the later period. Instead of artistic inspiration, death and frustrated love are the salient features. There is no happiness in the confidante-"center" relation, and gloom envelops the setting. On the other hand, the friendships in the last two stories are enriched by the spiritual understanding of the confidantes.

The importance of Mrs. Grose's role in "The Turn of the Screw" (1898) is determined by her being the only listener available, and is enhanced by her motherly sympathy, which encourages the governess's confidences. The scenes with the governess and herself occur at fairly regular intervals between passages of narration, which recaptiulate the governess's ruminations and encounters with the ghosts. As there are only a few brief scenes with the governess and the children, Mrs. Grose provides the chief means for dramatization.

Furthermore, her character presents the stolidity of the English serving class as a foil to the governess's acute sensibility. The governess herself discovers with satisfaction the absence in the housekeeper of imagination: " . . . she was a magnificent monument to the blessing of a want of imagination. . . ."[6] In the course of their relation, consequently, the governess comes to lean more and more on her confidante, and without her substantial support one feels that the young woman would have collapsed. But as this support is seen to be qualified by a latent opposition to the governess, the housekeeper reflects the conflicts and ambiguity of the whole nouvelle, which still attracts critical controversy. As it happens, little of that commentary has dealt with Mrs. Grose as confidante. The most attention she has received is from the psychological critics, who endeavor to prove the abnormality of the governess. In doing this, they refer to the housekeeper as the "victim of a palpable deception."[7] The best description of the housekeeper was written by Harold C. Goddard, before the trend in psychological criticism began:

. . . Mrs. Grose's character is shaped to fit the plot. If she is the incarnation of practical household sense and homely affection, she is utterly devoid of worldly experience and imagination. And she is as superstitious as such a person is likely to be. She can neither read nor write, the latter fact, which is a capital one, being especially insisted on. She knows her place and has a correspondingly exalted opinion of persons of higher rank or education. Hence her willingness, even when she cannot understand, to accept as truth whatever the governess tells her. She loves the children deeply and has suffered terribly for them during the reign of Quint and Miss Jessel. (Her relief on the arrival of Miss Jessel's successor, which the latter notices and misinterprets, is natural.) Here is a character, then, and a situation, ideally fitted to allow of the development of the governess' mania unnoticed.[8]

Taking for a moment Goddard's character analysis of the housekeeper, one notices at once the qualities found in other confidantes: the knowledge of her place and the devotedness to her charge. Her ignorance and admiration for those above her parallels Mrs. Wix's; and her simplicity resembles Miss Hurter's. At first glance, she is a truly perfect type to accept whatever a social superior tells her. On the other hand, her dependence does not prove the governess to be a deceiver or a maniac.

Besides, under James's pen even the simple souls are endowed with a depth of their own. Like Bob Assingham, Mrs. Grose may lack the accomplishments of a person of the world, but a natural fondness for the children, and a fear of getting embroiled make her rather hesitant in agreeing with the governess. Mrs. Grose is simple-minded, but stubborn; and one of her confider's terrors is that she might disbelieve her. At times the latter must reassure herself: "She believed me, I was sure, absolutely: if she hadn't I don't know what would have become of me, for I couldn't have borne the business alone" (p. 49). In this reliance on the housekeeper's concurrence, the governess is at pains to stress the emotional balance of her confidante, while sometimes doubting her own. They do agree on the necessity of keeping their heads, and the housekeeper finally concurs with the governess "as to its being beyond doubt that [she] had seen exactly what [she] had seen" (p. 37). Gradually Mrs. Grose produces information from the past that corroborates the surmises of her confider, except on one point—the moral corruption of the children. For the resistance which she offers to her confider arises from an instinctual desire to shield the children.

From the very beginning, every hint made by the governess against the character of the children is stubbornly countered by the housekeeper. The mere suggestion that Miles corrupted his schoolmates is rejected by her with a scornful, "odd laugh," and the question whether the governess fears he will corrupt her. Quint was blameworthy, yes, and so was Miss Jessel; but it was not the children's fault that they were so closely attached to the wicked pair: " 'Oh, it wasn't *him* [Miles]!' Mrs. Grose with emphasis declared. 'It was Quint's own fancy. To play with him, I mean—to spoil him' " (pp. 29-30). On several subsequent occasions the housekeeper vigorously defends the children, especially in Chapters VII and VIII.

As the tension mounts, and the governess's suspicion of immoral dealings between the dead servants and the children becomes clearer, Mrs. Grose turns a deaf ear to any such imputations. Her motives seem to arise from a sincere belief in the children; but they may be mixed with an ignorance or a dread of such horrible things. Fear plays a prominent part too, and she acknowledges it frankly when the governess accuses her of not stopping Quint's assumption of power at Bly. She has always tried to be neutral, and even now she attempts to gloss things over, and believe the best rather than the worst of the situation. Finally, when it becomes almost unbearable, she recommends sending for the uncle. But this throws the governess into such a panic that she threatens her confidante: " 'If you should so lose your head as to appeal to him for me—' She was really frightened. 'Yes, Miss?' 'I would leave, on the spot, both him and you' " (pp. 54-55). There is a latent hostility in this exchange, which flares up plainly in the showdown by the lake. After accusing Flora of seeing Miss Jessel, the governess suddenly realizes that she has

Mrs. Grose also, and very formidably, to reckon with. My elder companion, the next moment, at any rate, blotted out everything but her own flushed face and her loud shocked protest, a burst of high disapproval. "What a dreadful turn, to be sure, Miss! Where on earth do you see anything?" (p. 77).

Mrs. Grose's shock is justified by the previous agreement made with the governess never to mention the horrid names to the children. But the housekeeper is too much of an opportunist to show disapproval consistently. The next moment she is trying vainly to see the apparition also, and her "deep groan of negation, repulsion, compassion . . . [gives] a sense, touching to me even then, that she would have backed me up if she could" (p. 77).

This consolation is very brief, for Mrs. Grose enters "immediately and violently" into Flora's mood, seeking to quiet the child's outburst by denying the presence of the apparition. If there is any consistency in her subsequent attitude, it seems to favor Flora. The next morning she tells the governess of her inability to push Flora on the subject of the apparitions, and she reiterates the child's denials of having seen anything. The governess senses an alliance between Mrs. Grose and Flora against herself, and acts toward the eight-year-old as if she were an adult rival. Her fear of the child's influence on her brother against herself is even greater. Therefore, Mrs. Grose must be hustled away with the child at once. But Mrs. Grose is reluctant to go and leave Miles behind. The only thing that makes her go is the corruption she has heard in Flora's speech. In her anguish and dismay she challenges the governess's " 'Oh, thank God!',", agreeing bitterly that the child's profanity does justify the governess's position (p. 83). In this issue their opposition is quite clear. Mrs. Grose grieves over the child's language, whereas the governess triumphs at having found in it a concrete proof of her suspicions.

The thing that forces Mrs. Grose's capitulation more than

anything is Flora's unlady-like language: " 'It's beyond every-thing, for a young lady; and I can't think wherever she must have picked up—' " (p. 83). When the governess presses her, she finally concedes that Quint and Miss Jessel have corrupted the children: " 'I believe' " (p. 83). As a woman of the people she has never doubted the presence of revenants; but their presence alone does not suffice to shake her faith in the children's innocence. The evidence of debased class conduct is what overwhelms her trust in them. For as an English servant she clings to manners, the external elements that make for security within the social system. When these are disturbed the universe of Mrs. Grose crashes. And so, in her struggle, she believes and trusts the governess, at first through compassion, and later, on the evidence of her own offended sense of propriety. It extends to Miles as well: " 'I make out now what he must have done at school.' And she gave, in her simple sharpness, an almost droll disillusioned nod. 'He stole!' " (p. 84). The drop felt by the governess at this statement is ironical. All her accusations have fallen flat on the ears of this simple-minded woman. " 'He stole letters!' " she reiterates, trying to make an impression with her keenness (p. 84). It would certainly be an offense for a little gentleman to steal letters; and Mrs. Grose is satisfied with that, for she completely ignores the allusions to concealed vices. In any case, a confession from Miles, to which the governess looks forward, seems irrelevant to the housekeeper. " 'I'll save you without him!' " she calls in farewell (p. 84). Is this a hint to the governess to leave the boy alone?

If Mrs. Grose's attitude is at times inconsistent, it is due to her simplicity and cowardice, which boggle before the complexity of the affair. All through the nouvelle she hesitates and temporizes, hoping no doubt for some solution to turn up. Torn between pity for the governess and devotion to the children, she tries to compromise between them. But her efforts prove ineffective. All she has done is to listen to the young woman, who had made her a receptacle of lurid things, but there was an odd recognition of my superiority—my accomplishments and my function—in her patience under my pain. She offered her mind to my disclosures as, had I wished to mix a witch's broth and proposed it with assurance, she would have held out a large clean saucepan (p. 50).

In truth, the governess has offered such a broth to her confidante's attention; but her tranquillity is scarcely disturbed. That class consciousness which bids her respect and support the governess also makes her love the children and interpret their actions in her own limited way.

But for James, the opacity of Mrs. Grose's perceptions is functional in safeguarding ambiguity. His aim, as stated in the Preface to "The Aspern Papers," was to make "the situation . . . reek with the air of Evil."[9] He saw his task to give the sense "Of their being, the haunting pair, capable, as the phrase is, of everything—that is of exerting, in respect to the children, the very worst action small victims so conditioned might be conceived as subject to."[10] Consequently, Mrs. Grose is made to close her eyes to what may have gone on, and to have centered her objections mainly on Quint's stepping out of his class and ruling the house. Mrs. Grose is best considered as a peculiar phenomenon among the confidantes. On one hand, her technical role is absolutely essential to the dramatization of the nouvelle; but on the other, her character, being so limited by the exigencies of this role, leaves much to be desired. In composing the other three ghostly tales, James directed his attention to other problems in portraying the characters of the confidantes. The biggest problem that interested him was turning the confidante into a "second consciousness," and this he achieved in the last two stories.

The nameless lady in "The Altar of the Dead" (1895) who earns her living writing stories for inconsequential magazines, and who comes to share George Stransom's altar of the Dead in her own devotions, gradually assumes the role of confidante in his lonely life. At first, seeing her at his shrine, he is drawn in sympathy to her, hoping

that he had given her almost the contentment he had given himself. They worshipped side by side so often that there were moments when he wished he might be sure, so straight did their prospect stretch away of growing old together in their rites. She was younger than he, but she looked as if her Dead were at least as numerous as his candles. She had no color, no sound, no fault, and another of the things about which he had made up his mind was that she had no fortune.[11]

The fertile imagination of the typical Jamesian observer does not fail Stransom in divining much of this lady's background. But their acquaintance makes little headway until one day she informs him about her manner of living with an old aunt, and he observes that

She was not . . . in her first youth, and her vanished freshness had left something behind which, for Stransom, represented the proof that it had been tragically sacrificed. Whatever she gave him the assurance of she gave without references. She might in fact have been a divorced duchess, and she might have been an old maid who taught the harp (p. 208).

As time wears on, and they form the habit of leaving the church together, his confidences become intimate: ". . . there was never a word he had said to her that she had not beautifully understood. For long ages he never knew her name, any more than she had ever pronounced his own; but it was not their names that mattered, it was only their perfect practice and their common need" (p. 209). The peculiarity of this attachment has something of the ghostly character about it. Both friends are indeed so peculiar that they admit not caring for each other as people do in ordinary friendships. "Over this idea they grew quite intimate; they rallied to it in a way that marked a fresh start in their confidence" (p. 209). Their union lies in their devotion to their respective Dead; but so sacred do they hold them, that no names are ever mentioned. On this little detail the whole story hinges; for in the revelation of her Dead lies the shattering of his confidence.

In the meantime, however, they grow "old together in their piety. She was a feature of that piety, but even at the ripe stage of acquaintance in which they occasionally arranged to meet at a concert, or to go together to an exhibition, she was not a feature of anything else. The most that happened was that his worship became paramount" (p. 211). His greatest interest is not in her, but in himself. The shrine, he tells her, will not be full until the largest candle of all—his candle—will be lighted there, and his great consolation is to see her as "the priestess of his altar, and whenever he quitted England he committed it to her keeping. She proved to him afresh that women have more of the spirit of religion than men; he felt his fidelity pale and faint in comparison with hers" (p. 212). She is to guard the temple after his death, and administer the fund he will leave for that purpose. She may even light a taper for him, but to her serious question of who will light one for her there is no reply.

In the stories and novels from the 1890's on there is a marked rise in the degree of selfishness in James's confiders. The demands made upon this unnamed woman usher in the period of exploitation, of which Fleda Vetch, May Bartram, Maria Gostrey, Fanny Assingham, and Alice Staverton are the outstanding examples. When these confidantes make a request of their friends, they are quietly undeceived, or brutally ignored. The confidante in "The Altar of the Dead" guards her secret so well, that it takes Stransom "months and months to learn her name, years and years to learn her address" (p. 214). Not until her aunt's death does she permit him to enter her modest home, and discloses to him her shrine of devotion and the identity of her beloved Dead. It is Acton Hague, the man who wronged Stransom many years before.

The scene which follows—the only one in this story—provides the occasion for the mutual exchange of confidences. Her great secret, her love for Acton Hague and the enormity of his abuse, are revealed to Stransom. The nature of the abuse, however, she declines to reveal. On her probing, Stransom has to admit that although he has forgiven the man his injury, there is no candle for him on the altar.

"Ah, it's not true—you've *not* forgiven him!" she wailed, with a passion that startled him.

He looked at her a moment. "What was it he did to you?"

"Everything!" Then abruptly she put out her hand in farewell. "Good-by."

He turned as cold as he had turned that night he read of the death of Acton Hague. "You mean that we meet no more?"

"Not as we have met—not *there!*"

He stood aghast at this snap of their great bond, at the renouncement that rang out in the word she so passionately emphasized (p. 221).

In spite of his efforts to hold her, the spell is broken. He cannot make himself put up a candle for his enemy, and so his dismissal is final. The sense of loss seizes him like the chill of an ague. For him, it is the distant approach of the coldness of death. "He had ruthlessly abandoned her—that, of course, was what he had done" (p. 224). Alone, "fitting the unmatched pieces gradually together," he realizes how the coincidence had never before come to light: ". . . it was natural enough that of his previous life she should have ascertained only what he had judged good to communicate. There were passages it was quite conceivable that even in moments of the tenderest expansion, he should have withheld" (p. 225). Stransom is shaken by the contemplation of the wrong suffered by this lady. "A woman, when she was wronged, was always more wronged than a man, and there were conditions when the least she could have got off with was more than the most he could have to endure" (p. 226). Still, it is not enough to pity her; he must comply with her request if their friendship is to be resumed.

It was not in anger she had forsaken him; it was in simple submission to hard reality, to crude destiny. . . . She tried to make him forget how much they were estranged; but in the very presence of what they had given up it was impossible not to be sorry for her. He had taken from her so much more than she had taken from him (p. 228).

What strikes him most is that the woman with whom he has shared his dearest experience was shaped by the treatment of his enemy. "Moulded indeed she had been by powerful hands, to have converted her injury into an exaltation so sublime" (p. 226). And her injury—whatever it was—becomes another excuse for his not consenting to give him a taper.

The spiritual alienation from his confidante, in spite of his feeble attempts at communication, proves to be a greater privation than he can bear. It has two aspects: "the privation he inflicted," and "the privation he bore." For she never comes near his altar any more; while the refrain haunts his declining hours, "Just one more," and he struggles with the despair that no one will keep his altar after his own death.

Finally, moved by compunction to grant his confidante the joy he has been withholding from her, he makes a last effort to see her and tell her that one more candle will be lighted. Meeting her in the church again, where she has returned out of compassion for him, he expresses his change of mind. But seeing him so ill, ironically she misunderstands him, thinking the "one more" is to be for himself.

In spite of the morbidity of this story, the basic features of the confidante-"center" relation are recognizable: the dependence of the confider and the attempted exploitation of the confidante. Stransom fails in this attempt, only because someone else had preceded him into her sanctuary. She does succeed in leading him, however, in a way similar to that of her sister-confidantes: she leads Stransom to a deeper insight into himself, and to the recognition that the wrong he inflicts on her is not different in its motivation from the deed perpetrated by Acton Hague.

Like the next two stories, "The Altar of the Dead" deals almost exclusively with the inner life of man. That inner life is externalized somewhat through Stransom's contacts with the lady, whose minor role achieves major proportions. She is the only means employed by James to dramatize this tale, and in resisting Stransom she acts as an effective antagonist. Stransom is the only confider humiliated by a confidante who loves his enemy.

Several years later the author entertained similar ideas for a new story and recorded them in his *Notebooks*. May Bartram, the confidante in "The Beast in the Jungle" (1903), is the subject of these notes:

She has always loved him—yes, *that,* for the story, 'pretty,' and he, saving, protecting, exempting his life . . . has never known it. He likes her, talks to her, confides in her, sees her often—*la côtoie,* as to her hidden passion, but never guesses. She meanwhile, all the time sees his life as it is. It is to her that he tells his fear—yes, she is the '2d consciousness.' At first she *feels,* herself, for him, his feeling of his fear, and is tender, reassuring, protective. Then she reads, as I say, his real case, and is, though unexpressedly, *lucid.* The years go by and *she sees the thing not happen.* At last one day they are somehow, some day, face to face over it, and then she speaks. 'It *has,* the great thing you've always lived in dread of, had the foreboding of— it *has* happened to you.'[12]

Written just a year after the *Project* for *The Ambassadors,* this discussion of the confidante in "The Beast in the Jungle" has further similarities to the detailed outline of Maria Gostrey's role in the *Project.* The hidden love of the confidante for her friend and the sympathy with his fate, are constant in both May Bartram and Maria. The recognition on the part of the men is also similar; only the intensity of Marcher's discovery proves tragic, while Strether's quiet rejection of Maria's offer is only pathetic. "The Beast," however, is unique for the treatment of the confidante, for the whole story revolves on her relation with her friend. There are no other characters or interests. Nor is the object of their mutual concern concretized as in the children and the ghosts in "The Turn of the Screw." Like the nameless lady in "The Altar of the Dead," May Bartram is in fact the only source of interest in the story.

Marcher's reunion with May after a ten-year interval stirs in both a "feeling of an occasion missed."[13] The significant thing is that she remembers more than he does; most important of all, she recalls to his memory the great confidence he had made to her so long ago: " 'Has it ever happened?' " (p. 144). He is shocked at learning that he has imparted his deep secret; for at that time they were scarcely intimate.

". . . I had strangely enough lost the consciousness of having taken you so far into my confidence."
     "Is it because you've taken so many others as well?"
     "I've taken nobody. Not a creature since then."
     "So that I'm the only person who knows?"
     "The only person in the world."
     "Well," she quickly replied, "I myself have never spoken" (p. 144).

This bit of dialogue exposes the detail upon which the subsequent experiences of Marcher and May depend: she has guarded his secret all these years, but he has forgotten even confiding it to her, so slight was the impression she made. May is the receptive type of woman. She exemplifies a sublimation of woman as the vessel, a distinctive feature worshipped by the ancients. But Marcher is no ancient; he is instead a rather decadent modern, with no understanding for the sublime passivity of the woman in his life, because he is preoccupied with the possibility of profiting "perhaps exquisitely" by having confided in her. Marcher is blinded by egotism, although remorse of conscience does grip him occasionally. During their first interview he experiences a momentary pang:

To tell her what he had told her—what had it been but to ask something of her? something that she had given, in her charity, without his having, by remembrance, by a return of the spirit, failing another encounter, so much as thanked her. . . . So he had endless gratitude to make up (p. 145).

James disguises the following exposition with a natural desire of Marcher to know "just how he had figured to her." And so he asks her to recount the secret as it had been confided to her. She explains: " 'You said you had had from your earliest time, as the deepest thing within you, the sense of being kept for something rare and strange, possibly prodigious and terrible, that was sooner or later to happen to you . . .' " (p. 145).

Besides functioning in this way to recall the past, May Bartram is used—like Maria Gostrey—to analyze her friend and to prognosticate for him. She ascertains clearly that " 'Whatever it's to be . . . it hasn't yet come' " (p. 145). And he admits this, being now completely surrendered to her. What he most appreciates is that she takes him seriously. This is, of course, what all the confiders want, especially so, the closer they approach to mental aberration. Once certain of her seriousness, Marcher unfolds the nature of his apprehension to her, and his presumption that she, as spectator, is to be present when it happens. He appeals to her to watch with him, and again like Maria Gostrey, she pledges her companionship: " 'I'll watch with you' " (p. 147).

The pattern of this first chapter, consisting of part "picture" and part "scene," is followed in the following chapters, except the last, which consists of "picture" only. The balance maintained between "picture" and "scene" is more even than in "The Jolly Corner," because the confidante is more at the author's disposal. Marcher, the center of consciousness, relies on Miss Bartram, first for the recall of his past, second for the occupation of his present, and finally for the apprehension of his future. To all three functions she lends herself with equal grace. And Marcher keeps reminding himself that he must not impose on her, must not "see her as a mere confidant," but must be "careful to remember that she had, after all, also a life of her own, with things that might happen to *her* . . ." (p. 149). On the surface, these reflections seem admirably unselfish; but in reality they conceal deepest egotism. He is so concerned with letting her live her life, that the idea of marriage is categorically rejected: "His conviction, his apprehension, his obsession, in short, was not a condition he could invite a woman to share . . ." (p. 150). When she had suggested love as possibly *the* great event itself, he had promptly rejected the idea, as being inferior to his fate. He is too blind to see that her devotion over the years of separation was love indeed, and that she is eminently equipped and anxious to accompany him on his "tiger-hunt."

For her part, she encourages him in his search, assuring him that he is reserved for some "climax to so special a suspense" (p. 151). Also, she adapts her life more and more to his, occupying herself mainly with "watching" him. The pathetic irony of the story lies in Marcher's periodic qualms of conscience which occasion their discussions of whether her life is not slipping unprofitably away. In truth, that is taking place before his very eyes. She is waiting for him to recognize her love and return it; but she waits in vain. Gradually, her hints become broader; she refers to "the form and the way" in his case as they "were to have been," and to his courage, that he was to have shown her. After years of watching with, and listening to, this confirmed egotist, and of letting him wear her carpets bare with his perpetual pacing, she now feels his chance of recognizing love has passed. His watch is not at an end, she tells him. He guesses at last that she is withholding something from him—she knows his fate, and is afraid he will find out. To which she replies inscrutably, " 'You'll never find out' " (p. 156). He will never be able to come out of himself to recognize what he has missed.

The irony becomes more stinging for poor May Bartram when he questions her about their relation:

If he had practically escaped remark, as she pretended, by doing, in the most important particular, what most men do—find the answer to life in patching up an alliance of a sort with a woman no better than himself—how had she escaped it, and how could the alliance, such as it was, since they must suppose it had been more or less noticed, have failed to make her rather positively talked about? (p. 157).

The alliance, she assures him, makes her quite right: " 'It's all that concerns me—to help you to pass for a man like another' " (p. 157). In one of his "unselfish" moods, he responds handsomely, " 'How kind, how beautiful, you are to me! How shall I ever repay you?' " Her only answer is: " 'By going on as you are' " (p. 157). It is the closest he comes to finding out "the real truth" before he loses her in death. A dread of this impending catastrophe presents itself to him; yet he persists in thinking that it "yet wouldn't at all be *the* catastrophe" (p. 158). The thought of her dying before seeing his own fate consummated is intolerable to him; he supposes it must be so to her: "She had been living to see what would *be* to be seen, and it would be cruel to her to have to give up before the accomplishment of the vision" (p. 159). His sympathy for her impending loss, which scarcely approaches the grief he ought to have over her frustrated life, deepens the pathetic irony in Chapter III. Marcher's egotism is worse than Stransom's because of its blindness. Stransom at least knows what he ought to do to oblige his confidante; but Marcher's eyes are sealed until it is too late.

The second-last scene shows her as definitely separated from him, communicating with him "as across some gulf." In vain Marcher tries to force the revelation of her knowledge of his fate: " 'You know something I don't' " (p. 163). She cannot deny it, but it has not yet happened, it is only her idea. Still, if she doesn't communicate it, he insists, she is abandoning him.

"No, no!" she repeated. "I'm with you—don't you see?—still."
And as if to make it more vivid to him she rose from her chair—a

movement she seldom made in these days—and showed herself, all draped and all soft, in her fairness and slimness. "I haven't forsaken you" (p. 164).

It is her declaration of love, but again it falls on deaf ears; he can take her only "as capable still of helping him. It was as if, at the same time, her light might at any instant go out; wherefore he must make the most of it" (p. 164). Then, as if to emphasize the gift she is offering to him:

"It's never too late." . . . she stood nearer to him, close to him, a minute, as if still full of the unspoken. . . . It had become suddenly, from her movement and attitude, beautiful and vivid to him that she had something more to give him; her wasted face delicately shone with it—it glittered, almost as with the white lustre of silver, in her expression (pp. 165–166).

He only gapes in expectancy of the thing she might reveal. And his still so missing the point proves to be the thing they so long have expected. In the last scene she tells him: " 'You've nothing to wait for more. It *has* come.' " The sphinx, the sibyl has spoken: " '. . . your not being aware of it is the strangeness *in* the strangeness. It's the wonder *of* the wonder' " (p. 168). Marcher, and probably the reader with him, is baffled. Her final words are an injunction to him not to suffer. To that end she has borne her privation in silence. With one last effort she assures him that she would still live for him if she could.

The questions placed by James in Marcher's mouth are designed to produce just a little information at a time of May Bartram's feelings, and to enable her to skirt revealing "the real truth." All the clues to her love are made noticeable, one by one, and fall into place at the moment of Marcher's enlightenment at her grave. But on the surface, their communication seems to move through the intangibles of later Jamesian dialogue: the hints and allusions and dim perceptions from which only his characters are capable of extracting knowledge. Once the confidante is gone, all except private communing ceases for Marcher, and James hastens the conclusion. The last chapter is devoted only to the "picture" of his terrible discovery. His punishment is that, of all the Jamesian confiders, John Marcher misses his confidante the most.

Alice Staverton, the confidante in "The Jolly Corner" (1909), resembles May Bartram on a smaller scale. She shows the same sympathy with the protagonist, enters into his ideas with the same eagerness, and sees more deeply than he does. She too is exploited and unappreciated for her deepest devotion, until almost the end. Both women, although much in love, are pointedly shown as realists; whereas it is the men who dodge reality.

But Alice Staverton differs from May Bartram in the degree of pathos touched in her life. She is the onlooker, not at the unwitting frustration of her own love, but at another, equally unrewarding search—the efforts of a man to capture a glimpse of himself as he might have been. Like Miss Bartram, Miss Staverton complies with the desire of her confider that she should assist by lending her ear. Alice also differs in possessing an imagination of which her mild irony is born, and which is bold enough to have created an ideal for Spencer Brydon. This ideal she suggests to him: if he had stayed in New York he might have done great things in real estate. It is also mainly due to her suggestion that his years in Europe have accumulated "presences of the other age. . . ."[14] Her imagination further helps her to guess, "with a divination," that he prowls at night in his empty old home. "She listened to everything. She was a woman who answered intimately but who utterly didn't chatter. She scattered abroad therefore no cloud of words; she could assent, she could agree, above all she could encourage, without doing that" (p. 552). She touches lightly on the subject of a ghost of the past haunting his house. She has guessed his secret, but he pulls up before it and the subject is temporarily dropped.

In their next recorded conversation he confides to her that all things for him return to the question of what he personally might have been, how he might have led his life and 'turned out,' if he had not so, at the outset, given it up. And confessing for the first time to the intensity within him of this absurd speculation—which but proved also, no doubt, the habit of too selfishly thinking—he affirmed the impotence there of any other source of interest, any other native appeal (p. 554).

In this scene, Brydon, like the typical Jamesian confider, paces up and down before his confidante seated at her fireside. Uneasily he asks if she thinks his notion "a trifle." " 'I don't say it's a trifle,' Miss Staverton gravely interrupted" (p. 554). Like all the other confiders, Brydon is anxious not to be ridiculed, but to be understood. But she assures him of her acceptance of his idea and her belief in the outcome. With the penetration of the second consciousness she has shared his idea even before it was uttered.

"What you feel—and what I feel *for* you—is that you'd have had power."
  "You'd have liked me that way?" he asked.
  She hardly hung fire. "How should I not have liked you?" (p. 556).

Her faith would have accepted him if he had turned out differently—a billionaire immersed in the combats and vulgarities of amassing money, for instance—if he had remained those thirty-three years in New York. The woman's love penetrates surfaces; and in this penetration she sees his selfishness: " '. . . you don't care for anything but yourself' " (p. 557). He assents, yet qualifies. The man he would have been is a totally different person. " 'But I do want to see him,' he added. . . . 'And I shall' " (p. 557). To this she merely adds that she has already seen this other man in a dream, but she evades telling him what the fellow is like.
  These introductory conversations fill Chapter I. They are followed by the "picture" of Brydon haunting his house and

meeting the specter of his *alter ego* in Chapter II. Chapter III concludes the tale with another conversation between Miss Staverton and her confider. Alarmed by another dream, she has rushed to his empty house and found him unconscious on the floor. The sympathy of their minds makes her know intuitively what he knows from experience. Seeing his revulsion at the horrible sight, she tries to console him—no indeed, the creature he saw is not himself. But her final revelation repels Brydon. She could have liked this monstrous man: " '. . . to me . . . he was no horror. I had accepted him' " (p. 583). She had pitied the vision in his ravaged state. Why not, for if Brydon had remained in New York and turned out like that, he still might have given her the chance to marry him, which this way she has lost. Alice does not express this thought, but it might well be in her mind, when she defends the *alter ego*.

In spite of its brevity, "The Jolly Corner" is remarkable for the details of the confidante-"center" relation which it contains. Written several years after the last great novels with their fine portraits of the confidante, it is an example of the miniature artist at work. Alice Staverton has all of the prominent features of her role: she functions technically as a means of exposition and dramatization; as a character she is sympathetic to, and understanding of, the conflicts of her confider; her role is cast as the second consciousness, whose place it is to supplement the insights gained by the "center." In order to fill this role, her own intelligence is keen and her imagination vivid.

Above all, Alice Staverton ranks with those confidantes whose moral excellence distinguishes them in a gallery of exceptional women. As in the case of Mrs. Alsager and May Bartram, Alice's selflessness conceals a deep love for her confider. Together with Fleda Vetch, Maria Gostrey and Susan Stringham, these minor confidantes embody the ideals of friendship which James conceived in the later, and richest period of his creative work.

3. The Last Representatives:
"Crapy Cornelia" and The Outcry

"Crapy Cornelia" (1910) in large measure repeats the theme of earlier stories: the male protagonist and center of consciousness, White-Mason, cultured, meditative, almost effete, is balancing on the brink of an experience where a confidante joins him. They discuss the issue and reminisce together. But the marks of age are upon the hero's character as well as in the style of the "late James." White-Mason is more diffident than Christopher Newman, more egotistical than John Marcher. Less capable than any of the others, he covers up his failures with specious reasoning.

The undertaking which he faces is a marriage proposal to an extremely eligible young widow, Mrs. Worthingham. In Prufrockian fashion White-Mason reasons that his three previous rejections by other women were really blessings: it had been quite right "to have put himself forward always, by the happiest instinct, only in impossible conditions. He had the happy consciousness of having exposed the important question to the crucial test, and of having escaped, by that persistent logic, a grave mistake."[15] Feeling certain that he is much improved, both in fortune and in character, he proceeds toward the peculiar situation of making "the all-interesting inquiry" once again.

Ridiculous as this donnée appears, James's intention is serious. His protagonist retires from putting the question, and finally congratulates himself for having done so. Mrs. Worthingham is, after all, only a specimen of the new and vulgar opulence of New York, to which White-Mason, like Spencer Brydon, can never reconcile himself.

But the immediate cause of his remarkable change of mind is another woman, "a small black insignificant [and] oppressive stranger" (p. 192), a "mangy lion"—whom the widow has planted apparently with conscious intent as an obstacle in his

path. The ensuing recognition leads to a private interview between White-Mason and the shabby, crapy Cornelia Rasch. And
from there on, Mrs. Worthingham drops from view, and the
confidante, restored to White-Mason after many years, takes
over.

Crapy Cornelia is James's last version of a confidante who
understands yet is superior to her environment. Her very dress
and her few choice bits of art are diametrically opposed to the
values represented by Mrs. Worthingham. White-Mason and
Cornelia review their past since the early years of their friendship, and their mutual appreciation consoles them both. Meditat-
ing on "their rare little position, his and Cornelia's—position
as conscious, ironic, pathetic survivors together of a dead and
buried society" (pp. 209-210), the melancholy male observer
duplicates the traveller James who revisited his homeland in
1904 and viewed regretfully the changes wrought by vulgar
wealth.

The other bond uniting them is the confidence with which
White-Mason used to discuss his stillborn marriage proposals
with Cornelia. The occasion of this meeting is propitious for a
renewal of such confidences. "Poor crapy Cornelia" analyzes
her friend's state of mind regarding Mrs. Worthingham.
" 'You're so in love with her and want to marry her!' " she declares (p. 216). Then it flashes on him that this is a duplica-
tion of their discussion of Mary Cardew thirty years earlier,
and he picks up a photograph of the girl.

With a wave of delight, memories inundate him. It is Cornelia
who is rendering him this service, for she knows everyone and
everything of the blessed past. In this capacity Cornelia will do
beautifully, but not in any other. To her inquiry of whether he
wants to marry herself, White-Mason, speaking for all the
Jamesian male confiders, answers kindly in the negative. Her
purpose in his life will be to serve as his extended consciousness,
to know *for* him, to know with him.

Cornelia's true sentiments, however, are clear. After all these years she has returned—now that she is "old"—to visit him with perfect propriety, because she has always loved him. White-Mason understands, and promises to visit her daily. But what, she interposes, " 'since you can't marry me!—can you do with me?' " " 'Everything,' " he answers. " 'I can live with you—just this way.' To illustrate which he dropped into the other chair by her fire . . ." (p. 229).

The confiding male has once more made himself a nest in the home of his confidante—keeping her at a safe distance of friendship outside of marriage—yet using her sympathy and understanding as he desires. It is the same pattern as in *Roderick Hudson, The Ambassadors,* "The Beast in the Jungle," and "The Jolly Corner." In fact, the author always places the confidante at a safe distance from the confider, for the others are either safely married or are too old to qualify.

Besides Fanny Hurter, there is only one other exception, Lady Sandgate in *The Outcry* (1911), who marries in the end her confider and lover, Lord Theign. She differs also from her immediate predecessors by being a throwback to the simple *ficelle*. Her role is to be the peaceful hub of activity and controversy. Opposing parties confide in her, and her drawing room is a convenient rendezvous in the last part of the novel. But depth of character is lacking in both Lady Sandgate and the other figures in the novel. Furthermore, the lines of friendship are blurred by the obliqueness of dialogue, and the old theme of betrayal and frustration is mildly set aside in an ending originally designed to please the theatergoing public. The familiar devices of devotion to art and manipulation of fortune recur, but without their former luster.

The most that can be said for Lady Sandgate, with her forty-odd years, her modernity, beauty, and power of divination, is that she is a weak replica of Maria Gostrey and Fanny Assingham. Her portrait loses a good deal more by the dramatic form which James retained while converting the original play into a novel. As a consequence, no male protagonist-observer can give the reader his impressions of the lady; and such confidences as she does receive from Lord Theign are reserved mainly for the last book. Hence, the intensity and intimacy of the former confidante-"center" relations have disappeared, although the two are lovers. It becomes clearer than ever that the confidante-"center" relation is a proper vehicle for friendship, not mutual love.

The Outcry exemplifies the fruitless tinkering of the ageing author with one of his favorite techniques. There is no doubt that his best efforts had already been spent, and that the evolution of the minor confidante had passed its zenith. The last representatives demonstrate only the decline of a character and technique which had been handled with remarkable versatility. From the slight treatment in *Roderick Hudson* and the awkward fumbling with the role in *The American,* James had brought his minor confidantes through a richly varied development; and now, at the end of his career, it appears that he had actually exhausted her dramatic possibilities. In the evolution of the major confidantes there is a similar progression, only the technical variations are greater, the character traits are more pronounced, and the friendship is more thoroughly explored.

Part 2

THE

MAJOR

CONFIDANTES

Chapter 3

THE PORTRAIT OF A LADY

𝒯HE *Portrait of a Lady* (1881) is remarkable for many merits, including the indirect juxtaposition of two confidantes. The contrast between Henrietta Stackpole and Madame Merle, alluded to in the author's Preface, is more dramatic than the distinctions made between Mrs. Prest and Miss Tina Bordereau in "The Aspern Papers." In receiving fuller treatment, the confidantes in *The Portrait* are differentiated not only in their technical use, but also in their moral and cultural backgrounds.

In the Preface James gives more attention to Henrietta than to any other character, except of course the heroine herself. In discussing the function of Henrietta, he compares her with Maria Gostrey, "then in the bosom of time," and a better example of what Miss Stackpole sets out to be.[1]

Each of these persons is but wheels to the coach; neither belongs to the body of the vehicle, or is for a moment accommodated with a seat inside. There the subject alone is ensconced, in the form of its "hero and heroine," and of the privileged high officials, say, who ride with the king and queen. . . . Maria Gostrey and Miss Stackpole then are cases, each, of the light *ficelle,* not of the true agent; they may run beside the coach "for all they are worth," they may cling to it till they are out of breath (as poor Miss Stackpole all so vividly does), but neither, all the while, so much as gets her foot on the step, neither ceases for a moment to tread the dusty road (p. 55).

Although Miss Stackpole came to the author's mind along with the other characters, as "the definite array of contributions to Isabel Archer's history," yet her position remains inferior from the start: she is never a true agent in the drama of the novel (p. 53). James admits the incongruity between her ancillary function and her ample treatment, offering as an excuse "an excess of [his] zeal," an example of his weakness to *"overtreat,* rather than undertreat" his subject (p. 57), and an effort to embellish the novel by "cultivation of the lively. . . . Henrietta must have been at that time a part of my wonderful notion of the lively" (p. 57). It is true that this *ficelle* provides most of the humor in *The Portrait,* the rest of it being contributed by her friend, Mr. Bantling, by Mrs. Touchett, and by the Countess Gemini. But Henrietta's other function of confidante and admonisher of the protagonist is ignored by James in the Preface; it is simply left for the reader to discover for himself.

The basic difference between Henrietta and Madame Merle is indicated in the same part of the Preface: Henrietta is running beside the coach, while the latter lady, "seated, all absorbed but all serene, at the piano" at Gardencourt, presents to the heroine the sudden recognition of "a turning point in her life" (p. 56). To what extent Madame Merle becomes "the agent" in Isabel Archer's life will presently be taken up. Just now a remark on the contrasted mode of influence may be linked with James's own image of the coach. As Henrietta is running along on the outside, her influence can only be seen as external upon Isabel, whereas Madame Merle, seated within the coach—if one may extend James's metaphor—exercises a deep and thorough influence both exterior and interior, the full extent of which the heroine does not fathom until the end of the novel.

The great difference between the two confidantes originates

in their diverse purposes in the author's plan. Henrietta, who figures largely in the first part of the novel, which takes place in England and Paris, is used by James to analyze Isabel verbally and to be the first of her friends to predict her disaster. Equipped with utter frankness and fearlessness, Henrietta sees Isabel both from the outside and the inside. In spite of her warnings, however, she does not succeed in altering Isabel's life.[2] On the other hand, James's purpose for Madame Merle is to implement his heroine's downfall through the subtlety of her betrayal. Madame Merle dominates the later sections of the novel, before and after Isabel's marriage, which occur in Italy. The novel is a study of knowledge: knowledge gained through experience; knowledge hidden by deceit; knowledge distorted by prejudice. Isabel's tragic irony is the loss of happiness through knowledge. While Henrietta relentlessly uncovers ugly facts, it is in Madame Merle's interests to conceal them. Instead of criticizing Isabel, she builds up her already sublime ego. It is characteristic, and fateful, that the heroine should ignore the first and listen to the second confidante.

Seen with the critical eyes of Ralph Touchett, Henrietta's first appearance has the comic touches of the light *ficelle* the author meant her to be:

She was a neat plump person, of medium stature, with a round face, a small mouth, a delicate complexion, a bunch of light brown ringlets at the back of her head and a peculiarly open, surprised-looking eye. The most striking point in her appearance was the remarkable fixedness of this organ, which rested without impudence or defiance, but as if in conscientious exercise of a natural right, upon every object it happened to encounter. . . . She rustled, she shimmered, in fresh, dove-coloured draperies . . . she was as crisp and new and comprehensive as a first issue before the folding. From top to toe she had probably no misprint.[3]

The remarkable fixedness of her eyes is doubtless intended to symbolize the bumptiousness with which she makes her way across England and the Continent, and the general simplistic

American view of life, which James frequently satirized. Not only is Ralph critical of Miss Stackpole, but Mrs. Touchett objects strongly to the loudness of this enterprising woman:

"I don't like Miss Stackpole—everything about her displeases me; she talks so much too loud and looks at one as if one wanted to look at *her*—which one doesn't. I'm sure she has lived all her life in a boarding-house, and I detest the manners and the liberties of such places" (p. 88).

This blunt and tactless friend of Isabel does not succeed at first in obtaining any great confidences from the girl. Miss Archer is questing for a more profound experience of life—and Henrietta certainly is very easily understood. Still, she has been for "Isabel . . . a proof that a woman might suffice to herself and be happy" (p. 55). Her convictions about conscience and duty appeal to the heroine. In defending her to Ralph Isabel states:

"I'm afraid it's because she's rather vulgar that I like her. . . . it's because there's something of the 'people' in her. . . . she's a kind of emanation of the great democracy—the continent, the country, the nation. I don't say that she sums it all up, that would be too much to ask of her. But she suggests it; she vividly figures it" (pp. 86–87).

But Isabel finds that in an English setting, Henrietta can be very annoying. Her behavior at Gardencourt is often embarrassing; and her espousal of Caspar Goodwood's cause Isabel finds to be lacking in delicacy. Also, her criticism of Isabel's newly acquired ideas proves to be irritating to the independent girl. New ideas, Henrietta declares in a pontifical tone, " 'shouldn't interfere with the old ones when the old ones have been the right ones' " (p. 97). In her estimation, poor Ralph is suspect for his expatriate urbanity; and she holds forth to him on the American virtue of simplicity. " 'We take everything more naturally over there, and, after all, we're a great deal more simple. I admit that; I'm very simple myself. . . . I'm quite content to be myself; I don't want to change' " (p. 107).

That Isabel's new ideas are removing her from the state of simplicity causes alarm for her staunch American friend. To remedy this evil she applies to Ralph for help:

"You had better stir yourself and be careful. Isabel's changing every day; she's drifting away—right out to sea. I've watched her and I can see it. She's not the bright American girl she was. She's taking different views, a different colour, and turning away from her old ideals. I want to save those ideals. . . . I've got a fear in my heart that she's going to marry one of these fell Europeans, and I want to prevent it" (p. 108).

It will be prevented by getting Isabel to marry her old suitor from Massachusetts, who, with undashed hopes, has pursued her to Europe. " 'He's the only man I have ever seen whom I think worthy of Isabel' " (p. 109). " 'I know her well enough to know that she would never be truly happy over here, and I wish her to form some strong American tie that will act as a preservative' " (p. 110).

The sincerity of Henrietta's desire to save her friend " 'from drowning' " is very creditable. It springs from her innate simplicity, which dreads any change whatever. Also, her interest in Caspar's suit is prompted by a sincere sympathy for the young man, similar to the interest of Mrs. Tristram in her candidate. In her meddlesome way Henrietta even forces Ralph to invite Caspar Goodwood to Gardencourt. But despite her forwardness, Henrietta is not too obtuse to discover Ralph's love for Isabel. In pointing it out she serves the technical purpose of exposition, since Ralph would certainly never confess his feelings to anyone before doing so to Isabel herself on his deathbed.

One of Henrietta's big comic scenes is enacted with Lord Warburton before her departure from Gardencourt. Although it is one of James's digressions in favor of "the lively," and hence has nothing to do with Henrietta's role of confidante, a claim to its usefulness as an interlude can still be made, for it precedes a tense scene between Isabel and the Lord (Chapter XIV).

Miss Stackpole's subsequent and swift friendship with Mr.

Bantling in London adds more details to her comic role. In his appreciative company she simply effervesces. The men in whom Henrietta is interested, Goodwood and Bantling, are a commentary on her own character. As indicated in their revealing names, both men are paragons of Henrietta's cardinal virtue— simplicity. Isabel had called Caspar " 'very simple-minded' " (p. 90), and together Ralph and Isabel estimate Bantling as " 'a very simple organism' " and Henrietta as " 'a simpler one still' " (p. 128). These judgments made by Isabel on her first confidante and the latter's friends form the basis of contrast with her second confidante and her friend. To the reader this basis is quite clear; but to Isabel, ironically, the values of the second group are not so accurately defined.

Henrietta's simplicity is even more evident in the little ruse which she plays on Isabel to obtain a private hearing for Caspar. It is the entire extent of her plot to marry Isabel to the rugged young businessman, and in its naïveté scarcely compares with Madame Merle's machination. But it is true to her character, to which any deception is quite foreign. Her greeting to Isabel after the surprise interview with Caspar is: " 'Has he been here, dear?' the latter yearningly asked" (p. 143). The note of vicarious pleasure is unmistakable, which Isabel's annoyance does not in the least disturb. It is her mistake, however, to try to force confidences from Isabel:

"I hope you don't mean to tell me that you didn't give Mr. Goodwood some hope."

"I don't see why I should tell you anything; as I said to you just now, I can't trust you. . . ."

"You don't mean to say you've sent him off?" Henrietta almost shrieked.

"I asked him to leave me alone; and I ask you the same, Henrietta" (p. 144).

Isabel obviously is in no mood for recriminations, but Henrietta rides roughly over any precautionary considerations:

" 'Do you know where you're drifting? . . . You're drifting to some great mistake' " (p. 144). The seriousness of this warning is prompted by utter devotion of friendship, and the lively journalist, instead of indulging righteous anger at its rejection, humorously responds to Isabel's witty retort about Mr. Bantling's arrangements:

"Do you know where you're drifting, Henrietta Stackpole?". . . .
"I'm drifting to a big position—that of the Queen of American Journalism. If my next letter isn't copied all over the West I'll swallow my pen-wiper!" (p. 145).

But the confidante—still without obtaining confidences—is more than ever determined to pursue Mr. Goodwood's cause. In a short subsequent scene with Ralph she discloses her intention to " 'tell him not to give up. If I didn't believe Isabel would come round,' Miss Stackpole added—'Well, I'd give up myself. I mean I'd give her up!' " (p. 148). It is important for Henrietta's role that she should not give Isabel up. For near the end of the novel the author will use her sympathetic ministrations to his heroine when her need for a confidante is greatest. The present scene (Chapter 17) is the last to be dominated by Miss Stackpole for a long time. The following nine chapters are devoted, with only two exceptions, to the second confidante, Madame Merle.

Isabel had told Ralph that she liked " 'people to be totally different from Henrietta' " (p. 87), and in Madame Merle she undoubtedly finds such a person. The ideal represented by this woman instantly captivates her imagination:

Our heroine had always passed for a person of resources and had taken a certain pride in being one; but she wandered, as by the wrong side of the wall of a private garden, round the enclosed talents, accomplishments, aptitudes of Madame Merle. She found herself desiring to emulate them, and in twenty such ways this lady presented herself as a model. . . . It took no great time indeed for her to feel herself, as the phrase is, under an influence. "What's the harm," she wondered, "so long as it's a good one? The more one's under a good influence the better. The only thing is to see our steps as we take them—to understand them as we go. That, no doubt, I shall always do" (p. 163).

This aura of mystery surrounding Madame Merle, which Mrs. Touchett calls " 'her great fault,' " is enhanced by her classic appearance and aristocratic bearing:

It was a face that told of an amplitude of nature and of quick and free motions and, though it had no regular beauty, was in the highest degree engaging and attaching. Madame Merle was a tall, fair, smooth woman; everything in her person was round and replete. . . . Her grey eyes were small but full of light and incapable of stupidity —incapable, according to some people, even of tears; she had a liberal, full-rimmed mouth which when she smiled drew itself upward to the left side in a manner that most people thought very odd, some very affected and a few very graceful. . . . Madame Merle had thick, fair hair, arranged somehow "classically" and as if she were a Bust, Isabel judged—a Juno or a Niobe; and large white hands, of a perfect shape. . . . [She might have ranked] as . . . a baroness, a countess, a princess (pp. 151–152).

Just as Henrietta is decked out for high comedy, so her rival is endowed with the features and elegance of classical tragedy. Here is a woman capable of ruling kingdoms and destined to witness their collapse. So completely has she assimilated the traditions of the "old, old world," that no marked American trait remains visible. Her bid for Isabel's friendship on grounds of American origin falls flat. Isabel can only wonder "what Henrietta Stackpole would say to her thinking so much of this perverted product of their common soil, and had a conviction that it would be severely judged. Henrietta would not at all subscribe to Madame Merle; for reasons she could not have defined this truth came home to the girl" (p. 163).

Yet Madame Merle, she feels certain, would instantly "strike off some happy view" of Miss Stackpole; she "was too humor-

ous, too observant, not to do justice to Henrietta, and on becoming acquainted with her would probably give the measure
of a tact which Miss Stackpole couldn't hope to emulate" (pp.
163-164). Isabel's estimate of their mutual impressions is later
borne out during their actual meeting in Florence.

The extent to which Madame Merle captivates Isabel's confidence is determined by her striking singularity. The girl's romantic sense thrills because she

had never encountered a more agreeable and interesting figure than
Madame Merle; she had never met a person having less of that fault
which is the principal obstacle to friendship—the air of reproducing
the more tiresome, the stale, the too-familiar parts of one's own
character (p. 161).

There is an unconscious reference here to Henrietta, whose
sense of duty and staunch American independence are indeed
familiar parts of Isabel's own character. And the implicit comparison continues when Isabel notices that Madame Merle "was
not natural . . . her nature had been too much overlaid by custom and her angle too much rubbed away. She had become too
flexible, too useful, was too ripe and too final. . . . She was
deep . . ." (p. 165). In Madame Merle there is a totally new
creature to meet, and she becomes Isabel's only confidante until
the time of the latter's marriage. In spite of her silence over Lord
Warburton and Caspar Goodwood,

the gates of the girl's confidence were opened wider than they had
ever been; she said things to this amiable auditress that she had not
yet said to anyone. Sometimes she took alarm at her candour; it was
as if she had given to a comparative stranger the key to her cabinet
of jewels. These spiritual gems were the only ones of any magnitude
that Isabel possessed, but there was all the greater reason for their
being carefully guarded. Afterwards, however, she always remembered that one should never regret a generous error and that if
Madame Merle had not the merit she attributed to her, so much the
worse for Madame Merle (p. 161).

Undoubtedly, the measure of confidence bestowed by Isabel commits her in like measure to the power of the confidante. Madame Merle extracts more from Isabel in a few weeks than Henrietta does in years. This she does by showing keen interest in all that concerns Isabel, without however pumping her in the officious manner of Miss Stackpole.

She preferred for the present to talk to Isabel of Isabel, and exhibited the greatest interest in our heroine's history, sentiments, opinions, prospects. She made her chatter and listened to her chatter with infinite good nature. This flattered and quickened the girl, who was struck with all the distinguished people her friend had known . . . (p. 166).

The important thing in these confidences is not the factual details, but the laying bare of the girl's soul, which enables the older woman to read it most clearly. She gains knowledge of Isabel's idealism and generosity—both her strength and her weakness—and this knowledge gives her immediate power over the girl. Casually she leads into the topic of her American friend living in Italy, who is outstanding for nothing except his daughter: " 'But he has a little girl—a dear little girl; he does speak of *her*. He's devoted to her, and if it were a career to be an excellent father he'd be very distinguished' " (p. 169). These details she knows will influence Isabel's deeply sensitive heart: and the effect of the girl's first visit to his home later verifies her confidante's foreknowledge.

In presenting the picture of Madame Merle James does two things—he shows her impression made on Isabel, and he shows the reader the masks with which she makes that impression. Her most important masks are those of the trustworthy confidante, in whose heart secrets lie forever buried, and the sympathetic, just listener, who can find good in everyone, even the impossible Countess. Her dabbling in art and art-collecting is another mask. But the mask that underlies all the others is her small position among the great people of the world:

She had known great things and great people, but she had never played a great part. She was one of the small ones of the earth; she had not been born to honours; she knew the world too well to nourish fatuous illusions on the article of her own place in it. She had encountered many of the fortunate few and was perfectly aware of those points at which their fortune differed from hers. But if by her informed measure she was no figure for a high scene, she had yet to Isabel's imagination a sort of greatness. To be so cultivated and civilised, so wise and so easy, and still make so light of it—that was really to be a great lady, especially when one so carried and presented one's self (p. 164).

In the role of highly-trained lady-in-waiting upon the great, Madame Merle merits the applause of her youthful spectator, who notes in her life the functions pertaining to her role. When not engaged in her voluminous correspondence, nor in painting water-colors which she freely gives away, nor in playing the piano with perfect consideration for her listeners, she busies herself with rich embroidery, with playing cards, or in conversation. "She laid down her pastimes as easily as she took them up. . . . She was in short the most comfortable, profitable, amenable person to live with" (p. 165).

Another feature of Madame Merle's exterior masks is her philosophy of clothes:

"I know a large part of myself is in the clothes I wear. I've a great respect for *things!* One's self—for other people—is one's expression of one's self; and one's house, one's furniture, one's garments, the books one reads, the company one keeps—these are all expressive" (pp. 172–173).

It is the born actress discussing the histrionic value of her costumes and disguises; and it illuminates her use of masks throughout the novel.

In contrast with this lady and her masks, undisguised Henrietta, whose creed of honesty might be published in any headline, reappears briefly on the scene in Paris. Madame Merle has just shown the reader her controlled pleasure over Isabel's inheritance; Miss Stackpole's opinion on the contrary is that

"it will certainly confirm your dangerous tendencies . . . The peril for you is that you live too much in the world of your own dreams. . . . You're too fastidious; you've too many graceful illusions. Your newly-acquired thousands will shut you up more and more to the society of a few selfish and heartless people who will be interested in keeping them up. . . . you think you can lead a romantic life . . ." (pp. 184–185).

In renewing her warnings, Henrietta functions as the *ficelle* designed to prognosticate for the "center." Her arguments against the romantic life trouble and frighten Isabel, although they do not materially alter her course. Her reaction has nonetheless deepened since the scene in Pratt's Hotel when she listened to similar remarks. This change in Isabel's attitude marks a development in both her character and in her relation to her confidante. Her being frightened now foreshadows her confession of bitter sorrow later.

With the removal of the principals to Italy the activities of the two confidantes is considerably altered. Allowed only three brief appearances, simple Henrietta is relegated to her journalistic pursuits in other quarters; while Madame Merle closes in on Isabel in the realization of her plot. The reader feels that Isabel has moved out of Henrietta's sphere into the domain of the subtle expatriates. Mrs. Touchett and Ralph, having lived longer in Europe than Henrietta, are now used by the author as the more capable voices of warning to Isabel.

Madame Merle is given such free scope that she becomes the center of consciousness in the scene with Osmond (Chapter XXII).[4] The exposition given in this scene sets the stage for the unfolding of the plot to marry Isabel to Osmond. An air of intimacy is discernible in this private interview, yet the woman's motives lie so deeply concealed that her secret is safeguarded until the author is ready to reveal it to his heroine near the end of the novel. But cues are given to the reader here, which later fall in place. One of these is Madame Merle's pain over Pansy's not liking her. The depth of her deception in getting the girl to marry the father of her own child is equalled only by the suavity of her power of suggestion. In recommending him to Isabel's attention, she does not omit touching lightly on the girl's most vulnerable spot, her vanity:

He had his perversities—which indeed Isabel would find to be the case with all men really worth knowing—and didn't cause his light to shine equally for all persons—Madame Merle, however, thought she could undertake that for Isabel he would be brilliant. He was easily bored, too easily, and dull people always put him out; but a quick and cultivated girl like Isabel would give him a stimulus which was too absent from his life (p. 207).

When Osmond presents himself in the prearranged call on his ally in order to meet Miss Archer, James again resorts to the imagery of the theater to enhance the duplicity of the confidante:

Isabel took on this occasion little part in the talk; she scarcely even smiled when the others turned to her invitingly; she sat there as if she had been at the play and had paid even a large sum for her place. . . . They talked of the Florentine, the Roman, the cosmopolite world, and might have been distinguished performers figuring for a charity. It had all the rich readiness that would have come from rehearsal. Madame Merle appealed to her as if she had been on the stage, but she could ignore any learnt cue without spoiling the scene . . . (p. 209).

But Isabel is unaware of watching a rehearsed performance. She lacks the insight of Ralph who "had learned more or less inscrutably to attend, and there could have been nothing so 'sustained' to attend to as the general performance of Madame Merle" (p. 212). Through Ralph's consciousness, rather than Isabel's, the reader gains insight into Madame Merle's frustration. The beautiful classical type now appears merely as a small businessman's widow, who is accepted by people like the latest best-seller. James deliberately undercuts the earlier impression to prepare for the final revelation of her melodramatic involvement with Osmond. Her life is, after all, only bourgeois tragedy.

Madame Merle's ambitions, thwarted until now, converge with a quiet but fierce determination to see her plot through to consummation. In the third scene written from her point of view (Chapter 25) she engages the Countess Gemini in conversation, and coolly blackmails her into silence in respect to warning Isabel. Everywhere she is the self-possessed, suave contriver, who needs only to prevent obstacles from arising. Left to herself, Isabel will most probably enter into the marriage, and Madame Merle does leave her considerably to herself and to Osmond. She does, however, convey to Isabel in sympathetic terms the exposition of Osmond's and the Countess's background. In doing this she subtly injects the warning that one could not believe a word the Countess says. This is to safeguard the plot in case the Countess should try to betray it after all.

During this time Henrietta makes one of her brief appearances in Florence, and her meeting with Madame Merle gives only a sketchy and unilateral view of their differences:

Madame Merle surveyed [Henrietta] with a single glance, took her in from head to foot, and after a pang of despair determined to endure her. She determined indeed to delight in her. She mightn't be inhaled as a rose, but she might be grasped as a nettle. Madame Merle genially squeezed her into insignificance, and Isabel felt that in foreseeing this liberality she had done justice to her friend's intelligence (p. 236).

It may be inferred that Henrietta, having been squeezed into oblivion, fails to express her views of Madame Merle. The simplicity of the journalist is no doubt baffled by the consummate aplomb of the woman of the world. The contrast between the two confidantes, begun in their very names, and continued through the descriptions of their appearance, their manner and speech, culminates in the nature of their ambitions and the essential features of their characters. All these differences point up the distinction between their technical roles. Madame Merle, with all her skill sits at ease inside the coach, while Henrietta pants along on the outside. The deeply concealed alliance between Madame Merle and Gilbert Osmond complements the simple plan of Henrietta in favor of Caspar Goodwood. Isabel sees through the simple plan; but she never suspects duplicity in Madame Merle until it is too late.

Madame Merle however begins to doubt the beneficence of her plot before Isabel does. In the brief scene between herself and Osmond (Chapter 26), she reveals her terror at the abyss yawning at Isabel's feet—the abyss of Osmond's selfishness and cruelty: " 'I'm frightened at the abyss into which I shall have cast her' " (p. 239). It is the redeeming feature of Madame Merle's character that in spite of her readiness to exploit Isabel, she can still sympathize with her as a fellow victim. " 'That fine creature,' " the term she applies to her, indicates her admiration for the girl.

The two scenes between Madame Merle and Osmond reveal the character of the confidante more plainly than her scenes with Isabel. With her former lover, her masks are down, and the suppressed pathos wells up. Her role as betrayer requires these brief dialogues "behind the scenes," in order to keep the reader *au courant,* for revelation of the plot can scarcely be made through Isabel, the victim, who is the "center" throughout the greater part of the novel. These scenes also mark a progression in Madame Merle's own downfall. By this time the woman of many accomplishments and much social success has begun to doubt her greatest achievement. Osmond taunts her: " 'You can't draw back—you've gone too far.' 'Very good [she replies]; but you must do the rest yourself' " (p. 239).

James's study of the confidante-"center" relation in *The Portrait* revolves around his favorite theme of the American innocent acquiring experience. Isabel, the innocent heroine, stands midway between Henrietta, the isolationist armed with high-sounding prejudices, and Madame Merle, the expatriate who has surrendered to cosmopolitan cynicism. Through the confidential relation James facilitates the progress of his heroine from ignorance to disillusionment. As she moves out of Henrietta's orbit into Madame Merle's, the girl meets life and experiences the death of her idealistic ambitions.

Meanwhile the confidantes develop as well. Henrietta, the friend of Isabel's American years, outstrips her in coming to terms with Europe. They are her terms, certainly; but she finds on foreign soil the happiness and fulfillment which Isabel misses. In a reverse manner, Madame Merle, although versed in evil, discerns new depths in the sinister soul of Osmond. At the sight even she recoils. In this threefold way the author delineates the passage of the woman's heart from one stage to another. The progress of the confidantes is like an obbligato to the melody of the heroine's growth in awareness.

Because of the isolation created by Isabel's egotism, there is little collaboration between herself and her confidantes in their separate expansion of consciousness. Each one makes her way independently of the other. Still, Madame Merle, in using Isabel as her tool, does achieve her later understanding through the misery of the young woman. It is not, of course, a result of friendship. Once exploitation appears friendship dies. In most cases the Jamesian confidante is exploited. Here it is the confider. But the result is the same.

On the Eastern tour Isabel begins to discover the divergence in morality between Madame Merle and herself: ". . . our young woman had a sense in her of values gone wrong or, as they said at the shops, marked down" (p. 269). The consummate performance is slackening. Here and there the young woman notices that a corner of the curtain is never lifted on Madame Merle's past. In pondering this woman's depth she is now shocked, now dismayed, and increasingly filled with foreboding. Isabel's confidante—as none other—is an index of life. Minor satellites to Madame Merle are Mrs. Tristram, Mrs. Costello, and Lady Davenant. By studying these women their confiders could learn all they need to know about life; it is part of their tragedy that they lack a quick perception for clues of worldliness. James knew the smooth, hardened society woman very well. Many times he portrays the type in his international fiction. She is seldom a person to inspire confidence. As soon as Isabel awakens to this hardness in her friend her confidence begins to wane.

On her part, Madame Merle has shown herself an expert psychologist in estimating Isabel's need to confide. The confidences she elicits from the first days at Gardencourt until the end of the Eastern tour meet a psychological need on Isabel's part, and a strategic one on her own. In spite of her many friends, Isabel is always lonely. Isolated in part by her romantic ideals, in part by her egotism, she naturally allows admittance to her heart only to those who appeal to the ideals or flatter the egotism. Not until the end, when she has been purified by suffering, does she admit Henrietta and Ralph to her secrets; for up to this point she has resisted their advice and warnings.

After their return from the East the engagement takes place; and from then on Madame Merle's role in Isabel's life is wholly changed. An estrangement sets in between the two women; but Madame Merle interests herself more noticeably in Pansy. The first scene in this latter part of the novel showing Madame Merle transpires with Mr. Rosier, who begs her assistance in furthering his suit for Pansy. Madame Merle functions as Rosier's confidante, but offers him no sympathy and only scant advice. James also uses her to provide the reader with some information about the past three years which the narrative has skipped.

Madame Merle is next seen sailing through Isabel's drawing rooms as though claiming proprietorship:

The other rooms meanwhile had become conscious of the arrival of Madame Merle, who, wherever she went, produced an impression when she entered. How she did it the most attentive spectator could not have told you, for she neither spoke loud, nor laughed profusely, nor moved rapidly, nor dressed with splendour, nor appealed in any appreciable manner to the audience. Large, fair, smiling, serene, there was something in her very tranquillity that diffused itself, and when people looked round it was because of a sudden quiet (p. 307).

She continues to create her atmosphere, especially in conversation with Isabel's husband, the subject being, upon different occasions, a suitable husband for Pansy. Her assumption of authority in the matter is made obvious first to Rosier, then gradually to Isabel herself. The contrast now is not between confidantes, but between confidante and confider. As the former continues to shine upon others in the radiance of her cautious success, the lackluster of the latter deepens. Ralph perceives that "if [Isabel] wore a mask it completely covered her face. There was something fixed and mechanical in the serenity painted on it; this was not an expression, Ralph said—it was a representation, it was an advertisement" (p. 323).

Isabel notes the rift widening between herself and her old confidante. At first, the young woman had kept her admiration for the "rich sensibility" contained under the fine self-possession of her "highly cultivated friend," and more especially for her art of living "entirely by reason and by wisdom" (p. 331). But by the time Madame Merle has returned to Rome from her various travels, the third year of wedded life has elapsed for Isabel, and she has outgrown her admiration for Madame Merle's perfect demeanor.

She also perceives a difference, a detachment in her old friend. With her aunt's accusation that Madame Merle made her marriage still in mind, Isabel begins to wonder about her scrupulosity in keeping away. In any case, in her generosity Isabel is as yet unwilling to blame Madame Merle for her own unhappiness.

The serenity of Madame Merle's scenes comes, however,

closer to being shattered the nearer she approaches the subject
of Pansy's marriage to Lord Warburton. In Chapters 40 and
49 she engages her erstwhile confider in a verbal fencing
match over this issue. The first of these scenes follows directly
upon Isabel's surprising Madame Merle with Osmond in her own
drawing room, and receiving a new impression of their relation.
But before she has time to reflect on this new impression, Osmond has hastily withdrawn and Madame Merle has launched
into her exploratory discussion. Her aim is to discover the extent
of Warburton's attachment to Pansy. To Isabel she says:
" '. . . you've infinitely more observation of Lord Warburton's
behaviour than I.' " Isabel responds: " '. . . Lord Warburton
has let me know that he's charmed with Pansy.' " After stifling
her "treacherous impulse" to betray her mother's joy at this,
Madame Merle quietly resumes: " 'It would be very delightful;
it would be a great marriage. It's really very kind of him' " (p.
339).

Having declared she will no longer encourage Mr. Rosier,
for whose suit we know she had entertained some hope, Madame
Merle winds up:

"I want to see her married to Lord Warburton."
"You had better wait till he asks her."
"If what you say is true, he'll ask her. Especially," said Madame
Merle in a moment, "if you make him."
"If I make him?"
"It's quite in your power. You've great influence with him."
Isabel frowned a little. "Where did you learn that?"
"Mrs. Touchett told me. Not you—never!" said Madame Merle,
smiling.
"I certainly never told you anything of the sort."
"You *might* have done so—so far as opportunity went—when
we were by way of being confidential with each other. But you really
told me very little; I've often thought so since."
Isabel had thought so too, and sometimes with a certain satisfac-
tion. But she didn't admit it now—perhaps because she wished not
to appear to exult in it. "You seem to have an excellent informant
in my aunt," she simply returned (pp. 339–340).

Madame Merle then tells her how she learned from Mrs. Touchett of Isabel's declining the Lord's offer, and concludes with a glib suggestion: " 'But if you wouldn't marry Lord Warburton yourself, make him the reparation of helping him to marry some one else' " (p. 340). The grotesqueness of this suggestion is entirely a breach in Madame Merle's etiquette and a deep flaw in her polish. It indicates the violent urge of the mother's interest, which stops at nothing. Isabel has already perceived that she is "too much interested" in Pansy's love-affairs, and she resists the pressure exerted by both Madame Merle and Osmond.

Once more James clears the stage, and shifts the confidantes around. It is now Henrietta's turn to enter. She arrives, determined, "perfectly unchanged," "brisk and business-like," and calls on the Countess in Florence. James brings Henrietta to the Countess for expository purposes. She seeks preliminary information about Isabel's present predicament, but she does not gain much light from Amy's morally garbled views. Having herself felt Osmond's dislike, Henrietta is going to urge Isabel " 'to make a stand' " with her husband; and she will try to see for herself whether Isabel is unhappy. Another reason for this scene is to create colorful contrast between these two minor characters, thereby brightening the last part of the novel, which at this point is growing very dark and ominous. The frivolity and spitefulness of the Countess bring out in Henrietta Stackpole only more dignity, gravity, and determination to be of assistance. Even this woman's misery touches Henrietta's good heart: ". . . there was nature in this bitter effusion [of the Countess]" (p. 374).

The first, but lesser confidante then journeys to Rome to have her big scene with the protagonist. It is Isabel's confession of unhappiness, and marks the zenith of Henrietta's role as confidante.

She was a woman, she was a sister; she was not Ralph, nor Lord Warburton, nor Caspar Goodwood, and Isabel could speak.

"Yes, I'm wretched," she said very mildly. She hated to hear herself say it; she tried to say it as judicially as possible.

"What does he do to you?" Henrietta asked, frowning as if she were enquiring into the operations of a quack doctor.

"He does nothing. He doesn't like me."

"He's very hard to please!" cried Miss Stackpole. "Why don't you leave him?"

"I can't change that way," Isabel said.

"Why not, I should like to know? You won't confess that you've made a mistake. You're too proud" (pp. 399–400).

Isabel denies this and repeats that " 'One can't change that way.' " Henrietta counters: " 'You *have* changed, in spite of the impossibility' " (p. 400). It is her old theme—disaster is met in change, while safety lies in not changing. The only remedy for an unwise change is to change back again. By leaving Osmond Isabel would be able to return to America and freedom once more. Henrietta's own unchanged condition counterpoints with the imperturbability of Madame Merle on the one side, and the complete change in Isabel on the other. The utter honesty of her advice to her friend acts as a foil to the counsel offered by the Countess: "Don't try to be too good. Be a little easy and natural and nasty; feel a little wicked, for the comfort of it, once in your life!' " (p. 447). But Isabel rejects both the clean break advocated by the wholesome American newspaperwoman and the spiteful revenge suggested by the tainted expatriate. Besides illuminating further both women's characters, the function of this scene is to prepare for Isabel's final confession to Ralph.

The second visit of Miss Stackpole to Isabel proves unsatisfactory to herself. Not only does she fail to rescue Isabel, but distinctly she realizes the latter's desire to be rid of her. " 'Oh, you do give me such a sense of helplessness!' " (p. 410). That disappointment is very bitter for a woman of Henrietta's generous and efficient nature. She has listened to Isabel's confidences, but to no practical purpose. And the correspondent who put Europe in her pocket is nothing if not practical. The admirable woman who captivated Mr. Bantling and put him to work in the interests of the reading public, meets with complete failure in accomplishing anything for her friend. Technically, her role as *ficelle* is now finished.

But perhaps the saddest aspect of this scene is the moral rift widening between them. After recognizing that Madame Merle had a moral code differing from her own, Isabel could find some comfort in a superior feeling. But now, the other confidante is found to support an alien code as well: and Isabel is struck " 'with the offhand way in which [Henrietta] speak[s] of a woman's leaving her husband' " (p. 410). But Henrietta appeals for her justification to the practice common in " 'our Western cities, and it's to them, after all, that we must look in the future' " (p. 410). The freedom of the wife to abandon her husband rests on Henrietta's modern views of emancipation.[5] From the presentation of her arguments one feels that James inclines toward Isabel's choice of supporting the older code. Once she realizes her failure to convince Isabel, Henrietta wastes no time in packing up to leave; whereupon Madame Merle re-enters to have her last big scenes with her erstwhile confidante.

Returning from a visit to Naples she finds Lord Warburton departed and her dreams of a great marriage for Pansy wrecked. In Chapter 49 she accosts Isabel in their most critical scene. Madame Merle's smile "at the left corner of her mouth," that sign used several times by James to objectify the sinister element in her character, is noticeable as the scene opens. Isabel sees at once

that her visitor's attitude was a critical one. Madame Merle, as we know, had been very discreet hitherto; she had never criticised; she had been markedly afraid of intermeddling. But apparently she had only reserved herself for this occasion, since she now had a dangerous quickness in her eye and an air of irritation which even admirable ease was not able to transmute. She had suffered a disappointment which excited Isabel's surprise—our heroine having no knowledge of her zealous interest in Pansy's marriage; and she betrayed it in a manner which quickened Mrs. Osmond's alarm. More clearly than ever before Isabel heard a cold, mocking voice proceed from she knew not where, in the dim void that surrounded her, and declare that this bright, strong, definite, worldly woman, this incarnation of the practical, the personal, the immediate, was a powerful agent in her destiny. She was nearer to her than Isabel had yet discovered, and her nearness was not the charming accident she had so long supposed (p. 420).

This intuitional perception made by Isabel marks the approaching climax of her full insight into the character of her former friend. Although Isabel had really told her very little, still her confidences had sufficed to bind her to the woman who has been "a powerful agent in her destiny." The polished surface of this woman is cracking further than in the previous scene, forced open by "a nameless vitality" surging up within her being. It is perhaps the best dramatization of Madame Merle's character, and a scene that definitely gives her the advantage over her antagonist. Borne up by her vitality and spurred on by her acute disappointment, elated also by the strength of her position, she confronts Isabel in a new role—that of the truly superior being, superior not only in manner and bearing, but infinitely superior in the thing that next to money most ensures power: knowledge. This woman *knows* more than Isabel, whose fumbling for the clue she can easily afford to smile down upon. What Madame Merle knows is of course her own connection with Osmond and his child, and the exploitation she has made of Isabel. But one thing is lacking in her fund of information, something the knowledge of which will give her even more power over her tool. Unscrupulously she inquires:

"Just this: whether Lord Warburton changed his mind quite of his own movement or because you recommended it. To please himself I mean, or to please you. Think of the confidence I must still have in you, in spite of having lost a little of it," Madame Merle continued with a smile, "to ask such a question as that!" (p. 422).

Isabel will tell the truth if she says anything: never for a moment does Madame Merle doubt that, and by means of this honesty her enemy hopes to convict her out of her own mouth:

"And don't you see how well it is that your husband should know it? . . . it would make a difference in his view of his daughter's prospects to know distinctly what really occurred. If Lord Warburton simply got tired of the poor child, that's one thing, and it's a pity. If he gave her up to please you it's another. That's a pity too, but in a different way. Then, in the latter case, you'd perhaps resign yourself to not being pleased—to simply seeing your stepdaughter married. Let him off—let us have him!" (p. 422).

At the height of her power, seated grandly with her mantle gathered about her and "a faint, agreeable fragrance" around her person, Madame Merle delivers this, her finest speech, with theatrical effect. The weight of the accumulated impression is too much for Isabel. A horror has seized her:

"Who are you—what are you? . . . What have you to do with my husband? . . . What have you to do with me?" . . .
    Madame Merle slowly got up, stroking her muff, but not removing her eyes from Isabel's face. "Everything!" she answered.
    Isabel sat there looking up at her, without rising; her face was almost a prayer to be enlightened. But the light of this woman's eyes seemed only a darkness. "Oh misery!" she murmured at last; and she fell back covering her face with her hands. It had come over her like a high-surging wave that Mrs. Touchett was right—Madame Merle had married her (p. 423).

The relation between the confidante and her confider has reached its utmost stage. Madame Merle, who supplanted Mrs. Touchett in guiding Isabel into the ways of the great world, has finally brought her to the end of that "wonderful" road—to the brink of knowledge of good and evil—to the uttermost cleavage between loyalty and betrayal, between friendship and exploitation. The woman whose role began in the simple guise of confidante and guide, stands now fully revealed as the principal agent in the protagonist's life. Mrs. Tristram tries to function in this capacity, but fails. Mrs. Assingham tries, and for a time succeeds, but finally is relegated to the background. Madame Merle alone among James's confidantes remains supreme mistress of the protagonist's fate. Her shapely hand is discernible even in Isabel's final decision to return to Rome; for it was she who primed the latter to her selfless devotion to the child. Even though she fails in her last attempt to secure Lord Warburton, or to extract the answer from Isabel to her last question, she still triumphs over the latter's fate, and to the end she is almost completely mistress of herself.

The only time we see her falter much is in her third and last scene with Osmond (Chapter 49.). Broaching the subject of Isabel's state of shock as she has just observed it, Madame Merle suddenly bursts into passionate remorse:

"It was precisely my deviltry that stupefied her. I couldn't help it; I was full of something bad. Perhaps it was something good; I don't know. You've not only dried up my tears; you've dried up my soul.

You made me as bad as yourself.

Your wife was afraid of me this morning, but in me it was really you she feared" (pp. 427–428).

For Madame Merle herself this utterance represents a revelation of Osmond's character: " '. . . it's only since your marriage that I've understood you' " (p. 428). And with this understanding has come the most bitter recognition of the falseness and futility of her position. She has clung to Osmond for the good she could do him and the child. " 'It's that . . . that made me so jealous of Isabel. I want it to be *my* work,' she added, with her face, which had grown hard and bitter, relaxing to its habit of smoothness" (p. 429). But Osmond coldly counsels her to leave that to him, and departs. Madame Merle is left to face her frustration alone: " 'Have I been so vile all for nothing?' " (p. 429).

This last scene with Osmond shows a different Madame Merle from the self-assured lady who has glided through the novel. The author's sympathy with even this most unscrupulously designing woman is evident in these quiet touches to her character. Readjusting her masks, however, she appears in the parlor of Pansy's convent where she shares two final scenes with Isabel. Both women have come to visit Pansy, who has been sent back by her father to reflect more keenly on her duty of submission to himself. As Madame Merle enters, "Isabel saw that she was more than ever playing a part [yet] it seemed to her that on the whole the wonderful woman had never been so natural" (p. 449).

Isabel, knowing now her secret from the Countess, has no desire to speak to her; and so Madame Merle's first speech flows on

with much of the brilliancy of a woman who had long been a mistress of the art of conversation. But there were phases and gradations in her speech, not one of which was lost upon Isabel's ear. . . . She had not proceeded far before Isabel noted a sudden break in her voice, a lapse in her continuity, which was in itself a complete drama. This subtle modulation marked a momentous discovery—the perception of an entirely new attitude on the part of her listener. Madame Merle had guessed in the space of an instant that everything was at an end between them, and in the space of another instant she had guessed the reason why. The person who stood there was not the same one she had seen hitherto, but was a very different person—a person who knew her secret. This discovery was tremendous, and from the moment she made it the most accomplished of women faltered and lost her courage. But only for a moment. Then the conscious stream of her perfect manner gathered itself again and flowed on as smoothly as might be to the end (p. 450).

These lines begin the "picture" conveying the present relation between the unmasked confidante-traitor and her victim. It is one of the finest passages in the novel. It surveys a whole little drama of expectancy, loss of confidence, fear of exposure, on the part of Madame Merle; and the recognition, brief triumph, and passing revenge, on the part of Isabel. For the latter, however, the feeling of revulsion overflows all else as she sees how she was used as a common tool. Her only revenge is to remain

silent, so that "the cleverest woman in the world [was left] standing there within a few feet of her knowing as little what to think
as the meanest" (p. 451).

So, in the life-and-death game which has engaged these two
women—the struggle for superior knowledge—Isabel seems to
be the final victor. She "would never accuse her, never reproach
her; perhaps because she never would give her the opportunity
to defend herself" (p. 451). The "cleverest woman in the world"
has indeed been baffled, and she seats "herself with a movement
which was in itself a confession of helplessness" (p. 451).

But during the interval between the two scenes, while Isabel
is visiting Pansy, Madame Merle remains alone in the parlor.
When Isabel returns, the older woman has regained her poise
and has her last trump card ready. It is her last chance to reassert
her waning superiority, because it is one bit of information still
lacking to Isabel. Imparting it will set her at a definite and final
disadvantage, for it is calculated to infuse bitterness into the
last human relation offering Isabel comfort: the devotion of her
dying cousin.[6]

"Your cousin did you once a great service. . . . He made you a rich
woman."
    "*He* made me —?"
Madame Merle appearing to see herself successful, she went on
more triumphantly: "He imparted to you that extra lustre which was
required to make you a brilliant match. At bottom it's him you've to
thank. . . . Yes, it was your uncle's money, but it was your cousin's
idea."
Isabel stood staring; she seemed to-day to live in a world il-
lumined by lurid flashes. "I don't know why you say such things. I
don't know what you know."
    "I know nothing but what I've guessed. But I've guessed that"
(p. 456).

Isabel never learns that Madame Merle's guess was based on
information supplied again by Mrs. Touchett. The two weapons
wielded so effectively by her enemies, the knowledge of her re-

jection of Lord Warburton and now this guess of Madame
Merle's, constitute the irony of her suffering coming to her partially through the communicativeness of her taciturn aunt. With
supreme self-control she turns to her foe and speaks her only
words of revenge:

"I believed it was you I had to thank!"
Madame Merle dropped her eyes; she stood there in a kind of
proud penance. "You're very unhappy, I know. But I'm more so."
"Yes, I can believe that. I think I should like never to see you
again" (p. 456).

For Madame Merle to admit herself unhappy is to admit defeat. The announcement of her departure for America sounds
like a new adventure, quite stripped of its glamor. In this way
a dazzling role terminates. The "true agent" has accomplished
her work, but not in the way she had hoped. Her frustration
contrasts with the new life of promise beckoning to Henrietta.
    Isabel meets this lady upon her arrival in London. She finds
her the same devoted friend as ever; but a great change has at
last occurred in her, for Miss Stackpole is going to give up her
country. Again a flicker of comedy crosses the background of
gloom. Henrietta, the comedienne, manages to lighten the tone
in these last chapters. For her, the story does end as a comedy—
in marriage. And the contrast between herself and the other
confidante receives a final ironical twist in their reversed choices
of countries. Madame Merle, who has always disdained "funny"
America, will only "make a convenience" of it; but Henrietta
will now be able to penetrate the "inner life" of England which
heretofore has been closed to her. Isabel, briefly diverted, men-
tally criticizes this surprising step taken by the woman who had
always represented an ideal to her. But Henrietta is not worried
by having failed to measure up to her confider's romantic ideal.
Instead she proves to be a realist of considerable dimensions,
bright enough to change her prejudices when opportunity holds
out a promise to her. Her inveterate optimism sounds the final

note of the novel: " 'Look here, Mr. Goodwood . . . just you wait!' " (p. 482).

In keeping the confidantes separate, James was simplifying his treatment of each, and facilitating their separate influence on Isabel. A simultaneous action would only have defeated his purpose, for Madame Merle would, of necessity, have outshone Henrietta, and thus the "light *ficelle*" would have lost her role. Instead, James achieves the contrast of the two characters and roles by indirect reference and alternating shifts in scenes.

Henrietta's failure to save Isabel is compensated for by her own gratifying prospects. Besides Miss Hurter, she is the only confidante whose role terminates happily. Their function as comic figures explains this exemption from the customary frustration of the Jamesian confidante.

As for Serena Merle, her role as villainess in a tragedy destines her for a dark future. Her frustrations are more numerous than those of other confidantes: a loveless marriage; an episode in another man's life, from which she could emerge only as the loser; the sacrifice of her child for the sake of respectability; the failure to contract a brilliant, second marriage—all these are truly great disappointments. Ironically, pity is accorded to her only by her victim: " 'Poor woman—and Pansy who doesn't like her!' " (p. 445). The man for whom she has worked, plotted, and suffered, makes no secret of his being tired of her. Nothing, indeed, is spared her; and one is forced to admire the pride that can hold her head erect to the very end.

The difference in technical functions of "light *ficelle*" and "true agent" is consistently maintained throughout the novel. Henrietta watches Isabel from without; while Madame Merle shapes her fate from within. Both confidantes run the gamut of intimacy with, and estrangement from, their confider. But they differ in their tactics: the one is aggressive, the other suave. They differ also in their motives: the first is altruistic, the second selfish (for her child's sake). And finally they differ in their dramatic roles: Henrietta is only a foil for the more important rival confidante. The inadequacy of both women in their capacity of confidante is explained by their very characters. The American is too simple; whereas the subtle expatriate is too selfish and deep. Neither can help Isabel in her plight; even after her scene of remorse Madame Merle is incapable of begging pardon. When the confidantes fail, it is natural that the heroine's other friends should also fail to succor her. Much as Ralph and even Mrs. Touchett have tried, they are, for the most part, beyond the limits of Isabel's confidence.

The technical function of dramatizing exposition is not given to these two confidantes as exclusively as to those in the later novels. Madame Merle gives practically as much information about Osmond as Mrs. Tristram does about Claire de Cintré. In both novels, written in his early style, the author supplements this means of exposition by narration and subsidiary reporters; in *The Portrait* these reporters are old Mr. Touchett, Ralph, and the Countess Gemini. Henrietta supplies information about Mr. Goodwood and Mr. Bantling, both of minor interest. As for their eliciting information from the "center," this the confidantes do only to a limited extent; there is none of the complete recapitulation with which Strether, for instance, occupies himself in the presence of his confidante. Much of the interior analysis of Isabel's mind is carried on when she is alone, as in the famous Chapter 42.

Although Henrietta has been characterized as "simple" and Madame Merle as "subtle" and "deceitful," they are sisters in their human frailty. Miss Stackpole espouses a theory of matrimony that one hopes she will never practice on Mr. Bantling; and Madame Merle is sympathetically shown in her anguish of conscience and loss of what is dearest to her nature. Both are fully rounded characters. Their respective attitudes in regard to knowledge make their roles blend with the whole substance of the novel: Henrietta, with her prejudices, and Madame Merle with her power of knowledge, highlight in different ways their young confider, who has come to Europe to see and to learn.

Chapter 4

THE SPOILS OF POYNTON

*I*N HIS NOVELS, as in his short stories, James usually places the confidante in a position subordinate to the center of consciousness. There is, however, a notable exception to this practice, namely, Fleda Vetch in *The Spoils of Poynton* (1897). For James, the fusion of the two roles is an anomaly. Conceived primarily as a *ficelle,* or aid to lucidity, the confidante by nature of her calling was designed for a minor part. She was to be the recipient of information, not otherwise available to the reader. She was also to impart the fruits of her speculation, again for the reader's benefit. Now, in *The Spoils of Poynton,* James was to try another experiment. The center of consciousness, or the chief agent of lucidity, was to become the recipient of direct confidences of two secondary characters. Fleda herself confides very little. She does, however, fulfill the functions customary in all the confidantes, of interpreting and judging. Being the center of consciousness and the protagonist throws her moreover into greater dramatic prominence than the other confidantes.

This is the main difference between the roles of Fleda and Madame Merle. In *Poynton,* Fleda holds supreme sway as the protagonist and only center of consciousness, whereas Madame

Merle shares her function with other "registers," such as Ralph.[1] When compared with Susan Stringham, another partial "center," Fleda, like her, receives the information confided to her by her friend, and also registers impressions from the source of opposition; in Fleda's case, Owen, the opponent of Mrs. Gereth, becomes Fleda's second confider. These impressions are filtered through the register, arousing the appropriate emotional conflict in the woman receiving them, and with this coloration they reach the reader. In the cases of both Fleda and Susan, the confidante is wedged between her confider and the latter's antagonists. Making her observations from both sides, she cannot help being drawn in both directions. As Fleda is intimately committed to her friend, Mrs. Gereth, her emotional involvement increases with the progress of the story. Caught between two opposing forces, Fleda tries vainly to ameliorate her compromising situation. But Susan simply goes over to the enemy, in her innocent belief that this action is the best for her friend. For Fleda the issue can only demand resistance. From a sympathetic spectatorship she has been forced into the center of the fray. Unlike Madame Merle, she is helplessly involved, and never gets her hands on the reins.

Because of her dramatic prominence as center of consciousness, Fleda Vetch is more conspicuous than the other confidantes in their stories or novels. She is the center of all the scenes, and the subject of all the pictures. As confidante, therefore, she has the widest scope of all her sisters, since they are mostly limited to scenes with their confiders. Fanny Assingham, Susan Stringham, and to a lesser extent, Madame Merle, come closest to Fleda's dramatic importance of observer; though all of them are forced down, sooner or later, by superior contestants. To Fleda alone the reader of *The Spoils of Poynton* looks for appreciation, interpretation, and dramatization of the story. In a way, her security of knowledge is greater than Strether's, who must be led and advised; or than Isabel Archer's, who believing in her security, falls into a treacherous mistake, refusing advice and help. Fleda has the power which James adverts to again and again in his work: the power of insight and knowledge. From the very beginning she gauges the other characters accurately, because her insights are the author's only means of communication with the reader. When she makes a mistake in judgment, it is apparent to the reader from what has already been revealed.

Fleda's importance as center of consciousness is set forth by James in his Preface. The "things," he states, could obviously not be the center, since they are inanimate, and novels must have dialogue. Their significance would lie rather in the passions they stirred up, and in that respect they would enjoy "heroic importance." But Fleda

planted herself centrally, and the stroke, as I call it, the demonstration after which she couldn't be gainsaid, was the simple act of letting it be seen she had character. . . . Fleda's ingratiating stroke, for importance, on the threshold, had been that she would understand; and positively, from that moment, the progress and march of my tale became and remained that of her understanding.

From beginning to end, in "The Spoils of Poynton," appreciation, even to that of the very whole, lives in Fleda; which is precisely why, as a consequence rather grandly imposed, every one else shows for comparatively stupid; the tangle, the drama, the tragedy and comedy of those who appreciate consisting so much of their relation with those who don't. . . . The "things" are radiant, shedding afar, with a merciless monotony, all their light, exerting their ravage without remorse; and Fleda almost demonically both sees and feels, while the others but feel without seeing.[2]

The double endowment of intelligence and feeling makes Fleda's consciousness the suitable "reflector" needed by James for his story about art treasures. For her prominence she needs both, while Susan Stringham, with less intelligence, will do only for a minor center of consciousness. Mrs. Gereth, James continues, was not suitable as the center because "she was not intelligent, not distinctively able." Mrs. Gereth "is at best a 'false' character, floundering as she does in the dusk of disproportionate passion," hence "the very reverse of a free spirit" (p. 131).

In order to understand, Fleda has to be endowed with qualities that harmonize with the opposing forces. She must love beauty, as Mrs. Gereth does; but she must also appreciate common sense, as Mona Brigstock does. Mona, says James,

is *all* will, without the smallest leak of force into taste or tenderness or vision. . . . She loses no minute in that perception of incongruities in which half Fleda's passion is wasted and misled, and into which Mrs. Gereth, to her practical loss, that is by the fatal grace of a sense of comedy, occasionally and disinterestedly strays (p. 131).

Mona is what Bernard Shaw would call an agent of the Life Force, and in tacit recognition of this fact, James admits that everyone in the nouvelle is sterile except herself. Fleda, he concedes, loses matters close at hand by gazing into "blue perspectives," and Mrs. Gereth "drops half the stitches of the web she seeks to weave" (p. 132).

With the factual Mona on one hand, and the wildly imaginative Mrs. Gereth on the other, Fleda Vetch is caught in the middle. Yet James made her in such a way that she could shed light on both women, having both enough sense and imagination to appreciate and understand, as her role would require. The knowledge she possesses of the situation and its probable outcome is fed both by her intuition and the confidences she receives from both the mother and her son.

This power of knowledge becomes evident in her first scene with Mrs. Gereth. Seeing the horseplay between Owen and Mona, Fleda "took the measure of the shock inflicted on Mrs. Gereth."[3] Her impression of Mona at Poynton is more accurate than Mrs. Gereth's: "Mrs. Gereth contrived at the end of an hour to convey to Fleda that it was plain she was brutally ignorant; but Fleda more subtly discovered that her ignorance was obscurely active" (p. 29). Having a finer intelligence than Mrs. Gereth, Fleda is thereby isolated from everyone; for it is a foregone conclusion that Owen Gereth and Mona Brigstock are of even duller substance.

Another quick perception made by the girl is of the maniacal disposition of her benefactress. Brought to Poynton to admire the magnificent antiques gathered there by her hostess over twenty-six years, she is asked to commiserate with that lady over her impending loss of them to her son through the English inheritance laws. Fleda watches Mrs. Gereth prepare the house for the inspection of her future daughter-in-law, Mona. The crudity of the Brigstock taste both women have already sampled during their visit to Waterbath, and now

Mrs. Gereth, even as she whisked away linen shrouds, persuaded herself of the possibility on Mona's part of some bewildered blankness, some collapse of admiration that would prove disconcerting to her swain—a hope of which Fleda at least could see the absurdity and which gave the measure of the poor lady's strange, almost maniacal disposition to thrust in everywhere the question of "things," to read all behaviour in the light of some fancied relation to them. "Things" were of course the sum of the world; only, for Mrs. Gereth, the sum of the world was rare French furniture and Oriental china. . . . Almost as much as Mrs. Gereth's her taste was her life, but her life was somehow the larger for it (pp. 27–28).

The author is at pains to set Fleda aside from her acquaintances. Attracted herself by the beauty of the antiques, she yet perceives the narrowing effect they have had on Mrs. Gereth's mentality. The poor lady's "maniacal disposition," already evident to the observer, will soon develop into a monomania.[4] Fleda's love for beautiful things expands her erstwhile narrow horizon; and she can regard the constricted rage of her friend with growing apprehension. Fleda's salvation lies in her realism. Sprung from the middle class, she still has the matter-of-fact attitude of the people. To be lifted by her acquaintance with Mrs. Gereth into the world of elegance and art is a thrill immeasurable to her innate sense of beauty:

On that flushed and huddled Sunday a great matter occurred; her little life became aware of a singular quickening. Her meagre past fell away from her like a garment of the wrong fashion, and as she came up to town on the Monday what she stared at in the suburban fields from the train was a future full of the things she particularly loved (p. 11).

But the demands that will be made of her intelligent sympathy are foreshadowed in her "sense, partly exultant and partly alarmed, of having quickly become necessary to her imperious friend, who indeed gave a reason quite sufficient for it in telling her there was nobody else who understood" (p. 15).

Her embarrassment before Owen over her position adds to her uneasiness; for he treats her as the

domesticated confidant of his mother's wrongs with a simple civility that almost troubled her conscience, so deeply she felt that she might have had for him the air of siding with that lady against him. She wondered if he would ever know how little really she did this, and that she was there, since Mrs. Gereth had insisted, not to betray, but essentially to confirm and protect (pp. 21–22).

Fleda's interest in Owen's opinion of herself is but the first glimmering of stronger feelings, which gradually add to the complication of her predicament. Held frantically on the one side, by his mother, whose hypocrisy and odd wildness unsettle the girl; and drawn, on the other side, to sympathize with the young man himself, who temporarily disregards the vehemence of the passions around him, Fleda, with all her superior knowledge, is ironically perplexed over her situation. One thing, however, which she determines early in the story, is her withdrawal of confidence in Mrs. Gereth:

The future was dark to her, but there was a silken thread she could clutch in the gloom—she would never give Owen away. He might

give himself—he even certainly would; but that was his own affair,
and his blunders, his innocence, only added to the appeal he made
to her. She would cover him, she would protect him, and beyond
thinking her a cheerful inmate he would never guess her intention,
any more than, beyond thinking her clever enough for anything,
his astute mother would discover it. From this hour, with Mrs.
Gereth, there was a flaw in her frankness: her admirable friend
continued to know everything she did; what was to remain unknown
was her general motive (pp. 31–32).

But the reserve in which she seeks refuge avails her nothing
in the presence of Mrs. Gereth's hysterics. With "glittering eyes"
she proclaims the vital role the "things" have played in her life:

"They were our religion, they were our life, they were *us*! And now
they're only *me*—except that they're also *you*, thank God, a little,
you dear!" she continued, suddenly inflicting on Fleda a kiss apparently intended to knock her into position. . . . "They're living
things to me; they know me, they return the touch of my hand. . . .
I couldn't bear the thought of such a woman here—I *couldn't*. I
don't know what she'd do; she'd be sure to invent some deviltry, if
it should be only to bring in her own little belongings and horrors. . . .
They'd be thrust in here, on top of my treasures, my own. Who
would save *them* for me—I ask you who *would*?" and she turned
again to Fleda with a dry, strained smile. Her handsome, high-nosed,
excited face might have been that of Don Quixote tilting at a wind-
mill (pp. 35–36).

The author's intention is quite clear in this passage. Not in
themselves are the "things" excessively precious, but only in the
eyes of Mrs. Gereth, who is unmistakably placed in the exaggerated light of farce. The added image of Don Quixote clinches
the caricature. Not this lady with her aberration, but Fleda, the
calm and reasonable girl, is to be taken as the norm in *Poynton*.
And, although at first enraptured by the beauty of the "things,"
Fleda quickly gains the balance of common sense in estimating
their value in life. For her, the human attraction of Owen Gereth
soon proves to be of far greater interest; and only after she has

lost him at the end, does she return to her preoccupation with the "things." In other words, Fleda remains first a woman, and only secondly an aesthete. Mrs. Gereth, on the contrary, lost her womanly instincts long ago and replaced them by inanimate objects. The replacement has caused a mental derangement, which under James's pen, just skirts pathos, but retains the comic flare. The whole plan of making Fleda the center of consciousness implements this presentation of a woman gone mad over art collecting. Mrs. Gereth herself could not reveal her own flaw. It has to be observed by a realist, with intelligent sympathy. Fleda is intentionally made to be the only character who understands the fate of the mad aesthete, the other characters being too much on the far side of either intelligence or of sympathy.

The heightened degree of Mrs. Gereth's madness is seen in the violent manner in which she pushes Fleda at Owen. That Fleda should bitterly resent this is beyond her hostess's comprehension.

Mrs. Gereth was generously sorry, but she was still more surprised—surprised at Fleda's not having liked to be shown off to Owen as the right sort of wife for him. Why not, in the name of wonder, if she absolutely *was* the right sort? She had admitted on explanation that she could see what her young friend meant by having been laid, as Fleda called it, at his feet; but it struck the girl that the admission was only made to please her, and that Mrs. Gereth was secretly surprised at her not being as happy to be sacrificed to the supremacy of a high standard as she was happy to sacrifice her. She had taken a tremendous fancy to her, but that was on account of the fancy—to Poynton of course—Fleda herself had taken (pp. 42–43).

The girl's appreciation for the beautiful things has endeared her to the heart of Mrs. Gereth. It further qualifies her in that lady's eyes as the only possible custodian of the "things" and consequently the only possible choice for her son. Personal feelings on either side are entirely discountenanced by the frenzied woman. Her hatred for Mona Brigstock is purely in terms of aestheticism; for the girl's vulgarity of manner could scarcely upset a woman who stoops to like commonness in the parting scene:

"I'm not a bit the vague, mooning, easy creature I dare say you think. However, if you won't come, you won't; *n'en parlons plus*. It *is* stupid here after what you're accustomed to. We can only, all round, do what we can, eh? For heaven's sake, don't let your mother forget her precious publication, the female magazine, with the what-do-you-call-'em?—the grease-catchers. There!"

Mrs. Gereth, delivering herself from the doorstep, had tossed the periodical higher in air than was absolutely needful—tossed it toward the carriage the retreating party was about to enter (pp. 41–42).

Mona's skilled manner in catching the magazine in mid-air is loudly acclaimed by Owen, and scornfully noted by his mother, still unaware of her share in the burlesque. Her chief comic aspect is her ignorance of her own vulgarity, and her thoughtless abuse of others' rights. To sacrifice Fleda seems quite natural to her; Fleda surprises her in resenting it. "The truth was simply that all Mrs. Gereth's scruples were on one side and that her ruling passion had in a manner despoiled her of her humanity" (p. 43).

With only the dehumanized woman to occupy her fancy, Fleda finds it very easy to fall into friendly conversation with the very human son. In a short time she finds him confiding in herself:

"Naturally I want my own house, you know," he said, "and my father made every arrangement for me to have it. But she may make it devilish awkward. What in the world's a fellow to do?" This it was that Owen wanted to know, and there could be no better proof of his friendliness than his air of depending on Fleda Vetch to tell him (p. 49).

The other side of the conflicting parties is now unfolding its difficulties, hopes, and fears; and Fleda, the confidante, registers

Owen's arguments and personality, and distills them for the reader. In spite of having been alerted to his stupidity, to his slow and gaping cerebration, the reader, seeing him through Fleda's loving eyes, cannot help liking him. His embarrassment she can appreciate, being herself exposed to similar feelings; his fondness for Mona she does not resent, lacking the horror for her which Mrs. Gereth feels. Above all, his simplicity in placing both of them on an equal footing appeals to her sensitivity, so recently shamed by his mother's haughty treatment of the Brigstocks. Also, his helplessness makes the strongest bid for her sympathy; it was the first thing that had attracted her to Mrs. Gereth; but it had been smothered too soon in frenzied vituperations.

Still, Owen Gereth is not too helpless to secure a deliverer. The ready ear of Fleda soon receives the oppressive communication of the duty now imposed on her. She is to get Mrs. Gereth off the premises, without the furniture, into the little dower-house left to her by the deceased husband. The ugliness of this duty weighs heavily on Fleda:

It was odious to *her* to have to look for solutions: what a strange relation between mother and son when there was no fundamental tenderness out of which a solution would irrepressibly spring! Was it Owen who was mainly responsible for that poverty? Fleda couldn't think so when she remembered that, so far as he was concerned, Mrs. Gereth would still have been welcome to have her seat by the Poynton fire. The fact that from the moment one accepted his marrying one saw no very different course for Owen to take ... (p. 52).

And to escape momentarily from the onerous burden, Fleda indulges in some extravagant daydreaming.

That she is able to so indulge, shows a likeness in her to the essence of her hostess. Like Susan Stringham, Mrs. Gereth is a confirmed romantic, living in a world of ideals:

It was not the crude love of possession; it was the need to be faithful to a trust and loyal to an idea. The idea was surely noble: it was that of the beauty Mrs. Gereth had so patiently and consummately wrought. Pale but radiant, her back to the wall, she rose there like a heroine guarding a treasure. . . . Her fanaticism gave her a new distinction, and Fleda perceived almost with awe that she had never carried herself so well. She trod the place like a reigning queen or a proud usurper; full as it was of splendid pieces, it could show in these days no ornament so effective, as its menaced mistress (pp. 53–54).

In most instances, Fleda has only admiration for Mrs. Gereth's romantic zeal in defending undefiled beauty. Her spirit, as the author indicates, is strangely divided; her tenderness for Owen does not prevent her from marveling how a person used to Adela Gereth can adapt himself so easily to Mona Brigstock.

With such a mother to give him the pitch, how could he take it so low? She wondered she didn't despise him for this, but there was something that kept her from it. If there had been nothing else it would have sufficed that she really found herself from this moment the medium of communication with him (p. 54).

In his profound knowledge of the woman's heart, James touches the nerve of any feminine surrender—the urge to serve. Beyond her respect for the histrionics of Adela Gereth, beyond even her own admiration for "the works of art," as she calls them—beyond these strong attractions is the feminine urge to devote herself to the hopeless task of reconciling mother and son. Their friction bothers her tender heart. Her concern is like that of the other confidantes who are would-be lovers—of Alice Staverton, in her anxiety over Brydon's welfare, and of Maria Gostrey, in her fear of Strether's barren future. Fleda's admiration for Mrs. Gereth is romantic and imaginative, but her love for Owen is the realism of the human heart, which prompts action. It was this realism that made her resent being sacrificed on Mrs. Gereth's terms; it is the same realism that motivates her sacrificing herself to the hopeless task.

Realizing well the suffering on both sides—Mrs. Gereth

restive under the English law, and Owen under Mona's monitor-ship which "had already begun to make him do things he didn't like" (p. 60)—Fleda tries to picture herself involved in the dilemma. Already she compares Mona's highhanded treatment with the kind way she would have managed him, were she in Mona's place; and her sympathy mounts as the dilemma in-creases: "He was as touching in his off-hand annoyance as his mother was tragic in her intensity . . ." (p. 60). Her intensity prohibits her son from seeing her, and so, on his frequent visits to Poynton, he and Fleda are thrown together. The messenger between the two camps contents both parties with very meager news; and the deadlock continues.

What is happening to Fleda during the interim is that she is falling more deeply in love with Owen. Concealing this from his mother with greatest care, she finds her role of mediator growing exceedingly difficult. As the tension mounts around her, so her own nerves tighten. The game she must play to pacify Mrs. Gereth and yet try to facilitate her withdrawal without her being aware of undue influence is fearfully exacting for a young girl with relatively little social experience, and in her inadequacy she tries stalling for time by telling half-truths. She is too easily swayed by either party—influenced first by Mrs. Gereth's fanaticism, then by Owen's helplessness; and finally, she is caught between the parties she aspired to conciliate.

Owen, on his part, in his childish trust and unawareness, confides fully in Fleda. Now that his mother has turned aggres-sor and put aside all motherly feeling, he needs and finds a substitute. He never considers how Fleda may be feeling toward himself, until the moment when it would be useful to him to know.

His mother moves in the same self-absorption. Her mono-mania makes her prowl through the house, trying tormentedly to settle on what things she will remove to Ricks, her dower-house. To this compromise Fleda has finally brought the con-tending parties. Seen through her eyes, the poor woman's misery is genuine enough; for though comic, James does not intend her to be obnoxious to the reader. Fleda's understanding is the filter for the suffering on both sides. As the center, Fleda casts a haze of kindness over the glaring hostility and flagrant aberrations of the contending parties. Through her James raises the petty feud, fit for the scandal column, to a conflict in imperishable values—to a dispute with a votary of ideals who in herself is only a frail human vessel, filled with all manner of contradictory passions and base inclinations, but who nonetheless appears as pathetic and pitiable. It is Fleda's goodness of character that suffuses the picture with a pleasant glow—the glow that makes the difference between sordid newspaper squabbles and literary art.

Fleda having done what she decently can to effect a compromise, James removes her from the scene in order to further the plot. Behind her back Mrs. Gereth transports all the spoils of Poynton to her little house at Ricks. Arriving there some weeks later, Fleda is horrified by the sight. It is a shock; "it was as if she had abruptly seen herself in the light of an accomplice" (p. 83). To be invested with the trust of Owen, just recently impressed upon her in London, and then to have to visit the person who betrayed her own trust, clearly places the girl in a more awkward position than before. "It was farcical not to speak; and yet to exclaim, to participate, would give one a bad sense of being mixed up with a theft" (p. 84). The audacity of her hostess in purloining everything of value is matched only by her highhanded manner of receiving her guest: " 'Oh I know what you're thinking; but what does it matter when you're so loyally on my side?' It had come indeed to a question of 'sides,' Fleda thought, for the whole place was in battle array" (p. 85).

But what startles Fleda even more is the cynicism betrayed by Mrs. Gereth in her account of the removal, done "by as brilliant a stroke as any commemorated in the annals of crime" (p. 88). Her relation savors of religiosity: " 'Oh I was inspired —they [the packers] found me wonderful. I neither ate nor slept, but I was as calm as I am now. I didn't know what was in me; it was worth finding out' " (p. 89).

The exposition rendered by this intimate colloquy between Mrs. Gereth and her confidante illumines both characters more fully. Mrs. Gereth has given new evidence of her genius for composition; but she also reinforces Fleda's impression of her belligerency: "What indeed was her spoliation of Poynton but the first engagement of a campaign?" (p. 92). The issue also throws new light on Fleda's character: "She couldn't care for such things when they came to her in such ways: there was a wrong about them all that turned them to ugliness" (p. 92). The worst pang for her is the sadness Owen would be experiencing at his privation. In her outward manner she is still with Mrs. Gereth; but in her heart she is all on Owen's side now.

He had looked to her to help him, yet this was what her help had been. He had done her the honor to ask her to exert herself in his interest, confiding to her a task of difficulty, but of the highest delicacy. Hadn't that been exactly the sort of service she longed to render him? Well, her way of rendering it had been simply to betray him and hand him over to his enemy. Shame, pity, resentment oppressed her in turn; in the last of these feelings the others were quickly submerged. Mrs. Gereth had imprisoned her in that torment of taste; but it was clear to her for an hour at least that she might hate Mrs. Gereth (pp. 93–94).

She has made up her mind to abandon Mrs. Gereth forever, and so escape meeting Owen again, but circumstances quickly shake her determination, the most important of these being the sudden arrival of Owen himself at Ricks, and his request to see her. There follows the first big scene of the nouvelle, which up to this point has been a feat of foreshortening. James renders this scene fully because of its dramatic importance. It has been prepared for by their several summarized visits together at Poynton, which the author briefly described, and by their accidental meeting in the London street.

Owen's interest in his confidante is primarily and ostensibly his need for her help with his mother; here again his prime request is for Fleda to persuade Mrs. Gereth to return the "things." But behind this motive is a deeper one, which perhaps even to Owen himself is not fully clarified. He is falling in love with her, and she recognizes the fact at once. Her scruples over the propriety of an engaged man's wanting to buy her a present in the London stores, and walking through the park with her, had culminated in her fantastic escape from him down the Broad Walk. Now, however, her self-possession is more complete, and his excitement over the theft leaves a margin of interest between them not touching directly on the personal. This margin—the subject of the "things"—provides, on the other hand, a safe means of approach to familiarity, which Owen is not slow to use. As long as he can confess his troubles to her, he need not confess his admiration of herself: "He spoke not impatiently, but with a kind of intimate familiarity, the sweetness of which made her feel a pang for having forced him to tell her what was embarrassing to him, what was even humiliating" (p. 109). More than ever Fleda's desire is to help this poor man.

Her problem was to help him to live as a gentleman and carry through what he had undertaken; her problem was to reinstate him in his rights.
"I can't tell you what it is to me to feel you on my side!" Owen exclaimed.
"Up to this time," said Fleda after a pause, "your mother has had no doubt of my being on hers."
"Then of course she won't like your changing."
"I dare say she won't like it at all" (pp. 112–113).

His appeal to her generosity is quickly followed up by an appeal to her cleverness: " 'I don't know anything in the world half so well as you. If I were as clever as you I might hope to get round her' " (p. 114).

Fleda tries to dodge what she sees coming, by getting him out of the house, promising to influence his mother in his favor. But Owen quaintly eludes her tactics and brings the issue to a head:

"When I got into this I didn't know you, and now that I know you how can I tell you the difference? And *she's* [Mona] so different, so ugly and vulgar, in the light of this squabble. No, like *you* I've never known one. It's another thing, it's a new thing altogether. Listen to me a little: can't something be done?" It was what had been in the air in those moments at Kensington, and it only wanted words to be a committed act. The more reason, to the girl's excited mind, why it shouldn't have words; her one thought was not to hear, to keep the act uncommitted. She would do this if she had to be horrid (p. 118).

Her homelessness is the handle for him in making this oblique declaration of love:

He put out his hand now; and once more she heard his unsounded words. "With everything patched up at the other place, I could live here with *you*. Don't you see what I mean?"
Fleda saw perfectly. . . . That solution—of her living with him at Ricks—disposed of him beautifully, and disposed not less so of herself; it disposed admirably too of Mrs. Gereth. Fleda could only vainly wonder how it provided for poor Mona (p. 120).

With Mona's ultimatum in the air—either return the spoils or the engagement is off—Owen begins to wonder if it might not be a blessing in disguise. But Fleda proudly sees that she is paying for the public offer Mrs. Gereth had made of her at Poynton: ". . . if Mrs. Gereth had had more discretion little Fleda Vetch wouldn't have been in a predicament" (p. 121).

The unscrupulousness of Mrs. Gereth in trying to barter Fleda's future for her own selfish ends closely resembles the use made of their confidantes by John Marcher, Spencer Brydon, and Prince Amerigo. These four persons regard their confidantes simply as a means to their own gratification, either their

vanity or their cupidity. May Bartram and Alice Staverton submit with the graciousness of minor characters; but Fleda Vetch,
a fully developed personality and a woman of spirit, rebels.
Throughout the nouvelle she is contending with her two confiders for her independence. From the moment she conceals her
affection for Owen from his mother, the contest of wits is on.
With Owen himself her contest takes a similar form of conceal-
ment. At first it is a kind of hide-and-seek: escaping from him in
Kensington, pushing him out of the house at Ricks. It will soon
take on a different form. Fleda is perhaps the most untractable
of all the confidantes, and she is probably the most compromised. The unscrupulousness of Mrs. Gereth's using her is understandable enough, when viewed in the light of that lady's
mania. But the abuse the girl receives from her would-be lover
through his weakness of will is more painful still:

To know she had become to him an object of desire gave her wings
that she felt herself flutter in the air: it was like the rush of a flood
into her own accumulations. These stored depths had been fathom-
less and still, but now, for half an hour, in the empty house, they
spread till they overflowed. He seemed to have made it right for her
to confess to herself her secret. Strange then there should be for him
in return nothing that such a confession could make right! How
could it make right that he should give up Mona for another woman?
His attitude was a sorry appeal to Fleda to legitimate that. But he
didn't believe it himself, and he had none of the courage of his suggestion. She could easily see how wrong everything must be when
a man so made to be manly was wanting in courage (pp. 125–126).

If he fully understands what he is doing, Owen must be singularly lacking in sympathy for the girl he loves. He lets her know
that it lies in her power to break up his match with Mona, simply
in the way she represents his request to his mother. Mona will
certainly break off if the "things" are not restored; Mrs. Gereth,
with even the faintest hint of this, will cling to them forever.
Owen himself would not take the matter to court. So with a little manipulating, Fleda can have Owen for herself. It is, in

Jamesian language, a "devilish" predicament in which to put a girl. And it is this predicament that marks both her rise and her downfall. Reflecting on the situation after his departure, she sees that she

couldn't dream of assisting him save in the sense of their common honor. She could never be the girl to be drawn in, she could never lift her finger against Mona. There was something in her that would make it a shame to her forever to have owed her happiness to an interference. It would seem intolerably vulgar to her to have "ousted" the daughter of the Brigstocks; and merely to have abstained even wouldn't assure her she had been straight. Nothing was really straight but to justify her little pensioned presence by her use; and now, won over as she was to heroism, she could see her use only as some high and delicate need. She couldn't do anything at all, in short, unless she could do it with a kind of pride, and there would be nothing to be proud of in having arranged for poor Owen to get off easily (p. 127).

The "picture" of Fleda Vetch, which constitutes Chapter IX, and of which the last two quotations are excerpts, is a typical Jamesian analysis of character, neatly done in seven pages. It is the climactic moment of initial choice for his heroine. What follows is simply the result of this decision. Impelled by a strict sense of justice, Fleda's pride pulls up at what Owen places before her. In making her judgment of the case, however, she seems to abandon expansive common sense for narrow, strict logic: "She had nothing to do with his dislikes; she had only to do with his good nature and his good name. She had joy of him just as he was, but it was of these things she had the greatest" (p. 128). This obviously is Fleda's first love. She lacks the experience to know that once a woman takes on responsibility for a man, she takes it for all of him—his weakness and cowardice included. To see him through to marriage with Mona would be the honorable thing, according to strict justice, for her to do. In her eyes, it is also the heroic way. But to help him break off an already obnoxious engagement might be the only way really to save him from dishonor. She certainly does have something to do with his dislikes, since she has committed herself to him as his confidante. Knowing his weakness, she should realize his inability to break off by himself. Fleda's trouble arises partly from her stubbornly simplistic view of life, and partly from the confusion of her roles. The duties of confidante and the yearning of lover clash, leaving the issues too confused to admit of a simple yet successful solution. Fleda's mistake is to impose the simple solution by putting it all up to him. But, as will presently be shown, her hidden motivation is psychologically sound.

In the meantime three dramatized scenes between Fleda and Mrs. Gereth ensue. That lady is acute enough to divine Fleda's secret love; and with "an odd unwonted sense of age and cunning" she impresses the girl as suspiciously stalling for time (p. 140). Confidences on both sides have ceased. From now on it is a battle of wits, with Mrs. Gereth still determined to force the marriage of Fleda with her son, and Fleda evading her as best she can.

In these scenes (Chapters X-XII), the elderly lady takes the offensive from the start. Finding the indirect method ineffective, she resorts to frontal attack with two unequivocal utterances: " 'You don't in the least "hate" Owen, my darling. You care for him very much. In fact, my own, you're in love with him— there!' " (p. 149), and; " 'Save him—save him: you *can*!' " (p. 151). After securing an admission of Fleda's love, she presses her victim further for an indication of Owen's feelings. These Fleda tries hard to conceal:

> The girl hesitated an instant; she was conscious that she must choose between two risks. She had had a secret and the secret was gone. Owen had one, which was still unbruised, and the greater risk now was that his mother should lay her formidable hand upon it. All Fleda's tenderness for him moved her to protect it; so she faced the smaller peril (p. 154).

She admits what she was to have concealed from her hostess: that Mona has postponed the wedding until the "things" are returned. Mrs. Gereth jumps at this, and Fleda's weak assurance that Mona will never give him up has no effect on his mother: " 'Well, I'll keep them, to try her,' she finally pronounced; at which Fleda felt quite sick, as if she had given everything and got nothing" (p. 154).

From the beginning, poor Fleda has been playing a losing game, and her worst fear now is that Mrs. Gereth will discover her remaining secret—Owen's love for herself. She vividly visualizes the "brutality of good intentions" which her friend would exercise upon such a discovery:

One of the straightest of these strokes, Fleda saw, would be the dance of delight over the mystery Mrs. Gereth had laid bare—the loud, lawful, tactless joy of the explorer leaping upon the strand. Like any other lucky discoverer, she would take possession of the fortunate island. She was nothing if not practical: almost the only thing she took account of in her young friend's soft secret was the excellent use she could make of it—a use so much to her taste that she refused to feel a hindrance in the quality of the material (pp. 156–157).

This passage shows the innate vulgarity of Mrs. Gereth, besides her base opportunism and readiness at exploitation. In their third scene together she impudently puts the matter on Fleda's shoulders: " 'Deal with him in your own clever way—I ask no questions. All I ask is that you succeed. . . . he shall have everything in the place the minute he'll say he'll marry you' " (p. 157). Mrs. Gereth is just as adept in placing the whole responsibility on her friend as her son was. Never did a confidante pay more dearly for her initial generosity. It takes the dire threat of instant separation from Fleda to make Mrs. Gereth consent not to meddle herself. But before long she is to chisel at this promise and hasten the break-up.

Just now Fleda has all she can do to shield Owen from his mother's acuteness. His letter and its silence about the date of the nuptials provides the latter with another cause for jubilation. The longer she remains at Ricks, the more awkward Fleda's position grows. Being dependent on Mrs. Gereth's hospitality from the very beginning of their friendship, she is now in the even more disagreeable impasse of trying to keep her promise to Owen by influencing his mother to return the spoils. The whole dilemma has simply delivered her into her antagonist's power. Realizing her degraded state, she almost wishes herself back among the crude simplicity of West Kensington. A devotion to fine things is so clearly seen as a delusion, and Mrs. Gereth's conversation is becoming increasingly repulsive. She refers to rare attractions and a dangerous beauty in Fleda which are far from the truth: "These arts, when Mrs. Gereth's spirits were high, were handled with a brave and cynical humour with which Fleda's fancy could keep no step. . ." (p. 168). Her hostess's offensiveness reaches a climax when Fleda keeps assuring her that Owen loves Mona: " 'Do you mean to say that, Mona or no Mona, he could see you that way, day after day, and not have the ordinary feelings of a man?' " (p. 168).[5] This offensiveness is another detail in the realistic portrait of Mrs. Gereth. James's enjoyment in adding stroke after stroke to her picture can be gleaned from such asides as: "What did the Post exist for but to tell you your children were wretchedly married?—so that if such a source of misery was dry, what could you do but infer that for once you had miraculously escaped?" (p. 167).

Finally, however, Fleda makes the break and returns to her father's place in London, only to discover that "The lady of Ricks had made a desert around her, possessing and absorbing her so utterly that other partakers had fallen away" (p. 171). The spoliation of Poynton has entered into the young woman's life. Mrs. Gereth, who went in and out of Fleda's soul at will is a type of tyrannical friend who devours the confidante.[6] The remarkable thing about Fleda is that she perseveres in her loyalty to Mrs. Gereth, and preserves her individuality and her freedom. In the Preface, James makes a point of Fleda's freedom: ". . . the free spirit, always much tormented, and by no means always triumphant, is heroic, ironic, pathetic or whatever, and as exemplified in the record of Fleda Vetch, for instance, 'successful' only through having remained free."[7]

But freedom of spirit is no safeguard from isolation; rather it usually leads to it. Forgotten by her friends, barely tolerated by her father, Fleda "wandered vaguely in the western wilderness or cultivated shy forms of that 'household art' for which she had had a respect before tasting the bitter tree of knowledge" (p. 172). James could hardly state it more clearly that the worship of "things" can turn into a curse; for that tree grew for Fleda in the garden of beautiful things, and Mrs. Gereth taught her to develop her taste for them. This taste for beauty increases her alienation from her father, who "was conscious of having a taste for fine things [old brandy-flasks, penwipers, ash-trays] which his children had unfortunately not inherited" (p. 173). Poor Fleda is doomed to that isolation which she, as confidante, tried to remedy for her friends. Her future is a blank of anxiety.

James has technical reasons for separating Fleda from Mrs. Gereth. The first reason is to shed a milder, more compassionate light on that lady, through the girl's fancy; and secondly, to facilitate an undisturbed interview between Fleda and Owen. Owen resumes their relation on their old basis of confidante-friend, and ignores Fleda's discouraging manner. The scene furthers the action by his confessing to having been tipped off by Mrs. Gereth as to Fleda's whereabouts. This perfidy of her other friend rankles in the girl's heart. Mrs. Gereth simply cannot leave matters alone. Fleda informs him of the reasons for his mother's delay, and elicits in turn from him the exposition regarding Mona's present attitude. Functionally, the scene parallels and extends the previous one between the young people at Ricks. Only, James avails himself amply of the contrast in settings, and of Fleda's humiliation over her fall from Ricks to West Kensington. The brief descriptions of the smutty maid are excellent. To Owen, however, these things are as nothing, when he faces his bedeviled state. Particularly he blames Mona for coming down on him in her disappointment. Fleda seeks refuge from her own feelings by defending Mona. But she is brutally brought round by the sudden disclosure of Mona's jealousy: " 'She said you were not honest' " (p. 196). Owen's childlike simplicity is evident in the glibness with which he repeats conversations. His childish dependence comes to the fore in the twice repeated question: " '*Am* I to tell my solicitor to act?' " (p. 197). This solution offers Fleda

the great chance of her secret. If she should determine him to adopt it she might put out her hand and take him. It would shut in Mrs. Gereth's face the open door of surrender: she would flare up and fight, flying the flag of a passionate, an heroic defence. The case would obviously go against her, but the proceedings would last longer than Mona's patience or Owen's propriety. With a formal rupture he would be at large; and she had only to tighten her fingers round the string that would raise the curtain on that scene (p. 198).

The only thing that makes her hesitate is that he has told Mona he loves her. " 'What in the world has become, in so short a time, of the affection that led to your engagement?' " (p. 198). The honor involved in repudiating declarations of love is of great consequence to Fleda, with her natural inclination to idealism. But beneath her altruistic concern for Owen's honor is her feminine care for her own self: if he could so easily assure Mona Brigstock he loved her, and then so easily renounce it, what chances would little Fleda Vetch stand of securing the permanence of his love? Just now he leans heavily on her support and advice; but is he by nature inconstant? The rapid flow of his next speech, leading up to the point of declaration of love to herself is expressed in the thought and idiom of a child—from blaming Mona, to quoting Mona, and hiding behind "nice old Mummy." The speech is essentially comic, and James can only rescue his serious heroine from her impasse by breaking off the declaration with a device typically used in comedies: the sudden entrance of an irate parent. Footfalls and voices announce the impending disaster, and Fleda can think only of Mrs. Gereth, who would gloat. But James betters the comic surprise by ushering in Mrs. Brigstock.

The note of high comedy is kept throughout the following scene, Mrs. Brigstock providing James with an opportunity of refreshing contrast with Mrs. Gereth. Fleda tries to be brilliant, but only blunders as badly as Owen in his embarrassment. When he takes up her defense it only spoils whatever chance Fleda had to right herself with Mrs. Brigstock.

After this there is but one thing for Fleda: "to abandon Owen, to give up the fine office of helping him back to his own" (p. 215). Arriving at her sister's home in a "stupid little town," she soon receives word of Owen's pursuit. He arrives, and they engage in their third and final big scene. Her duty is still her foremost excuse for allowing him to come; only on his mentioning it in a letter does she submit to the inevitable: " 'You owe me something, you know, for what you said you would do and haven't done . . .' " (p. 217).

Owen's first concern is to assure Fleda of his practical freedom from the engagement, all but the formal break having taken place. The scene transpires first to give exposition of the Brigstock position, then to dramatize the lovers' conflict.

"She said our relation, yours and mine, isn't innocent."
"What did she mean by that?"
"As you may suppose, I particularly inquired. Do you know what she had the cheek to tell me?" Owen asked. "She didn't better it much: she said she meant that it's excessively unnatural."
Fleda considered afresh. "Well, it is!" she brought out at last.
"Then, upon my honor, it's only you who make it so. . . . by the way you keep me off" (pp. 221–222).

But he cannot understand her anxiety over his easy repudiation of his former love.

"Can you take such pleasure in her being 'finished'—a poor girl you've once loved?"

Owen waited long enough to take in the question; then with a serenity startling even to her knowledge of his nature, "I don't think I can have *really* loved her, you know," he replied (p. 224).

He will not be put off. To her objection that Mona will hold tight, he pleads with her to save him from her. Fleda of course understands his weakness and his simplicity which alone could prompt a man to make such a plea. The confidante however remains superior to her lover. She sees the impossibility of his request, and the strain makes her break down into a confession of her own feelings. An ecstatic sequence follows, but it cannot avert the hour of decision. To Fleda's logical mind Owen's freedom is not yet real: " 'You're not all right—you're all wrong!' Fleda cried in despair. 'You mustn't stay here, you mustn't!' she repeated with clear decision" (p. 230).

The issue forces her to face her own contrariness. She had urged him before to leave the initiative to breaking the engagement to Mona, so nothing could be said against him; now she accuses him of not breaking it himself. In self-defense he checks her, and she retracts:

". . . I don't know what nonsense you make me talk! You *have* pleased me, and you've been right and good, and it's the only comfort, and you must go. Everything must come from Mona, and if it doesn't come we've said entirely too much. You must leave me alone —forever" (pp. 230–231).

"Good-bye, good-bye! If she doesn't let you off it will be because she *is* attached to you" (p. 234).

The pain she feels over this possibility is rendered in a brief description:

It was his betrayal of his need of support and sanction that made her retreat—harden herself in the effort to save what might remain of all she had given, given probably for nothing. The very vision of him as he thus morally clung to her was the vision of a weakness somewhere at the core of his bloom, a blessed manly weakness of which, if she had only the valid right, it would be all a sweetness to take care (p. 235).

The weakness which drew him to her originally, and prompted his confidences, makes him in the moment of parting still depend on her for guidance. He demands if she would make him marry a woman he hates:

"No. Anything is better than that."

"Then, in God's name, what must I do?"

"You must settle with her. You mustn't break faith. . . . The great thing is to keep faith. Where *is* a man if he doesn't? If he doesn't he may be so cruel. So cruel, so cruel, so cruel!" Fleda repeated. "I couldn't have a hand in *that,* you know. . . . You offered her marriage: it's a tremendous thing for her." Then looking at him another moment, "*I* wouldn't give you up!" she said again (pp. 236-237).

As before, his confidante makes the decision for him, and he, like a little boy, meekly returns to Poynton, where, upon return of the spoils, Mona swiftly gets him. In trying to assess Fleda's choice, one should consider two things—her dependence as confidante, and her independence as a woman. In the former capacity she takes the simple view of Owen's duty: he must keep faith. In the latter position she wants him exceedingly; but a deep concern for herself warns her against encouraging him to break faith, for she has seen his want of manly courage. Also her self-respect rejects the thought of implication. The difference in the motives goes back to the distinction in the two roles.

In the meantime, Mrs. Gereth, who upon divulgence from Mrs. Brigstock has supposed the whole affair settled between Owen and Fleda, has sent everything back to Poynton. The news is crushing to Fleda. The noble trust invested in her by her friend is overwhelming, and she sees Mrs. Gereth again in a new light:

And what most kept her breathless was her companion's very grandeur. Fleda distinguished as never before the purity of the passion; it made Mrs. Gereth august and almost sublime. It was absolutely unselfish—she cared nothing for mere possession. She thought solely and incorruptibly of what was best for the things; she had surrendered them to the presumptive care of the one person of her acquaintance who felt about them as she felt herself . . . (p. 258).

The enormity of her mistake dawns slowly upon Mrs. Gereth, as Fleda miserably stutters out the grim fact of Owen's absence, her own adoring love for him, and the vague hope that he will soon get his release from Mona. Her listener receives this broken speech in portentous silence. Then her wrath breaks. Disappointment, frustration, and loss of her treasures make her heap abuse on the quaking girl. Keenly she touches the latter's sorest spot, her duty as confidante: " 'Good God, girl, your place was to stand before me as a woman honestly married!' " (p. 266). Knowing her confidante thoroughly, Mrs. Gereth berates her folly roundly, and Fleda, inconsistently, at once regrets having sent Owen away.

"Owen's a blockhead," she repeated with a quiet, tragic finality, looking straight into Fleda's eyes. "I don't know why you dress up so the fact that he's disgustingly weak."

Fleda hesitated. . . . "Because I love him. It's because he's weak that he needs me," she added.

"That was why his father, whom he exactly resembles, needed *me*. And I didn't fail his father," said Mrs. Gereth. She gave Fleda a moment to appreciate the remark; after which she pursued: "Mona Brigstock isn't weak; she's stronger than you!" (p. 272).

As time passes, their growing recognition of Mona's victory reunites the two women in their need for mutual support. The older woman's exhaustion after having removed the "things" to Poynton, besides her present grief, reduce her in a matter of hours to near helplessness. Now that Fleda has ceased being a tool, her role as confidante is once more welcomed by her friend. And Fleda promises:

". . . whatever you ask, whatever you need, that I will always do."

"I shall need your company," said Mrs. Gereth. Fleda wondered an instant if this were not practically a demand for penal submission—for a surrender that, in its complete humility, would be a long expiation. But there was none of the latent chill of the vindictive in the way Mrs. Gereth pursued: "We can always, as time goes on, talk of them together."

"Of the old things? . . . Never!" she exclaimed (pp. 282-283).

Suffering has reunited them, because it has purified both and made Mrs. Gereth less demanding on her confidante.

In the sequel Fleda seems to go through an interior revolution. The poignant sense of having betrayed Mrs. Gereth's trust by failing to secure Owen for herself seems to obliterate her former justification in turning him away. Time now passes for her in silent religious communion with the memory of the beautiful things that have returned to Poynton. "She greeted them with open arms; she thought of them hour after hour; they made a company with which solitude was warm . . ." (p. 285).

The next scene with Mrs. Gereth (Chapter XX) provides some of the remaining exposition. The latter has been down to Poynton to see her son and has ascertained two facts: that he has been privately married, and that he hates his wife. Still denying that there had been any obligation on her son's part to Mona, she declares that the girl took action only when the spoils began to arrive. After that they were quickly married. Mona did what Fleda wouldn't, she hustled him to the registrar. Mrs. Gereth misses no opportunity to underscore her friend's mistake. But Fleda has regained her self-possession.

After this the two women form a new relation, shaped

almost wholly on breaches and omissions. Something had dropped out altogether, and the question between them, which time would answer, was whether the change had made them strangers or yokefellows. It was as if at last, for better or worse, they were, in a clearer, cruder air, really to know each other. Fleda wondered how Mrs. Gereth had escaped hating her: there were hours when it seemed that such a feat might leave after all a scant margin for future accidents. The thing indeed that now came out in its simplicity was that even in her shrunken state the lady of Ricks was larger than her wrongs (p. 307).

For her part, Fleda succeeds in submerging her feelings by occupying herself with the actual need of her confider:

... his mother's bare spaces demanded all the tapestry the recipient of her bounty could furnish. There were moments during the month that followed when Mrs. Gereth struck her as still older and feebler, and as likely to become quite easily amused (p. 308).

The religious devotion with which Fleda had secretly communed with her memories of the spoils, is revived by the letter from Owen, offering her one of them as a remembrance. Filled with rapture she makes her pilgrimage to Poynton. Her devotion to the Maltese cross, mentioned before and named specifically by Owen, forms the brightest image as she travels into the country. But disaster has overtaken Poynton and its treasure. Fire robs Fleda of the only recompense offered to her for her painful role of confidante.

In that role Fleda Vetch has acquitted herself in a dubious fashion. Having tried hard to please both confiders, she has soon found her position untenable; but escape proved inadequate. The bullying of Mrs. Gereth has forced her to betray her feelings for Owen: but his attentions have not helped her predicament either; and the possibility of being caught in the future trap of denial by an inconstant husband has alarmed her as well. Nevertheless, as the center of consciousness, she sustains the biggest part accorded to a confidante by Henry James. The author seems to have lavished on her character the qualities he most cherished in a woman: fidelity, in spite of her weakness; tenderness, intelligence, and independence. The main difference between her role and that of the other confidantes is in her being the "center," which means that exposition is provided principally by her confiders to her, instead of in the opposite manner as in *The Ambassadors*. Being the "center" she controls all of the scenes, and indeed the success of the nouvelle depends largely upon the artistic merits of her character. The minor perfections of the work, those of clash of characters, contrast of settings, and dramatic suspense, all enhance the success with which

the central character is portrayed. A thoroughly human personality, equivocating when trapped, making mistakes in spite of
her intelligence, and taking the blame perhaps too supinely,
Fleda ranks as one of the most successful confidantes, both for
her dramatic prominence and for the appeal of her character.
James's own fondness for her can be gathered from the space he
gives to her in his Preface, where she gets more direct reference
than any other confidante elsewhere, except Maria Gostrey in
the *Project* for *The Ambassadors*.

The theme of betrayal, which affects the roles of Susan Stringham and Madame Merle, is alluded to in regard to Fleda, whose
hypersensitive conscience accuses her of this guilt. Her deep
concern for strict justice and honor is presented in the form of a
slightly oversimplified moral code, which brooks no exceptions
or modifications. Yet this firm surface conceals a deep personal
anxiety and dread for her own future. Her dread lest the danger
of rejection might come near her as it does to Mona, is probably
the clue to her momentous decision. Still, the diversity between
her opinion and Mrs. Gereth's in this matter leaves the whole
question open for the reader. It is a fitting denouement for a
complicated role played almost continually at high tension, but
played, from the dramatic viewpoint, so successfully that it
never strains credibility.

Chapter 5

WHAT MAISIE KNEW

For *What Maisie Knew* (1897) James created in Mrs. Wix a special confidante. She is a character whose last appearance is at complete variance with her first one, and whose technical function expands from the simple confidante of the protagonist through an active championship, to the final stage of potential corrupter and rival of the child. As confidante she performs the usual functions hitherto discernible in the role: she interprets, advises, prophesies, judges, and in turn confides in the protagonist. Most of these functions serve expository purposes. Since the protagonist is a child, the confidante's interpretations and prophecies are necessary for elucidation. The functions that are peculiar to her individual role are those of intrigue and armed conflict. These become apparent and increasingly prominent from the middle of the novel onwards. Another feature of Mrs. Wix is her class, which bars her socially from those whom she serves, but which her redoubtable character seeks to surmount. The disparity between her and Sir Claude is greater than that between the governess and Mrs. Grose.

Maisie's first glimpse of Mrs. Wix, her governess at her mother's establishment, is of "a still more frightening old woman, a figure awaiting her on the very doorstep. . . . Mrs. Wix took her and, Maisie felt the next day, would never let her go."[1] This first feeling of the child foreshadows the fierce struggle to ensue between Mrs. Wix and the various claimants of Maisie's guardianship. Transferring at once to the little girl her frustrated love for her own dead child, the elderly governess makes Maisie feel that "she had been, with passion and anguish, a mother, and that this was something Miss Overmore was not, something (strangely, confusingly) that mamma was even less" (p. 34). At once Mrs. Wix is contrasted with the two other chief women characters; and the salient feature of her character is her motherliness. It is what ensures her ultimate dominion over Maisie, and because instinctual, rather than intentional like Mrs. Beale's strategy, it wields the greater force. For the moment, however, the fierceness of mother love is muted and channelled, and embraces the child's aching desire in a soothing safety, which charms the little girl more "than papa, than mamma . . . than Miss Overmore, on whose loveliness, as she supposed it, the little girl was faintly conscious that one couldn't rest with quite the same tucked-in and kissed-for-the-night feeling" (p. 36).

This instinctual sympathy of the dowdy old woman for Maisie soon relegates the outward obstacle of appearance to the background. Her greasy grey hair, done in an old-fashioned "glossy braid, like a large diadem, on the top of the head, and behind, at the nape of the neck, a dingy rosette like a large button," her "melancholy garb . . . with the added suggestion of her goggles [which] reminded her pupil of the polished shell or corslet of a horrid beetle," make her look at first "cross and almost cruel"; but eventually Maisie grows aware of "her being in the eyes of the world a figure mainly to laugh at. She was as droll as a charade, or an animal, toward the end of the 'natural history'—a person whom people, to make talk lively, described to each other and imitated" (pp. 35-36). Her insect and animal-like queerness indicates exteriorly her aboriginal interior traits. They complement amusingly her romantic fancies and total lack of education. Her romantic imaginings compensate for her private frustrations and public humiliations, and color her own drab existence.

She took refuge on the firm ground of fiction, through which indeed there curled the blue river of truth. She knew swarms of stories, mostly those of the novels she had read; relating them with a memory that never faltered and a wealth of detail that was Maisie's delight. They were all about love and beauty and countesses and wickedness. Her conversation was practically an endless narrative, a great garden of romance, with sudden vistas into her own life and gushing fountains of homeliness. These were the parts where they most lingered; she made the child take with her again every step of her long, lame course and think it beyond magic or monsters (p. 37).

The bent of Mrs. Wix's imagination finds ample scope in her plans for the future of Maisie, Sir Claude, and herself. Having lost her own husband "ages" ago, and heaping on him, as Maisie notices, no florid reminiscences, Mrs. Wix discovers in Sir Claude, Maisie's stepfather, an ideal and idol. At first this admiration is conditioned merely by his well-bred condescension to the lowly governess;[2] but after receiving a new dress, a "five pound note and the history of France and an umbrella with a malachite knob," besides many a chaffing "till she was purple with the pleasure of it" (pp. 67-69), Mrs. Wix gives herself up to total devotion so that "[Maisie's] lessons these first days and indeed for long after seemed to be all about Sir Claude" (p. 67), and it was a settled question that his gentlemanliness exceeded every other in the world.

Marius Bewley seems to be the first critic to note the true relation which Mrs. Wix adopts toward Sir Claude. He writes:

Elderly, ugly, fantastic as she is, Mrs. Wix falls in love with Sir Claude. The fact isn't insisted on, and it might even be possible to interpret in non-erotic terms her passionate avowal to Maisie that she 'adores' Sir Claude, although I doubt it. . . . Although the allusions are veiled [in Twenty-four], Mrs. Wix's behaviour and speeches are such as to be understandable only in terms of an utter infatuation for the young man, and there are moments when our belief in her disinterestedness wears thin. Her desire to keep Sir Claude and Mrs. Beale separated, if it arises primarily from her concern for Maisie, seems at some points not to be untouched by sexual jealousy.[3]

The evidence is preponderantly in favor of Mr. Bewley's observations. From the simple satisfaction she derives at Maisie's childlike avowal of loving Sir Claude (Nine) to the furious struggle to keep him (Twenty-four), Mrs. Wix shows clear signs of infatuation; but to her own eyes they are hidden. She remains throughout in perfect good faith. Encased by her "old-fashioned conscience" and her "dingy decencies," as she is encased by her beetle-like shiny old dress, Mrs. Wix stays unaware of the humiliating nature of her aggression. Fortified by her insistence on the "moral sense," she becomes, under James's pen, a pathetically ironical figure, rather than the character she is usually taken to be by the critics.[4] A close study of the novel will furnish the evidence, supporting a sounder judgment of Mrs. Wix's character, upon which her function as confidante depends so fully.

The mutual confidence established at once between Maisie and Mrs. Wix provides the means of communication with the reader.[5] In showing "what Maisie knew," James avails himself of the confidante's words and actions as a catalyst. Her interpretations of the actions of the other adults greatly further the instruction of the child in the ways of the world. James subtly underscores this in the casual reference to Maisie's education in the sordid life around her. And while the governess attests to scruples in discussing these topics with a child, she manages to exonerate herself: " 'It isn't as if you didn't already know everything, is it, love?' and 'I can't make you any worse than you *are,* can I, darling?' " (p. 71).

The clash between her old-fashioned decencies and interior relish in the indecent seems clearly imputed to the governess by the narrator. Her very need to justify herself is incriminating.

However objectively innocent, if the child is "bad" in Mrs. Wix's sense and is encouraged in her badness, this procedure certainly does not exculpate that person. If Maisie were not "bad," what indeed could Mrs. Wix talk about?[6] Mrs. Wix's conscience never quite rests in peace. Near the end of the novel it again rises up, accusing her of her lost innocence. For the present, however, scruples are easily brushed aside, and the two engage in an analysis of why women fall in love with Sir Claude, which abruptly culminates in Mrs. Wix's solemn declaration:

. . . Maisie, receptive and profound, suddenly said to her companion: "And you, my dear, are you in love with him too?"
    Even her profundity had left a margin for a laugh; so she was a trifle startled by the solemn promptitude with which Mrs. Wix plumped out: "Overhead and ears. I've *never,* since you ask me, been so far gone" (pp. 71–72).

No distinction is made between her case and those of the other women. To be smitten by his merits is a great thing, its only drawback being the wife's consequent jealousy. Maisie herself is startled by Mrs. Wix's seriousness. And during the times of their abandonment in the empty house

Mrs. Wix reminded her disciple on such occasions—hungry moments often, when all the support of the reminder was required—that the "real life" of their companions, the brilliant society in which it was inevitable they should move and the complicated pleasures in which it was almost presumptuous of the mind to follow them, must offer features literally not to be imagined without being seen (p. 72).

The child's uninitiated state and the old woman's facile admiration combine to create their mutual awe; and Mrs. Wix's vicarious pleasure is plainly ironical. It links her with Mrs. Tristram and Mrs. Assingham, who, although society women, find themselves deprived of certain fulfillments. Actually, in dramatic importance, Mrs. Wix is a close competitor with these meddling confidantes. The manner in which she takes over the reins after her arrival in Boulogne is perhaps partly due to the minority of the protagonist; but it is also unmistakably a result of her domineering character and instinctual drives. Once again, James adapts the role of the confidante to the exigencies of her character.

The novel does not really get under way until Maisie's parents have separated and begun new liaisons. The scene in her father's house when Mrs. Wix is sent by Mrs. Farange to coax Maisie back with Sir Claude's photograph (Seven) provides the moment of initial interest. It is the first confrontation of Mrs. Wix with Mrs. Beale, and it foreshadows the bigger scenes to follow. As repeated later, the child becomes the obvious pawn of the contending parties. But a subtler pawn introduced into this scene is the photograph of Sir Claude; and in claiming it, Maisie prefigures a contention of another kind. With great reluctance Mrs. Wix relinquishes the precious object, which was sent to her by Maisie's mother. James satirizes the poor woman's agony by describing how her "straighteners" and her ancient pelisse enter into the struggle.

The germ of the issue is already clear, though not fully grown: Mrs. Wix has enlisted as Sir Claude's champion, and because Mrs. Beale (née Miss Overmore) holds aloof, not yet having felt his charm, the only opponent is the child. But the word "surrender" is too strong for any doubt as to Mrs. Wix's attachment. Maisie, still in her innocence, presents no formidable opposition that an older and wiser girl or a woman would offer; hence Mrs. Wix's relatively easy relinquishment. But, nevertheless, this scene strikes up the theme of rivalry between the old woman and the child, into which the more threatening bid of Mrs. Beale will presently obtrude. The passion with which Mrs. Wix defends Ida and Sir Claude to Mrs. Beale reveals her as an antagonist to reckon with. James emphasizes her pathos by making the contrast so apparent between her impulses and her unprepossessing exterior. Doomed from the start to the ridicule of Mrs. Beale and the contumely of Mrs. Farange, she has only the natural rejection of Sir Claude to look forward to.

This final affront, however, is far from her mind, as she blissfully adopts the role of his confidante in his marital troubles.
Sir Claude's frequent visits to the schoolroom and his likewise
frequent "private" and "earnest" conversations with Mrs. Wix
are for a time the notable subjects of Maisie's awareness.

He led [a domestic life] after all in the schoolroom, and there were
hours of late evening, when she had gone to bed, that Maisie knew
he sat there talking with Mrs. Wix of how to meet his difficulties.
His consideration for this unfortunate woman even in the midst of
them continued to show him as the perfect gentleman and lifted the
subject of his courtesy into an upper air of beatitude in which her
very pride had the hush of anxiety. "He leans on me—he leans on
me!" she only announced from time to time; and she was more surprised than amused when, later on, she accidentally found she had
given her pupil the impression of a support literally supplied by her
person (p. 88).

The subject of these conversations being Sir Claude's future,
Mrs. Wix inevitably feels herself called upon to plan it for him.
" 'He's a wonderful nature, but he can't live like the lilies. He's
all right, you know, but he must have a high interest' " (pp. 88-
89). The "high interest" presumably corresponds to his getting into Parliament, a goal of Mrs. Wix's own devising, and
it crops up eventually as also a means of "saving him." Although
noncommittal to Maisie's inquiry, the governess can mean only
the other women besetting him, particularly Mrs. Beale, who,
two chapters back, was already recognized as the "chief" difficulty in Sir Claude's life.

The idea of Parliament, however, is only a small scratching
before the plans for Sir Claude's future are fully hatched. These
are amply divulged in Twelve, the scene with Maisie, Mrs. Wix,
and Sir Claude. He asks:

"Do you mean leave this house and take up my abode with you?"
"It will be the right thing—if you feel as you've told me you feel."
Mrs. Wix, sustained and uplifted, was now as clear as a bell.

. . . "It's your happy thought that I shall take a house for you?"

"For the wretched homeless child. Any roof—over *our* heads—will do for us; but of course for you it will have to be something really nice" (pp. 92–93).

The plan of a separate menage, just for the three of them, supports Bewley's comment: "And the ugly possibility arises in the reader's mind that Mrs. Wix's attachment to Maisie may match Mrs. Beale's in this: that for them both, and however much they may like Maisie for herself, the little girl provides a means of closing in on Sir Claude."[7] With his awakening to her plans, Sir Claude begins his attempts at evasion and withdrawal. Later Maisie realizes that his weakness is his fear of possessive women. Here, already, although Maisie is still unaware of it, his fear of Mrs. Wix begins.

That person, blinded by infatuation, keeps pressing her point: " '. . . the whole point's our being together' " (p. 94). Even Maisie can grasp the force of Sir Claude's objection to "bolting with Mrs. Wix," although the good lady urges it as a salutary escape from a certain bad woman.

Again, although Maisie cannot catch the allusion, both Sir Claude and the reader infer the bad woman to be Mrs. Beale. As for herself, the child is preoccupied with Mrs. Wix's eloquence, and the impact of seeing "Mrs. Wix come out as Mrs. Wix had never come before—not even on the day of her call at Mrs. Beale's with the news of mamma's marriage. On that day Mrs. Beale had surpassed her in dignity, but nobody could have surpassed her now" (p. 95). The poor old governess has clearly been metamorphosed into the inspired guide of the hesitant man. She can now nod recognition to her fellow guides, Mrs. Tristram, Maria Gostrey, and Fanny Assingham. In all of them self-interest is a concealed yet powerful motive; but the latter three lack the high moral tone of the battered governess in pleading:

"We can help each other. What you'll do for our young friend here I needn't say. That isn't even what I want to speak of now. What

I want to speak of is what you'll *get*—don't you see?—from such an opportunity to take hold. Take hold of *us*—take hold of *her*. Make her your duty—make her your life: she'll repay you a thousandfold!" (p. 95).

The earnestness with which she makes her appeal must also be seen in the light of her own insecurity. Practically devoid of education herself, and apparently all alone in life, her position, threatened as it is by jealous Ida for conversing with her husband, is at best precarious. "It took her pupil but a moment to feel that she quivered with insecurity . . ." (p. 91). And, "Maisie expressed in her own way the truth that she never went home nowadays without expecting to find the temple of her studies empty and the poor priestess cast out" (p. 99).

At any rate, the fervor of her appeal to Sir Claude bears her up under the marked hatred of his wife, until one day Maisie finds her utterly crushed. She looks so ill that the child fears her mother has done her worst. But it is only Mrs. Wix's discovery that Sir Claude has been lying to conceal his meetings with Mrs. Beale.

The pathetic figure which the Jamesian confidante sometimes cuts is repeated in Mrs. Wix, fighting desperately for herself. Her using Maisie as a shield is quite obvious in this scene; and in her eyes it is a legitimate way to guarantee her own preservation. Without the child and a share in her being provided for, she has absolutely no prospects. And the tenuousness of her position becomes clearer to Maisie after Sir Claude has arranged for her removal to Mrs. Beale's: " 'But when I'm here what will Mrs. Wix do?' 'Ah you should have thought of that sooner!' said her companion with the first faint note of asperity she had ever heard him sound" (p. 106).

It signals the disappearance of that poor woman for ten chapters, and her noticeable drop from Maisie's consciousness. When she returns to view, in Twenty-two, the second half of the novel is well under way, and it is to be more dominated by the governess than the first half was. Whereas she only appeared in approximately every second chapter then, her scenes recur now in every chapter, with the single exception of Thirty, in which she is just as present to the minds of its actors, Maisie and Sir Claude, as if planted directly before them.

After a long obscurity, then, Mrs. Wix makes a startling reappearance. Like Maisie's first meeting with her, this second one is summarized in a Jamesian picture, but in a very different manner. She lands with victory assured by the "power [given by Sir Claude] to have 'changes' . . . of the most intimate order, adapted to climates and occasions so various as to foreshadow in themselves the stages of a vast itinerary" (p. 189). A sly humor plays through the ironic description of her landing at Boulogne, financed by the man whom she has come to "save." Mrs. Wix has not come over to listen to Sir Claude's witticisms. The redness of her face may be the result of *petits verres*—Maisie involuntarily associates it with measles and "habits"—but it also indicates the high degree of her determination.

Like Henrietta Stackpole, Mrs. Wix unwittingly provides the lighter side to the story. A good sign of James's intention to be witty at the expense of his confidante is her dangling in an ironical position, where, in spite of her attempts to carry it off successfully, she yet seems ridiculous. In one of these predicaments Mrs. Wix finds herself upon landing. Having made a stormy Channel crossing, she arrives in a state "that Maisie scarce knew whether to suppose the depth of prostration or the flush of triumph. The lady on [Sir Claude's] arm, still bent beneath her late ordeal, was muffled in such draperies as had never before offered so much support to so much woe" (p. 189). The details mentioned in Mrs. Wix's outfits contrast with those in Mrs. Assingham's. In the latter's case clothes are made redolent with exotic airs; in Mrs. Wix's place clothes are made to be demeaning: ugly when shabby, ridiculous when elegant. "The incongruity of her smartness, the circumference of her stiff frock, presented her as really more ready for Paris than any of them" (p. 193). Together with her own self-deception as to her aims, her appearance continually exposes her to the indulgent smiles of the reader. James seems to be playing a game with this confidante. Although few, if any, of the confidantes finally achieve their most cherished desires, Mrs. Wix is still outstanding in her poverty and ignominy. No one, except the child, takes her seriously. Besides, she makes a fool of herself by chasing a young man and lacks the intelligence to realize it.

Her arrival heralds the high point of her aggression. She "rose from her chair and, as if to take more of a stand, placed herself, not without majesty, before the fire" (p. 193). Fortified with Ida's backing, she delivers the burden of her message. "Mrs. Wix was now bold enough for anything. 'She [Ida] wants me to persuade you to get rid of the person from Mrs. Beale's' " (p. 193). Susan Ash, the maid from Mrs. Beale's with the low IQ, whom Sir Claude had brought over with Maisie, is a danger signal of Mrs. Beale's own imminence. She is therefore to be summarily dismissed. When Sir Claude humanely suggests taking her home, Mrs. Wix, the woman whose "moral sense" critics extol, retorts: " 'Pay her fare and give her a sovereign. . . . If she goes wrong on the way it will be simply because she wants to . . .' " (p. 194). This startling bit of advice surprises Maisie, who notes a novelty in the tone that matches the newness of Mrs. Wix's cap. One guesses that this fuss is an attempt to keep Sir Claude from meeting the maid's mistress. Either the "moral sense" is in abeyance, or it is betraying its fallaciousness.

Demonstrating his disinclination to fight, Sir Claude courteously changes the subject. He has sized up Mrs. Wix's altered condition—her determination and her flushed face—and from now on his strategy will be passive resistance. This emissary of Ida's is a formidable opponent in her own right. Ida and her injunction are merely an alibi for Mrs. Wix:

"What she meant was to make me know that you're definitely free. To have that straight from her was a joy I of course hadn't hoped for; it made the assurance, and my delight at it, a thing I could really proceed upon. You already know now certainly I'd have started even if she hadn't pressed me; you already know what, so long, we've been looking for and what, as soon as she told me of her step taken at Folkestone, I recognised with rapture that we have. It's your freedom that makes me right"—she fairly bristled with her logic. "But I don't mind telling you that it's her action that makes me happy!" (p. 195).

Mrs. Wix exposes—unintentionally—the true nature of her motives by the key words in her speech: "my delight," and "we've been looking for," "we have," "me right," and "me happy." It is quite plainly a confession of love. Her joy is fused in one breath with the pronoun, first person plural, and it does not include Maisie. Rather, it is the "we" who had the midnight colloquies over his prospects. His freedom justifies her position, not as governess, which needs no justification as long as he has the child, but as a companion on his travels. It is hard to determine how far her prospects at this moment go; but her very attire testifies to her readiness to follow him anywhere. Her manner of speaking to him further indicates her assumption of a status equal to his. Like a wife-to-be, she is already laying down the law. Nevertheless, her declaration of his being "definitely free" from Ida will later be flatly contradicted when she sees him eluding her grasp.

The coolness with which he receives this effusion, and the disregard for her "we's" do not, however, stem the tide of her feelings. Rather, they rise higher upon his cold inquiry concerning her sudden alliance with Ida. She defends that woman's sudden change in her regard. The real reason for her forgiving Ida everything is of course their common resistance to Mrs. Beale. " 'It's to *keep* you—I won't say from yourself, because in yourself you're beautiful and good! It's to save you from the worst person of all. I haven't, after all, come over to be afraid to speak of her!' " (p. 197).

As he quietly defends Mrs. Beale, the discussion quickly mounts into a heated argument. In the thick of the fray little Maisie lucidly plumbs the depths of Sir Claude's problem. Mrs. Wix accused him of fearing Mrs. Beale; but the child recalls

smoothing over the artificial connectedness between the two characters charmed him into developing Maria's figure into "something of the dignity of a prime idea" (p. 324).

James's first feat in "smoothing over" is accomplished in making the initial meeting between Strether and Maria appear as natural as possible. They had "the appearance of having accepted each other with an absence of preliminaries practically complete. . . . It was almost as if she had been in possession and received him as a guest. Her acquaintance with the place presented her in a manner as a hostess. . . ."[2] The ease and spontaneity of her manner help dispel any awkwardness on his part resulting from a scruple of propriety. Her leading "him forth into the world" counts for him as "his introduction to things" (p. 23).

Another device used by James at this juncture to disguise his *ficelle* is her previous acquaintance with Waymarsh. Although the latter disclaims any recognition, the acquaintance serves Maria as an index to Strether and his connections. As confidante, she is at first obliged to share her function with Waymarsh. But before long the lady has superseded the gentleman in Strether's confidence. Her immediate influence on Strether is what James alluded to in the Preface as her "function [which] speaks at once for itself, and by the time she has dined with Strether in London and gone to a play with him her intervention as a *ficelle* is, I hold, expertly justified."[3] This intervention is her entering into the plans and apprehensions of Strether with the tact and insight of an accomplished lady and sympathetic friend. It is indeed these qualities of character which join "the seams or joints of Maria Gostrey's ostensible connectedness" with Strether.[4] And it is her rounded character that lends dramatic credibility to the otherwise awkward role imposed on her. A lone American woman living in Europe who picks up a slightly dazed elderly American gentleman bound for Paris on a strange mission does need some justifying on grounds of dramatic probability and seriousness. This probability James sought and found in the intersubjectivity between his center of consciousness and the confidante. As Leon Edel has pointed out, in turn referring to the *Notebooks,* James had no need to hesitate to choose artificial situations, or factitious solutions, because the realism he achieved was in making such unrealities seem real.[5] Like Flaubert, James believed that reality lay in the creative process.

The first justification offered by James is Maria's position of globetrotter and *femme du monde.* In an era of invasions of Europe by wealthy American travellers, she combines the versatility of cicerone with the availability of a travellers' agency. Like Madame Merle, she has made it her business to please. " 'I'm a general guide—to "Europe," don't you know? I wait for people—I put them through. I pick them up—I set them down. I'm a sort of superior "courier-maid." I'm a companion at large. . . . I never sought it—it has come to me. It has been my fate, and one's fate one accepts' " (p. 26). Hers is an unfailing knowledge of shops, prices, theaters, plays. So at once her great usefulness in such a delicate matter as ordering Waymarsh's breakfast puts a priority on her presence. Strether has just begged her "not to break away at the very moment she had created a want" (p. 35). Already an awareness of his need is discernible, although for the moment it remains on the mundane level.

Later on, as Waymarsh's defection in sympathy will become more and more apparent, Strether's need for Miss Gostrey will reassert itself; but just now her relationship with him is being solidified by her own appearance and personality. The "positive high picture" of Maria dining with Strether at a small table with lighted candles and rose-colored shades, which opens Book Second, depicts the critical hour of his inner surrender. He had already "given himself up" to her and she had taken over the "job" of his problem before they left Chester; but this meal in the London "public place" followed by the scene in the theater sets the seal upon his commitment. The fine impression made on his mind of the distinction between Mrs. Newsome and Maria is accentuated by his conscious identification of both women with fated queens—Queen Elizabeth and Mary Stuart. Maria's appearance is so impressive that "he had in addition taken it as a starting point for fresh backward, fresh forward, fresh lateral flights" (p. 43). It is the real beginning of his adventure. Maria, the first agent of his initiation, is now securely in the lead.

Powerful as the impression of Miss Gostrey's experience and appearance is, the greater influence on Strether nonetheless is exerted by her character. As usual, James endows his important lady with exceptional intelligence and intuition. Hardly has the acquaintance begun before her analysis pierces him to the quick: " 'Your failure's general. . . . The failure to enjoy. . . . I wish you *would* let me show you how.' " He replies, " 'Oh I'm afraid of you!' " (p. 25). But this she confidently denies. Very soon her power of divination exposes to Strether his own terror of Waymarsh. At the theater she further uncovers the secret of his mission: " 'I seem with this freedom, you see, to have guessed Mr. Chad. He's a young man on whose head high hopes are placed at Woollett; a young man a wicked woman has got hold of and whom his family over there have sent you out to rescue' " (p. 45). Dramatic suspense is greatly enhanced by her guessing the situation from hints he has let fall. Also, her perceptiveness evokes his admiration, thereby binding him closer to herself.

The scene which follows is the first large segment of dramatized exposition between Strether and Maria. It is preceded somewhat earlier by a shorter, less informative scene between Strether and Waymarsh in the Chester hotel. The two scenes contrast with each other especially in the relation of the speakers. In the earlier scene, Waymarsh and Strether are fencing: the thrust is aimed at eliciting information which the parry tries to conceal. But in the theater scene with Maria these positions are abandoned. Maria's illuminations seize upon the facts, which Strether has only—weakly or bravely, as best he can—to admit. One feels his helplessness, his state of deliverance into her hands. But the sympathy and kindness of his interrogator, as well as her own confidence inspire the poor man himself with trust.

However ignorant of women in general, Strether has experienced plenty of domination at the hands of Mrs. Newsome. Hence his initial fear of trusting himself to Maria's illuminations. By now, however, it has passed over into complete confidence. What in the first interview she had promised—to show him how "to enjoy"—is already beginning to take shape: he is enjoying the most "extraordinary [thing that] has ever happened to him"—the having fallen utterly into her hands (p. 25).

The fact is that Strether is quite unprepared for the encounter with Miss Gostrey. Having married "so young as to have missed the natural time in Boston for taking girls to the Museum" he lost his wife early (p. 44). For years thereafter "he had never taken any one anywhere" (p. 44). When eventually the friendship with Mrs. Newsome developed, the initiative was on her side, both in the publication of the Review and in the commissioning of the ambassador.

Strether's relation with Maria contrasts with both of the preceding ones. He cannot refrain from contrasting her with Mrs. Newsome. First the image of the queens hovers before him; then he observes: " 'Mrs. Newsome . . . hasn't moreover your courage on the question of contact.' " But she rejects this: " 'I've mere battered indifference' " (p. 47). James makes much of Maria's battered state in his *Project* of the novel written for Harpers:

This young woman—young as a slightly battered unmarried woman of five-and-thirty can be—is a study, as it were, of a highly contemporary and quasi-cosmopolite type, and has her high utility in my little drama. . . . An American spinster left by the accidents of life free to wander, and having wandered and re-wandered from an early time, Miss Gostrey, clever, independent, humourous, shrewd, a little battered, a little hard, both highly unshockable and highly incorruptible, and many other things besides, is above all full of initiations and familiarities, full of Europe, full of ways and means, full of everything and everywhere. . . . She is inordinately modern, the fruit of actual, international conditions, of the growing polyglot Babel.[6]

Were James writing in the 1960's, he would perhaps have designed Maria as a member of "the marginal sex."[7] Clearly she has "knocked about" so long over so vast a territory that her battered condition is only the outward manifestation of her inner isolation. She has not the force of the Newsome personality; and yet Strether finds in her what the Woollett lady lacks: an interest in "the human predicament," a "divination of it and a semi-cynical helpfulness *about* it."[8] It is a question of either wideness or narrowness of vision. The wider the vision, the greater the sympathy. Mrs. Newsome, rigid in the American matriarchal tradition, still ironically lacks "courage on the question of contact." To which Maria adds an incomparable bit of elucidation: ". . . if your friend *had* come [instead of Strether to Europe] she would take great views, and the great views, to put it simply, would be too much for her" (pp. 47-48). In other words, Mrs. Newsome avoids contacts that might derogate from her acknowledged superiority. That an aggressive woman is usually afraid, is what Maria in effect is saying; and what the aggressive provincial woman fears most is the confrontation with great, with *new* ideas; whereas Maria, the cosmopolite, is at home in the widest circles, and for all her battered condition, still dazzles the provincial Strether.

The importance of the theater scene lies, therefore, first in the full exposition rendered in dialogue between Strether and Maria, and second, in the complete contrast in Strether's eyes between Maria and Mrs. Newsome. The third significance achieved by this scene is in the triple function of Maria, here set forth for the first time, and later to be repeated and embellished at greater length.

The first aspect of her function synchronizes with that of the other *ficelles*: to be a listener, to draw expository facts, from the center of consciousness for the benefit of the reader. Maria ranks with Madame Merle and May Bartram in her talent for eliciting personal confessions. Quickly she probes into the nature of Strether's reward; and although balked temporarily by his evasions, she will eventually guess the full truth and present it to him: "I've never believed, you know, that you did propose. I always believed it was really she—' " (p. 364). And Strether does not deny it.

The second part which Maria plays is to predict the future. One of two things, she suggests, may have happened to Chad: " 'One is that he may have got brutalised. The other is that he may have got refined' " (p. 54). For Strether this *is* a novelty, since he has not yet been introduced to "the wonderful place" of Chad's residence. But Maria knows her Paris, and easily divines a transformation for the better in the suspect young man.

Thirdly, Maria turns her powers of analysis on Strether himself. In this respect she complements the narrator's internal analysis of Strether's consciousness. " 'You're a depth of duplicity!' " she volunteers when for the second time he evades her probing into his possible marriage with Mrs. Newsome (p. 56). Before launching the third and final attack, she sums up her impressions of his character: " '*You'll* save [Chad]. That's who'll save him,' " she declares. " 'Oh but with Mamie's aid,' " he rejoins. " 'Unless indeed you mean . . . that I shall effect so much more with yours!' " " 'You'll do more—as you're so much better—than all of us put together,' " she answers, still leaving the door open for herself and the aid she may yet give. " 'I think I'm only better since I've known *you!*' " he bravely and sincerely counters (p. 57). Though inexperienced in the cosmopolis, Strether is not naïve. Already he senses that a transformation in him has begun, initiated by this interesting little woman. But this frank avowal does not yet lay him open to her persistent clue-hunting regarding his personal gain. For a third time, just before they leave the theater, Miss Gostrey tries to elicit the admission from him:

"You've spoken to me of what—by your success—Mr. Chad stands to gain. But you've not spoken to me of what you do."

"Oh I've nothing more to gain," said Strether very simply.

She took it as even quite too simple. "You mean you've got it all 'down'? You've been paid in advance?"

"Ah don't talk about payment!" he groaned.
.... "What—by failure—do you stand to lose?"
He still, however, wouldn't have it. "Nothing!" he exclaimed. . . .
.... "What do you stand to lose?"
Why the question now affected him as other he couldn't have
said; he could only this time meet it otherwise. "Everything."
"So I thought. Then you shall succeed. And to that end I'm
yours—"
"Ah, dear lady!" he kindly breathed.
"Till death!" said Maria Gostrey. "Good night" (pp. 57–58).

Strether's commitment to Maria is ratified by her dedication
to his cause. It is a deliberate pact made by mature persons with
the air of subscribing to a great venture—"till death!" In itself,
the trip to Paris to persuade a young *bon vivant* to return to his
duties is no such momentous task. But in the consciousness first
of Strether, then by empathy, of Miss Gostrey, it is an issue of
far-reaching consequences. " 'Everything' " has been staked by
the man, and he needs a woman to see him through. Reality is
less in the plot than in the reactions of the characters. The impression of his need made on Maria's keen mind is so lasting
that her dedication—as will be seen—is actually a total offering of herself.

After the London episode, Miss Gostrey delays her arrival
in Paris for a week, and in the light of her future strategy this
delay must be considered as intentional. She has let Strether
take the plunge alone. While he was taking it, James made use
of Waymarsh as confidant. In the scene between the two men
which opens Book Third Strether goads the dour New Englander
with startling gaiety and unconcern over his nondiscoveries
regarding Chad's affair. Upon Waymarsh's exasperated demand, " 'Then what the devil *do* you know?' " Strether's disconcerting reply is, " 'Well, . . . I guess I don't know anything!' "
And the narrator adds, "His gaiety might have been a tribute to
the fact that the state he had been reduced to did for him again
what had been done by his talk of the matter with Miss Gostrey
at the London theater. It was somehow enlarging . . ." (p. 74).

So enlarging has the effect been of his first week in Paris that by the time he steps into Maria's little *entresol* his sensibilities are completely harmonized with his surroundings. "He might have been a little scared at the picture of how much more, in this place, he should know himself 'in' hadn't his friend been on the spot to measure the amount to his appetite" (p. 81). Her dwelling offers him a further induction into the mysteries of European culture.

James frequently made use of houses and possessions to illustrate his characters. The same is true of the homes of Chad, Maria Gostrey, and Madame de Vionnet. Each in turn adds to the more wonderful impression made on their guest. Like the role she plays, Maria's domicile prepares Strether's sensibilities for the encounters with Madame.

Her compact and crowded little chambers, almost dusky, as they at first struck him, with accumulations, represented a supreme general adjustment to opportunities and conditions. . . . The life of the occupant struck him of a sudden as more charged with possession even than Chad's or than Miss Barrace's; wide as his glimpse had lately become of the empire of "things," what was before him still enlarged it; the lust of the eyes and the pride of life had indeed thus their temple. It was the innermost nook of the shrine—as brown as a pirate's cave (pp. 81–82).

The impact on Strether of his friend's home is quietly conveyed in inverted religious imagery. In his Woollett days Strether doubtless heard many a preacher inveigh against the concupiscence of the eyes and the pride of life. It was in a temple of the Lord where he received these denunciations. Now the church setting has turned topsy-turvy. The honest New Englander has entered not only the temple where the objects of greed and pride are worshipped; but he has penetrated to the very sanctuary of these idols. And then comes the shock from yet another quarter: the "shrine" is "brown as a pirate's cave." Maria, who at first was pictured in bird imagery as innocently picking up her rarities and conveying them to her "final nest," stands suddenly exposed in Strether's eyes as surrounded by the riches of piratical plunder.

Another outstanding feature of James's portraiture of Maria is the use of color. In London, her broad red velvet throat band with its antique jewel set her apart from Mrs. Newsome in her ruche and black silk gown. There is a wealth of implication in the two colors worn by these women. Black of course was the favorite Puritan color for centuries; whereas red suggests the opulence of the Renaissance—an allusion that will later be amplified in connection with Madame de Vionnet. Now Maria, the skilled *femme du monde* and antithesis to Mrs. Newsome, appears in her own setting, her lovely little pirate's cave, whose brownness gleams with "glints of gold," and "patches of purple." The whole place is low, dusky, old with the venerability of antiquity and rarity. No oppression, however, is felt here. Rather, "the circle in which they stood together was warm with life, and every question between them would live there as nowhere else" (p. 82). Not only is her home a center of priceless works of art like Madame's, it is also a haven of life, like Gloriani's garden. By such subtle innuendoes does James point up Maria's function as go-between. Although her fireside welcomes Strether as a home in foreign parts, it will be at the other woman's where he will find ultimate satisfaction. Maria's influence is transitory; she is only the highly accomplished lady on a limited scale; Strether, though unknowingly, yet waits for another. Although the description of her little home shows Maria as the priestess, not the goddess, at the shrine of culture, still her complexity of character is sufficient to fascinate Strether with new insights as he stands in her charmed circle of life. "She was the blessing that had now become his need, and what could prove it better than that without her he had lost himself?" (p. 82). The guide, the commentator, has returned. Now Strether can escape Waymarsh's growing suspicion of his motives; he can fly to the little shrine in the Quartier Marboeuf for sympathy and enlightenment.

In the lively dialogue which ensues Strether recapitulates for Maria his new acquaintance with little Bilham and Miss Barrace. With a few brief questions she ascertains the degree of his changed attitude toward Paris and toward his embassy. "*She* saw, however, still other things [than he did], though in an instant she had hidden them" (p. 83).

Upon her agreement to meet the members of Chad's group in an attempt to gauge them for him, he arranges a meeting with little Bilham in the Louvre. Her comment, " 'Oh he's all right—he's one of *us*!' " dropped quietly to Strether reassures him immensely; for he assumes it to mean what his New England conscience interprets: here is another intense American—just "a special little form of the oldest thing they knew [which] justified it at once to his own vision as well. He wanted to be able to like his specimen with a clear good conscience, and this fully permitted it" (p. 85).

" 'He's one of *us*!' " is however an ambiguous statement. Maria may well have meant it to signify "he's one of our cosmopolitan set," which would have been quite different from Strether's understanding of the phrase. In this light it closely resembles her earlier statement: " 'They've [Chad's friends] *been*, in effect, wonderful' "—a statement which Strether had accepted—wonderful in their taste, their cleverness, their polish, their charm (p. 84). James had used the word in this sense many times in *The Awkward Age*. The reader easily makes the connection between "wonderful" and "all right . . . one of us"; but Strether's comprehension shrinks suddenly from its newly acquired Parisian breadth to the erstwhile confines of the Woollett conscience. If Maria does not mean what Strether assumes, who can her first person plural pronoun include but the American expatriates and their French liaisons? But if she identifies herself with them, where does that leave Strether? And what does she really mean by "all right"?

Assuming for the moment that "one of us" means one of the Parisian set, and remembering what Maria has heard from

Strether, that Chad's woman is "Base, venal—out of the streets," then naturally "all right" must mean *not* base, not venal, but wonderful. That this interpretation is really what she means is borne out by little Bilham's defense of Chad's "virtuous attachment." Bilham is an accomplished man of the world; he does belong to the "wonderful" set; and by claiming him as "one of us," Maria is identifying herself with the same set, with the result that Strether has given himself up to the standards of Paris from the very beginning. From Woollett's point of view, therefore, the *ficelle* is just as sinister a character as "the woman" in Chad's life. Her identifications in education and friendship with Marie de Vionnet later explain the resemblance. It will later become apparent how James uses Maria as a foil for Madame.

Having met little Bilham twice, Maria finally delivers her oracular pronouncements. Seated with Strether and Waymarsh in a box at the Français, she begins by praising the young man as " 'far and away, you know, the best of them' "—of the long procession of young and old she has met coming to Europe from America (p. 88). Bilham can be trusted: " 'He won't do the least dreadful little thing.' " But what follows refers indirectly to Strether: " 'I've had my disappointments—the poor things are never really safe; or only at least when you have them under your eye. One can never completely trust them' " (p. 89). How indeed Strether will disappoint her is told at the conclusion of the novel.

Presently she begins to interpret for Strether the tactics of the others. "Though she disclaimed the prophetic vision she was at this instant the nearest approach he had ever met to the priestess of the oracle. The light was in her eyes. 'You must face it now' " (p. 90). Bilham was acting under orders from Chad, who had purposely absented himself from Paris. Strether faces it.

"So that Chad has done the whole thing?"

"Oh no—not the whole. We've done some of it. You and I and 'Europe.' "

"Europe—yes," Strether mused.

"Dear old Paris," she seemed to explain. . . . "But the idea you speak of," she said, "won't have been his best. He'll have a better. It won't be all through little Bilham that he'll work it."

This already sounded almost like a hope destroyed. "Through whom else then?"

"That's what we shall see! . . . [Then, as a gentleman enters the box:]. . . . "Why, through this gentleman!". . . . Miss Gostrey had said more than she knew. They were in presence of Chad himself. (pp. 90–91).

Maria as prophetess was already announced in the London theater. In the Paris theater she makes her formal pronouncement, although as the narrator observes, it is as yet without full insight on her part. Her momentary blindness does not however derogate from her oracular powers; for the oracle of Delphi was none the wiser for what she said. Chad will indeed "work" Strether's change through himself, but even more so through Madame de Vionnet. This fact Maria will in due time perceive before anyone else. So far, she does know and admits having herself a hand in Strether's recent change.

Just as Miss Gostrey had deferred giving Strether her full opinion of little Bilham, so she hesitates regarding Chad. "His impression of Miss Gostrey after her introduction to Chad was meanwhile an impression of a person almost unnaturally on her guard. He struck himself as at first unable to extract from her what he wished. . . . He repeatedly knocked at her door to let her have it afresh that Chad's case—whatever else of minor interest it might yield—was first and foremost a miracle almost monstrous" (p. 109). In his attempts to name its cause he gropes for terms: " 'It's a plot. . . . It's a plant! . . . Call it then life' " (p. 109). But Maria holds off and watches him struggle with the mystery. Though withholding her opinion, "her silences were never barren, nor even dull" (p. 109). Like Miss Wenham, May Bartram and so many others, Maria is a good listener.

Finally, Strether succeeds in pinning her down: Will Chad return to Woollett? And to a forthright question she gives a forthright reply:

"No—he won't," she said at last. "He's not free."

The air of it held him. "Then you've all the while known—?"

"I've known nothing but what I've seen; and I wonder," she declared with some impatience, "that you didn't see as much. It was enough to be with him there—[in the box]" (p. 110).

The following dialogue delicately unfolds what both of them have divined—Maria having perceived of course more than Strether, drawing as she can on her vast experience. She points out to him that the cause of Chad's miraculous change is a woman—a " 'good' " woman—an " 'excellent' " woman. One feels her espousing the woman's cause. " 'Consider her and judge her only in Chad. . . . Don't make up your mind. There are all sorts of things. You haven't seen him all' " (p. 111).

Strether at once recognizes how this policy may compromise his mission. This she grants, but adds that if he will only bide his time, Chad will "shake her off" in due course, for " 'He's not as good as you think!' " (p. 111). The oracle has spoken once more. This warning remains prominent in Strether's consciousness, causing an even greater turmoil in his feelings over the question of Chad's innocence or guilt. The very thought of Chad's "effort to sink her" appears to him as the basest ingratitude: " 'After all she has done for him?' " This sentiment Miss Gostrey rewards with "a wonderful smile" (p. 111). Here, at least, is a man who will value a woman's gifts and service.

A few days after little Bilham's assurance of the "virtuous attachment," a scene between Strether and Miss Gostrey takes place. It is a typical scene of analysis, wherein the two actors endeavor to clarify each other's views. Strether has not asked Chad the name of his lady. This omission is a tactical necessity for James, who is saving this climactic revelation for Book Fifth, with its three great scenes in Gloriani's garden. So as yet Miss Gostrey is herself still guessing as to the nature of the "attachment." Some new information is however added by Chad's having asked Strether to meet the lady and her daughter. In their resulting debate, Strether and Maria speculate as to which of the two ladies is Chad's special friend. The scene gains in interest by their lucid conclusions, namely: the attachment is of long standing, and Strether himself has been on probation before meeting *ces dames*. Finally, Strether throws his doubt right at her:

> "You don't believe in it!"
> "In what?"
> "In the character of the attachment. In its innocence."
> But she defended herself. "I don't pretend to know anything about it. Everything's possible. We must see."
> "See?" he echoed with a groan. "Haven't we seen enough?"
> "*I* haven't," she smiled.
> "But do you suppose then little Bilham has lied?"
> "You must find out."
> It made him almost turn pale. "Find out any *more*?"
> He had dropped on a sofa for dismay; but she seemed, as she stood over him, to have the last word. "Wasn't what you came out for to find out *all*?" (p. 122).

In all her clairvoyance, Maria is outstanding for her discretion. Her hesitation to make a pronouncement on little Bilham and Chad is matched by her reticence in judging the lady involved. Ever conscious of the ancillary part she must play, she keeps reminding Strether of what he must discover for himself. The latter of course is dimly aware of her deep suspicion of Chad. Still, she does not mar Strether's growing awareness by making categorical predictions. Of necessity this *ficelle* is a person of consummate tact and prudence. The moment Maria learns the identity of the lady, she withdraws from the scene in order to let Strether "find out" for himself. But her withdrawal is not effected before she renders him the service which her honor will permit, that of telling him the history of Madame Vionnet. "It was a relief, Miss Gostrey hinted, to feel herself no longer groping; she was unaccustomed to grope and as a general thing, he might well have seen, made straight for her clue. With the one she had now picked up in her hands there need be at least no waste of wonder" (p. 142).

The story of the Countess is rendered indirectly in a vivid "picture" "so freely sketched" by Maria, preceded and followed by lively dialogue between herself and Strether. The picture method is particularly well adapted to this otherwise lengthy narration, for it telescopes a life-story; and refracting its rays through Strether's consciousness it endows the story with a "taste of history." Marie, the child of an international marriage, with foreign education and polyglot abilities, is admittedly difficult to name and place. Furthermore, an unhappy marriage has changed her, although a person of her stamp "would have headed straight" after her separation. The picture turns into dialogue with Maria's brisk comment, " 'I saw that . . . that night at the Français; it came out for me in three minutes. I saw *her*—or somebody like her' " (p. 145). For Maria, the pieces of the puzzle fit together now; and for Strether she has two important revelations. One is that the Countess has brought up Chad for her daughter. It is the good French mother's duty. The other is that Madame de Vionnet may try to use Strether himself. " 'Yes—she counts on you. . . . Are you disappointed she isn't worse?'. . . 'Yes. If she were worse she'd be better for our purpose. It would be simpler' " (p. 146).

Miss Gostrey's previous aloofness which puzzled Strether upon occasion recurs at this time in the form of a blow: she is leaving Paris.

"I mean that if she comes to see me I shall—now that I've pulled myself round a bit after the shock—not be home."

Strether hung poised. "You call it—your recognition—a shock?"

She gave one of her rare flickers of impatience. "It was a surprise, an emotion. Don't be so literal. I wash my hands of her."

Poor Strether's face lengthened. "She's impossible—?"

"She's even more charming than I remembered her."

"Then what's the matter?"

She had to think, how to put it. "Well, *I'm* impossible. It's impossible. Everything's impossible."

He looked at her an instant. "I see where you're coming out. Everything's possible. . . . Why don't you mean to receive her?"

Her answer in an instant rang out. "Because I wish to keep out of the business."

It provoked in him a weak wail. "You're going to abandon me *now*?"

"No, I'm going to abandon *her*. She'll want me to help her with you. And I won't" (pp. 142–143).

James places this important declaration *before* the account of the Countess's life because he wishes to end the scene with Maria on a note that will lead directly into the next one with Chad. The shock to Strether of Maria's impending departure and the attendant suspicion have to be absorbed by the pleasant tale of the Countess's life, and final assurance on Miss Gostrey's part that she trusts Madame up to a point: " 'I'm not afraid for myself. . . . I trust her. There's nothing she'll say about me. In fact there's nothing she *can*' " (p. 147). In giving the other woman credit, she immediately takes it away. Her own reputation is safe in the latter's hands, only because it would be safe anywhere. Strether's amazed comment is, " 'Oh you women!' " " 'Yes—' " she retorts, flushing, " 'there we are. We're abysses' " (p. 147). In the light of future developments, an unexpressed fear is seen to be mingled in her reason for leaving.

Strether has now reached a perilous position poised between two interested women. A man of his inexperience may well have been daunted. Maria, in deference to discretion and, ultimately, to loyalty to Strether, has withdrawn from the field. Since Madame had adopted tactics for winning Strether over to her side, there remained nothing to Maria but evacuation. Open hostility to the other woman would have proved worse than useless. As for Strether's safety, she has given him all the warnings she feasibly could. And, in the last analysis, he must work out the problem for himself. It is a greater decency in her to leave him than to betray his confidence, a course to which Madame, with her previous right to allegiance, could oblige Maria to take. What she avoids has already been demonstrated by little Bilham, on whom the task devolved of telling "the lie."[9] Maria knows that Bilham's subservience to gentlemanly mores would not be accounted sufficient by Madame if Maria stayed around to cast a possible doubt on the "virtuous attachment."

That is the reason adduced from Maria's character. But the technical reason for removing Maria, disguised in Jamesian fashion by the former, is that the *ficelle* suddenly becomes superfluous. Strether has been initiated and led by his guide up to the critical moment of his introduction to the famous woman. Now it is James's purpose to leave his protagonist fully exposed—without other recourse—to the influence of this woman. As confidant Waymarsh has withdrawn almost completely, and his relations with Strether are entirely severed in Book Seventh, just before Miss Gostrey's return (p. 191). Even Chad makes himself unobtrusive.

Madame de Vionnet, now left in possession of the field, wastes no time coming to the point of her rival:

"Why has Maria so suddenly gone? Do you know? . . . She's absent—with all respect to her sick friend, though I know indeed she has plenty—so that I may not see her. She doesn't want to meet me again. Well," she continued with a beautiful conscious mildness, "I liked and admired her beyond every one in the old time, and she knew it—perhaps that's precisely what has made her go—and I dare say I haven't lost her for ever." Strether still said nothing; he had a horror, as he now thought of himself, of being in question between women—was in fact already quite enough on his way to that. . . . She soon went on: "I'm extremely glad of her happiness." But it also left him mute—sharp and fine though the imputation it conveyed. What it conveyed was that *he* was Maria Gostrey's happiness . . . he drew back as well, with a smothered inward shudder, from the consideration of what women—of highly-developed type in particular—might think of each other (pp. 168–169).

Some time later she queries:

"Maria's still away?"—that was the first thing she had asked him; and when he had found the frankness to be cheerful about it in spite of the meaning he knew her to attach to Miss Gostrey's absence, she had gone on to inquire if he didn't tremendously miss her. There were reasons that made him by no means sure, yet he nevertheless answered "Tremendously"; which she took in as if it were all she had wished to prove. Then, "A man in trouble *must* be possessed somehow of a woman," she said; "if she doesn't come in one way she comes in another" (p. 185).

So now, as James would put it, "it is out" between them. Strether does not deny his relation with Maria. But he is shrewd enough not to discuss her with the newer acquaintance. On the other hand he is gradually becoming enmeshed in the net of Madame de Vionnet. This further involvement does not cause him however to desire to break with the lady of his first acquaintance. The reason for his attitude is the essential difference between the relations. Strether's friendship with Maria is fostered by his need of her; whereas his growing attachment to the Countess is based on his sense of her need of him. As far as he is momentarily concerned, both ladies think differently. Maria has worked for Strether's independence; Marie seeks to subject him. And neither woman is anxious for the presence of the other. The words of Madame quoted above are full of feminine duplicity. Her expression of gladness on behalf of her old friend suggests the very opposite. When the speaker eventually reveals more of her depth, this duplicity is clearly seen. Her jealousy of Maria Gostrey comes to the fore in the scene with Sarah Pocock, when she teases Strether indirectly by telling Sarah of "dear old Maria . . . the wonderful woman" whom Strether hides from every one else (p. 235). The *double entendre* of these witty remarks reveals for wondering Strether something in Madame which he is as yet unprepared to explain.

In contrast to the Frenchwoman's duplicity the honesty of Maria, the American, is striking. " 'She'll want me to help her with you. And I won't' " (p. 143). It is indeed in the role of foil that Miss Gostrey's character attains its fullest dimensions. The contrast between the two women begins with their physical appearance and concludes with their integrity. It is principally to this end that the last half of Maria's story is devoted.

Upon her return to Paris Strether at once resumes his conferences with her. But the face of their relation has changed; and
Maria—honest and forthright as she is when certain of herself
—declares:

"My absence has helped you—as I've only to look at you to see.
It was my calculation, and I'm justified. You're not where you were.
And the thing," she smiled, "was for me not to be there either. You
can go of yourself."

"Oh but I feel today," he comfortably declared, "that I shall
want you yet."

She took him all in again. "Well, I promise you not again to leave
you, but it will only be to follow you. You've got your momentum
and can toddle alone."

He intelligently accepted it. "Yes—I suppose I can toddle" (p.
199).

She does nevertheless accept his renewed confidences about
events leading up to the present situation: Waymarsh's defection, Chad's reversal in favor of returning home, and counter-
reversal, upon Strether's urging, to remain after all. Technically
speaking, James could dispense with such a scene of recapitulation until this moment, because he was engaged throughout
Book Sixth and part of Seventh in presenting the dramatization
of Strether's and Madame's growing friendship, besides one important scene with Chad, Book Seventh, II. Everything was experienced in the present, even Strether's reverie in Notre Dame,
Book Seventh, I. Now the story has leaped ahead, and Maria is
brought back to facilitate recapitulation and prognosis. To the
old service of making Strether feel "his sense of things cleared
up and settled" she lends herself as usual with good grace (p.
203).

But it is in an altered capacity that she does so. Her keen insight perceives that his "toddling" amounts to such a state of
preparedness which not even the advent of the Pococks can per-
turb. " 'You *are* magnificent!' " she declares (p. 203). She further divines the degree of importance Madame de Vionnet has
by now attained in his life, though at first they dodge mentioning

her name. The change in their relation is eventually distilled through Strether's consciousness in retrospect:

His relation with Maria as well was, strangely enough, no longer quite the same; this truth—though not too disconcertingly—had come up between them on the renewal of their meetings. It was all contained in what she had then almost immediately said to him; it was represented by the remark she had needed but ten minutes to make and that he hadn't been disposed to gainsay. . . . The time seemed already far off when he had held out his small thirsty cup to the spout of her pail. Her pail was scarce touched now, and other fountains had flowed for him; she fell into her place as but one of his tributaries; and there was a strange sweetness—a melancholy mildness that touched him—in her acceptance of the altered order (p. 205).

This passage and the one following beautifully portray the image of the woman facing rejection. It is not the type of mutual agreement made by Madame Merle with Osmond; nor is it quite the total rejection of May Bartram by John Marcher. Less business-like than the first and less poignant than the second, it nonetheless contains its own element of pathos. The woman's altruistic joy comes to an end because her service will soon be no longer required. Maria's helplessness, yet unselfish consent, enhance the beauty of her character. None of this is lost on Strether:

It marked for himself the flight of time, or at any rate what he was pleased to think of with irony and pity as the rush of experience; it having been but the day before yesterday that he sat at her feet and held on by her garment and was fed by her hand. It was the proportions that were changed, and the proportions were at all times, he philosophised, the very conditions of perception, the terms of thought. . . . It was as if she had shrunk to a secondary element and had consented to the shrinkage with the perfection of tact. This per-fection had never failed her; it had originally been greater than his prime measure for it; it had kept him quite apart, kept him out of the shop, as she called her huge general acquaintance, made their com-merce as quiet, as much a thing of the home alone—the opposite of the shop—as if she had never another customer. She had been wonderful to him at first, with the memory of her little *entresol,* the image to which, on most mornings at that time, his eyes directly opened; but now she mainly figured for him as but part of the bristling total—though of course always as a person to whom he should never cease to be indebted. It would never be given to him certainly to inspire a greater kindness. She had decked him out for others, and he saw at this point at least nothing she would ever ask for. She only wondered and questioned and listened, rendering him the homage of a wistful speculation. She expressed it repeatedly; he was already far beyond her, and she must prepare herself to lose him (pp. 205–206).

Closely upon this recognition follows Strether's supreme disclosure of confidence:

"I began to be young, or at least to get the benefit of it, the moment I met you at Chester, and that's what has been taking place ever since. I never had the benefit at the proper time—which comes to saying that I never had the thing itself. I'm having the benefit at this moment; I had it the other day when I said to Chad, 'Wait'; I shall have it still again when Sarah Pocock arrives. It's a benefit that would make a poor show for many people; and I don't know who else but you and I, frankly, could begin to see in it what I feel. I don't get drunk; I don't pursue the ladies; I don't spend money; I don't even write sonnets. But nevertheless I'm making up late for what I didn't have early" (p. 207).

He concludes this speech by pointing out Chad and Madame de Vionnet as "my pair": " 'The point is that they're mine. Yes, they're my youth; since somehow at the right time nothing else ever was. What I meant just now therefore is that it would all go—go before doing its work—if they were to fail me' " (p. 207). The vicarious pleasure he gets from the "innocent attachment" is what buoys him up on the wide waters presently to be so troubled. For after he left Maria's little pail, the wide waters of experience have received him.

All this Maria accepts bravely, not refraining, nevertheless, to score a point on her own behalf:

"Don't you remember how in those first days of our meeting it was *I* who was to see you through?"

"Remember? Tenderly, deeply. . . . You're just doing your part in letting me maunder to you thus."

"Ah don't speak as if my part were small; since whatever else fails you—"

"*You* won't, ever, ever, ever?"—he thus took her up. "Oh I beg your pardon; you necessarily, you inevitably *will*. Your conditions —that's what I mean—won't allow me anything to do for you."

"Let alone—I see what you mean—that I'm drearily, dreadfully old. I *am,* but there's a service—possible for you to render—that I know, all the same, I shall think of."

"And what will it be?"

This, in fine, however, she would never tell him (p. 207).

One observes her trying to hide her pain. Pride, **however**, asserts her claim to resume her offices should he ever "come to grief." Yet this same pride prevents her disclosing the nature of those offices. Strether, in his blindness, can envision only a situation where she will abandon him because he cannot do something for her. Her "conditions" of independence, courage, and *savoir-faire* contrast in his opinion unfavorably with Madame de Vionnet's apparent helplessness and gentle appeals. It seems that this is the basic distinction which Strether makes between the two women. In the time of testing he prefers the helpless woman to the omniscient guide. Both have their charm; but it is a mark of his maturity and manliness that he prefers the former to the latter. Neither must the fact of the Countess's greater beauty be overlooked.

Maria of course is thinking of the one supreme thing he could do for her, namely offer marriage: " '. . . there's a service—possible for you to render—' " which she hopes for, in spite of her age, that exaggerated factor in both women's lives. Actually, hers is the advantage of being the Countess's junior by three years. The topic of his service recurs, but never does either one speak more explicitly. Pride and tact on her side, reserve and a secret preference for the other woman on his, make them avoid the naked issue.

In Books Ninth, Eleventh, and Twelfth, when Maria does

appear at all, it is in the diminishing role of the listener who is
"out of it." "He walked over [to Maria's] of course much less
than usual. . . . He was sorry again, gratefully sorry she was so
out of it—she who had really put him in; but she had fortunately
always her appetite for news. The pure flame of the disinterested
burned in her cave of treasures as a lamp in a Byzantine vault"
(p. 253). James's image here does two things: it ties in with
the image of the pirate's cave, and it richly expresses his own
admiration for his *ficelle*. Geared to a difficult role, this little
lady is playing it brilliantly, even to the dimming of her lights
at the end. No wonder the author rejoiced anew over her when
writing his Preface. The "string," the "stage trick" has lent herself to a characterization both demanding and self-sacrificing.
And in her James puts forward another one of his unselfish
women. Filling a smaller role than Isabel, Maria yet holds her
own by showing greater skill at adaptation.

Two scenes, in Book Ninth and Book Eleventh, serve as the
many predecessors did—for recapitulation, analysis, and
prognosis. Maria patiently attends to Strether's concern over
Chad and the Pococks, Sarah and Mamie in particular. " 'Well,
you owe more to women than any man I ever saw. We do seem
to keep you going,' " is a small, but typical Gostreyan observation dropped during one of these discussions (p. 255).

In the second of these two scenes she again reverts to the fact
of her uselessness. The mention of Madame de Vionnet in almost the same breath cannot be overlooked as a contributing
factor.

"They go, the five, as I understand you, and you and Madame
de Vionnet stay."

"Oh and Chad." To which Strether added: "And you."

"Ah 'me'!"—she gave a small impatient wail again, in which
something of the unreconciled seemed suddenly to break out. "*I* don't
stay, it somehow seems to me, much to my advantage. In the presence of all you cause to pass before me I've a tremendous sense of
privation."

Strether hesitated. "But your privation, your keeping out of everything, has been—hasn't it?—by your own choice."

"Oh yes; it has been necessary—that is it has been better for you.
What I mean is only that I seem to have ceased to serve you" (p.
309).

His reply to that is to ask her insistently to remain now with him;
and then to ask the real reason for her sudden departure from
Paris. Her reply is again characteristic in cautiousness, for as
yet it is not the complete answer:

"Well then I dashed off, as you say, so as not to have the confusion
of being there if Marie de Vionnet should tell you anything to my
detriment. . . . I owe her thanks. Whatever her temptation she didn't
separate us. That's one of my reasons," she went on, "for admiring
her so."
"Let it pass then," said Strether, "for one of mine as well. But
what would have been her temptation?"
"What are ever the temptations of women? . . . She would have
had you, with it, more for herself. But she saw she could have you
without it" (p. 310).

Maria openly recognizes the superiority of her rival, in spite
of Strether's "handsome" assurance, " '*You* . . . would have had
me at any rate *with* it' " (p. 310). In the almost painful analysis
which she then makes of his relation with Madame one sees her
brave struggle "to keep it up":

"Don't really be afraid to tell me if what now holds you *is* the
pleasant prospect of the empty town, with plenty of seats in the shade,
cool drinks, deserted museums, drives to the Bois in the evening, and
our wonderful woman all to yourself." And she kept it up still more.
"The handsomest thing of *all,* when one makes it out, would, I dare
say, be that Mr. Chad should for a while go off by himself. It's a
pity, from that point of view," she wound up, "that he doesn't pay
his mother a visit. It would at least occupy your interval" (p. 313).

A sustained note of bitterness and perhaps masochism can be
detected in this detailed picture. Her open acknowledgement of

Chad's being no longer Madame's hero can but indicate her recognition of Strether's having taken his place. Also, Maria has an ulterior motive. She wants to pin him down—if possible —to an avowal of his attachment to the Countess. But Strether evades her nicely each time. If Mrs. Newsome still is willing to forgive him, would he be ready to give up Madame de Vionnet? " 'If it doesn't do—at any rate, to deny that Marie's charming, it will do at least to deny that she's good.' 'What I claim is that she's good for Chad.' 'You don't claim'—she seemed to like it clear—'that she's good for *you*?' But he continued unheeding" (p. 317).

Her last attempt to search him is made with unusual abruptness:

"Mr. Newsome and Madame de Vionnet may, as we were saying, leave town. How long do you think you can bear it without them?"

Strether's reply to this was at first another question. "Do you mean in order to get away from me?"

Her answer had an abruptness. "Don't find me rude if I say I should think they'd want to!"

He looked at her hard again—seemed even for an instant to have an intensity of thought under which his colour changed. But he smiled. "You mean after what they've done to me?"

"After what *she* has."

At this, however, with a laugh, he was all right again. "Ah but she hasn't done it yet!" (p. 318).

He confesses to nothing. The very next chapter takes him out to the country where he has his complete revelation of the true nature of the "virtuous attachment."

Book Twelfth gathers together the loose threads of the story of the confidante. Her post as guide is now definitely resigned to him, a proof of which is the uncle-niece imagery with which James describes Strether and Maria wandering through the Paris streets. To fill up time, "he proposed amusements to her . . . and he had thus, for several days, an odd sense of leading her about Paris . . . that might have belonged to a kindly uncle doing the honours of the capital to an intelligent niece from the country. . . . while she, on her side, was, like the country maiden, all passive modest and grateful—going in fact so far as to emulate rusticity in occasional fatigues and bewilderments" (p. 344).

This little game which she plays to humor his sense of leadership is another sign of her kindness and concern for him. Furthermore—

> She left questions unasked—she who for so long had been all questions; she gave herself up to him with an understanding of which mere mute gentleness might have seemed the sufficient expression. She knew his sense of his situation had taken still another step—of that he was quite aware; but she conveyed that, whatever had thus happened for him, it was thrown into the shade by what was happening for herself. This . . . was the major interest, and she met it with a new directness of response, measuring it from hour to hour with her grave hush of acceptance. Touched as he had so often been by her before, he was, for his part too, touched afresh. . . . It was all he needed that she liked him enough for what they were doing . . . the essential freshness of a relation so simple was a cool bath to the soreness produced by other relations. . . . an hour with his present friend . . . [had] something of the innocent pleasure of handling rounded ivory (p. 345).

This delicate summary of the situation of Strether—who has " 'come to grief' " as she foresaw—leaning once more on his confidante, without however confiding—is another fine picture of her generosity in rising to meet his crises. At this point the supreme demand is made of her altruism by her rival, who pleads for her intercession with him. James finds one more important function for his star *ficelle*. It is like the "slight rise" just before the catastrophe in a Greek tragedy. A new, slight turn to events keeps the last lap of the story from dragging. The rival, now feeling at a disadvantage, cleverly manipulates the woman still in favor. So the confidante becomes go-between for the erstwhile friends, who were doing, until recently, so beautifully without her. Poor Maria's position is increasingly laden with irony. But her toughness of character sees her through.

The incident provides her as well with the opportunity of stating at last the full truth about her departure from Paris. It is characteristic in its independence and honesty.

"I didn't want to have to lie for her. I felt that to be too much for me. A man of course is always expected to do it—to do it, I mean, for a woman; but not a woman for another woman; unless perhaps on the tit-for-tat principle, as an indirect way of protecting herself. I don't need protection, so that I was free to 'funk' you—simply to dodge your test. The responsibility was too much for me. I gained time, and when I came back the need of a test had blown over" (p. 549).

Strether accepts this. She follows it up with a final analysis of himself, which reveals more of her concern than has been hitherto glimpsed.

"What I see, what I saw," Maria returned, is that you dressed up even virtue [the "virtuous attachment"]. You were wonderful—you were beautiful, as I've had the honour of telling you before: but if you wish really to know," she sadly confessed, "I never quite knew *where* you were. There were moments," she explained, "when you struck me as grandly cynical; there were others when you struck me as grandly vague."
Her friend considered. "I had phases. I had flights."
"Yes, but things must have a basis."
"A basis seemed to me just what her beauty supplied."
"Her beauty of person?"
"Well, her beauty of everything. The impression she made. She has such variety and yet such harmony."
She considered him with one of her deep returns of indulgence—returns out of all proportion to the irritations they flooded over. "You're complete" (pp. 349–350).

Her admission of previous doubt shows up her objectivity in contrast to his subjectivity. Was he cynical, or just vague? The question had disturbed honest Maria, for "things must have a basis." The *ficelle* is used here as a norm of moral evaluation. As Strether confesses, he had been guided by his impressions of Madame. As man, he had reacted subjectively. It is sometimes easier for a woman than for a man to be objective where another woman is concerned. Maria must be given credit for treating her rival fairly throughout. In pleading for her now she is really admirably objective. As presently shown, her judgment is balanced by a strong sense of solidarity for her own sex, and an identification of the Countess's loss with her own. " 'Those things are nothing when a woman's hit. It's very awful. She was hit' " (p. 350). And, " 'Poor dear thing!' " (p. 351).

But for the practical woman that Maria is, words of sympathy alone do not suffice. "Miss Gostrey, in short, offered herself for service to the end" (p. 351). Could she not tell Madame de Vionnet that Strether does not judge her after all?

> "She thinks you and she might at any rate have been friends."
> "We might certainly. That's just"—he continued to laugh—"why I'm going."
> It was as if Maria could feel with this then at last that she had done her best for each. But she had still an idea. "Shall I tell her that?"
> "No. Tell her nothing" (p. 351).

The last scene of the novel is given to Strether and his faithful confidante. Their relation has come full circle. They recall their first days together. James evokes once more the charm of her home: ". . . the place had never before struck him as so sacred to pleasant knowledge, to intimate charm, to antique order, to a neatness that was almost august" (p. 361). Strether calls it "a haunt of ancient peace," and she replies, " 'I wish with all my heart . . . I could make you treat it as a haven of rest.' On which they fronted each other across the table, as if things unuttered were in the air" (p. 361).

The unuttered things are her renewed offer of herself to him. After ascertaining the finality of the break with Mrs. Newsome, she asks:

> "To what do you go home?"
> "I don't know. There will always be something."

"To a great difference," she said as she kept his hand.

"A great difference—no doubt. Yet I shall see what I can make of it."

"Shall you make anything so good—"

. . . He had sufficiently understood. "So good as this place at this moment? So good as what *you* make of everything you touch?" He took a minute to say, for, really and truly, what stood about him there in her offer—which was as the offer of exquisite service, of lightened care, for the rest of his days—might well have tempted. It built him softly round, it roofed him warmly over, it rested, all so firm, on selection. And what ruled selection was beauty and knowledge. It was awkward, it was almost stupid, not to seem to prize such things, yet, none the less, so far as they made his opportunity they made it only for a moment. She would moreover understand—she always understood (p. 365).

This passage of internal analysis conveys more perfectly than dialogue could, the sense of shelter offered to the lonely man by this woman's devotion.[10] It marks also the distance Strether's appreciation has come. From his first impression of the lovely little "pirate's cave" full of art treasures, this place has grown so into his sensibility that now its strongest appeal for him is as a home. In using the simple images of "pail," and "cool bath," in connection with Maria, James has built up to the full effect of this passage. Strether's deepest need is, after all, not for art alone, but for beauty combined with the security of a home.

Yet Strether cannot accept the offer, because as Maria said, "things must have a basis," and his relation with her lacks for him the ultimate basis of love. The reason he gives her is best calculated to save her pride: " 'That, you see, is my only logic. Not, out of the whole affair, to have got anything for myself' " (p. 365). Aside from his attempt to save her pride, he is doubtless still held back by a strict Calvinist sense of justice: success—reward; no success—no reward. Like Maria, the guide, Strether, the ambassador, receives no payment. Perhaps also, there is the unconscious fear of ridicule from Woollett: he could not save Chad; much less could he save himself. The scene with Madame de Vionnet before Sarah when Waymarsh leaped to Strether's defense should not be forgotten in all its painfulness for the latter. Were not the Countess's refined taunts calculated to cut short his relation with her rival?[11]

The whole complex relation of Maria Gostrey with Strether and Madame de Vionnet; her vivid contrast with this lady, as well as with Mrs. Newsome and Sarah Pocock; and finally her own accomplishments and desires, all contribute both scenically and pictorially to the creation of her character, and to the successful disguise of her role as *ficelle*. She is indeed James's most important *ficelle*. As confidante, guide, and spiritual mother dispensing food and drink and offering a home to the wandering protagonist, she fills the biggest role of all the confidantes who are not centers of consciousness. In predicting the future she crowns the forecasts of Mrs. Costello, Madame Grandoni, Mrs. Prest, and Henrietta Stackpole. By analyzing the character of her confider, she complements the insight of Henrietta and May Bartram. Her frequent scenes with Strether from Book First through Book Twelfth are spaced almost symmetrically, in conjunction with the precise pattern of the whole novel. In no other long novel does James hinge the progression of his story so closely and so frequently upon the regular appearance of the confidante. Maria is also the best-disguised *ficelle,* because of her independent existence as a person, and her dramatic part as foil. Furthermore, in her are summed up the foregoing confidantes who functioned on one or two levels only, serving technical ends, and either taking a moral stand, while listening sympathetically, or suffering rejection as a lover. Maria functions on all four levels. She differs, moreover, from three of her more prominent predecessors, Mrs. Tristram, Madame Merle, and Mrs. Wix, by refusing to take a hand in the action, thereby serving the technical purpose of elimination of a secondary character in favor of a principal one. Succeeding Maria Gostrey are Susan Stringham and Fanny Assingham, who in technical aspects resemble each other more closely than they do Maria.

$\mathcal{Chapter}$ $\mathcal{7}$

THE WINGS OF THE DOVE

$\mathcal{R}$EGARDLESS OF THE large number of confidantes James had already created by 1901, much variety still remained from which he could realize the character of Susan Stringham. Appearing right after Maria Gostrey in the order of composition, she demonstrates the artist's versatility that suffered no diminution after so great a creation as Maria. In her role as partial center of consciousness Susan has some features in common with her predecessors, Madame Merle and Henrietta Stackpole, and to a lesser extent, with Fleda Vetch. A middle-aged, little New England widow, with a "charming face" and "bright little nippers," Susan is concretely individualized, and plays a rather exciting role in *The Wings of the Dove* (1902). This excitement is alluded to by the author in his Preface:

If [the heroine's] impulse to wrest from her shrinking hour still as much of the fruit of life as possible, if this longing can take effect only by the aid of others, their participation (appealed to, entangled and coerced as they find themselves) becomes their drama too—that of their promoting her illusion, under her importunity, for reasons, for interests and advantages, from motives and points of view, of their own. Some of these promptings, evidently, would be of the highest

181

order—others doubtless mightn't; but they would make up together, for her, contributively, her sum of experience, represent to her somehow, in good faith or in bad, what she should have *known*. Somehow, too, at such a rate, one would see the persons subject to them drawn in as by some pool of a Lorelei—see them terrified and tempted and charmed; bribed away, it may even be, from more prescribed and natural orbits, inheriting from their connexion with her strange difficulties and still stranger opportunities, confronted with rare questions and called upon for new discriminations.[1]

Mrs. Stringham was definitely "appealed to, entangled and coerced" by the striking, yet odd New York heiress, whom she had met the winter before in Boston. There "the young lady . . . had, on the spot, deeply, yet almost tacitly, appealed to her, dropped into her mind the shy conceit of some assistance, some devotion to render."[2] Mrs. Stringham is exceptionally well adapted to such an appeal, being by nature a kindly person, and by profession a writer of short stories for "the best magazines," and having what she fondly believes to be her " 'note,' the art of showing New England without showing it wholly in the kitchen" (p. 119).[3] As a writer and critic, she does not lack discrimination and imagination; but her little talent is taken unaware by the strange encounter with Milly Theale.

But this imagination—the fancy of a possible link with the remarkable young thing from New York—*had* mustered courage: had perched, on the instant, at the clearest lookout it could find, and might be said to have remained there till, only a few months later, it had caught, in surprise and joy, the unmistakable flash of a signal (p. 117).

It is Susan's imagination which responds so quickly to Milly's appeal; and this faculty has an exceptionally strong romantic tendency. The removal from the kitchen of which her stories treat, is humorously paralleled in their little author's own breathtaking flight from home, to which her young friend pressingly invites her. James uses Susan as a center of consciousness in order to reflect her enthusiastic impressions of Milly Theale. Susan's point of view is given in Book Third, part of Fourth, and part of Seventh. In Book Third she recalls her first acquaintance with the girl and their setting forth into the world together. Her romantic flair sees Milly in almost incongruous imagery, and it is well to remember when reading it, that these are Susan's, not James's thoughts:

It was [Milly's] nature, once for all—a nature that reminded Mrs. Stringham of the term always used in the newspapers about the great new steamers, the inordinate number of "feet of water" they drew; so that if, in your little boat, you had chosen to hover and approach, you had but yourself to thank, when once motion was started, for the way the draught pulled you. Milly drew the feet of water, and odd though it might seem that a lonely girl, who was not robust and who hated sound and show, should stir the stream like a leviathan, her companion floated off with the sense of rocking violently at her side (p. 126).

This is what James refers to in the Preface, Susan's being "bribed away . . . from more prescribed and natural orbits." The European tour develops into a grand venture, presaged by the little woman's view of Milly as the great ship. It takes her to orbits she had never dreamed of—Mrs. Lowder's magnificent London house, and the old Venetian palace. The possible literary interest she may have had when starting, gives way before the poignant human interest in which she presently finds herself involved. With "promptings . . . of the highest order" and in perfect "good faith," Mrs. Stringham attaches herself to the striking, lonely girl. Better than all the novelists put together, is "the real thing, the romantic life itself. That was what she saw in Mildred—what positively made her hand a while tremble too much for the pen" (p. 120)—and "the real thing" beggars "the thin trickle of a fictive 'love-interest' " of her stories in the magazines (p. 121).

Typical of this romantic human interest, Susan Stringham soon abandons the clumsy ship image in favor of a more appropriate one—Milly in her eyes appears, with her "crown of old gold," as the "heiress of all the ages," who affects her

as the princess in a conventional tragedy might have affected the confidant if a personal emotion had ever been permitted to the latter. That a princess could only be a princess was a truth with which, essentially, a confidant, however responsive, had to live. Mrs. Stringham was a woman of the world, but Milly Theale was a princess, the only one she had yet had to deal with, and this in its way, too, made all the difference. It was a perfectly definite doom for the wearer—it was for every one else a perfectly palpable quality (p. 134).

Susan honestly believes that Milly's royalty is palpable for others, but from later contacts it is doubtful whether anyone besides Merton Densher even suspects it. In the case of Densher, too, the appreciation of the girl is more for her goodness, simplicity, and pitiable doom, than for her possible regality. Susan's incorrigible romanticism colors everything she meets; it fairly transmutes the "slim, constantly pale, delicately haggard, anomalously, agreeably angular young person" from New York (p. 118). Before the end of Book Fourth, James stresses Susan's romantic tendency four times, and Milly's twice.

The mystery enveloping Milly is part of her romantic aura, and from the beginning of their friendship Mrs. Stringham has set herself to observe it:

During the breathless minutes of her watch [on the mountain] she had seen her companion afresh; the latter's type, aspect, marks, her history, her state, her beauty, her mystery, all unconsciously betrayed themselves to the Alpine air, and all had been gathered in again to feed Mrs. Stringham's flame (p. 140).

As for Milly, she clearly perceives Susan's romantic bent and her "positive need" to treat her confider as a princess. Such an attitude on the part of the confidante requires the setting and behavior of court-etiquette. With her knowledge of history, Susan has formed definite ideas of how a princess should be treated.

Susan had read history, had read Gibbon and Froude and Saint-Simon; she had high-lights as to the special allowances made for the class [of princesses], and, since she saw them, when young, as effete and overtutored, inevitably ironic and infinitely refined, one must take it for amusing if she inclined to an indulgence verily Byzantine. If one *could* only be Byzantine!—wasn't *that* what she insidiously led one on to sigh? Milly tried to oblige her—for it really placed Susan herself so handsomely to be Byzantine now. The great ladies of that race—it would be somewhere in Gibbon—weren't, apparently, questioned about their mysteries. But oh, poor Milly and hers! Susan at all events proved scarce more inquisitive than if she had been a mosaic at Ravenna. Susan was a porcelain monument to the odd moral that consideration might, like cynicism, have abysses. Besides, the Puritan finally disencumbered—! What starved generations wasn't Mrs. Stringham, in fancy, going to make up for? (pp. 279–280).

It does not take Milly long to evaluate her companion's romanticism, and in her reflections given above, a note of amused impatience is clearly struck.[4] "Milly tried to oblige her," but after all, what mysteries does Milly have other than her illness and her liking for Merton Densher? The images of the Ravenna mosaic and the porcelain monument are a trifle amusing, so incongruous are they with the real situation of the New York girl, yet so apt in describing her companion's artificial attitude of deference. Susan's living in an unreal world is emphasized by the references to her reading, in terms of which she tries to place her idol:

Our couple had at all events effected an exchange; the elder friend had been as consciously intellectual as possible, and the younger, abounding in personal revelation, had been as unconsciously distinguished. This was poetry—it was also history—Mrs. Stringham thought, to a finer tune even than Maeterlinck and Pater, than Marbot and Gregorovius (p. 124).

Mrs. Stringham's literary passions throw much light on her character. The romanticism of Maeterlinck, who admired Novalis and Emerson, his emphasis on the inner life of man,

as well as his medieval cast of mind, would appeal to a com-
patriot of Emerson and Longfellow. His original views on art
together with Pater's aestheticism balance nicely with the anti-
quarianism of Gregorovius, the histories of Froude and Gibbon, and the social doctrine of Saint-Simon. Susan is a well-
read woman of her century. The interest in the Middle Ages and
Renaissance can be seen as a fine thread running through
Maeterlinck, Pater, Gregorovius, and Froude. Gibbon is close
to Gregorovius in his work on Rome. Marbot alone seems unlike
the others in his works, until one considers the romantic subject
of his *Memoirs,* the excitement of his generalship in some of the
most famous battles of history. For such a well-read woman, and
author in her own right, "this was poetry—it was also history—"
to meet Milly Theale. Her dead family is transformed in Susan's
eyes as

the luxuriant tribe of which the rare creature was the final flower,
the immense, extravagant, unregulated, cluster, with free-living ancestors, handsome dead cousins, lurid uncles, beautiful vanished
aunts, persons all busts and curls, preserved, though so exposed, in
the marble of famous French chisels—all this, to say nothing of the
effect of closer growths of the stem, was to have had one's small
world-space both crowded and enlarged (p. 124).

An enthusiastic historian of a great dynasty would write in
language like this. And the last scion of the dynasty bears, in
Susan's misty eyes, all the marks of public life:

This was her own way of describing a face that, thanks, doubtless,
to rather too much forehead, too much nose and too much mouth,
together with too little mere conventional colour and conventional
line, was expressive, irregular, exquisite, both for speech and for
silence. When Milly smiled it was a public event—when she didn't
it was a chapter of history (p. 132).

Milly, as center of consciousness in Book Fifth, easily grasps
her companion's romantic flair and her unconscious desire to

figure in a Byzantine setting. They are now in London, entertained at the resplendent court of Maud Manningham Lowder,
who as a schoolgirl even, had been "large, high-coloured . . .
florid, exotic and alien—which had been just the spell—even
to the perceptions of [Susan's] youth" (pp. 155-156). What this
girl has developed into, the reader has already learned through
the consciousness of Kate Croy:

> She would have been meanwhile a wonderful lioness for a show,
> an extraordinary figure in a cage or anywhere; majestic, magnificent,
> high-coloured, all brilliant gloss, perpetual satin, twinkling bugles
> and flashing gems, with a lustre of agate eyes, a sheen of raven hair,
> a polish of complexion that was like that of well-kept china. . . .
> [with] her florid philistinism, her plumes and her train, her fantastic
> furniture and heaving bosom, the false gods of her taste and false
> notes of her talk . . . (pp. 34–35).

Kate Croy, being one of the finer Jamesian intelligences, penetrates Aunt Maud's false gloss; but harmless Susan is properly
awed by the spectacle, which deliciously feeds her romantic
imagination. As Milly is aware, in poor Susan's fancy the
starved Puritan generations are having their vicarious fling. As
for Mrs. Wix, Maria Gostrey, and Fanny Assingham, there is
a vicarious pleasure for Susan to be sought and found in the
reflected glory of her friend. Susan literally triumphs in presenting Milly Theale to London society. The condescension of Maud
for Susan in contracting an unpromising marriage is now to be
avenged by

> the poetic justice, the generous revenge, of her having at last some-
> thing to show. Maud, on their parting company, had appeared to
> have so much, and would now—for wasn't it also in general, quite
> the rich law of English life?—have, with accretions, promotions, ex-
> pansions, ever so much more. Very good; such things might be; she
> rose to the sense of being ready for them. Whatever Mrs. Lowder
> might have to show—and one hoped one did the presumptions all
> justice—she would have nothing like Milly Theale, who constituted
> the trophy producible by poor Susan (pp. 157–158).

And as Milly's success does not fail Susan's anticipations, the reflected glory which illumines the confidante glows all the more splendidly. The impact of their success lifts them "by the incalculable strength of a wave that was actually holding them aloft and that would naturally dash them wherever it liked" (pp. 185-186). Susan's own "exaltation" holds Milly's attention: "Susie glowed in the light of her justified faith" (p. 186). All she needs is "the fine floating gold-dust, something that threw over the prospect a harmonising blur" cast by "Maud's fidelity to a sentiment. That was what Susie was proud of, much more than of her great place in the world, which she was moreover conscious of not as yet wholly measuring" (p. 186).

Leaving aside, for the moment, Susan's impression of Maud's sentiment, one can see in the New Englander the willingness to be impressed by European panoply, summed up so neatly in the narrator's description of her as "the pilgrim from Boston." Like Strether, Susan Stringham is on her journey of devotion, although the nature of their trips is hidden at first from these seekers for beauty. Susan however is not sure

that what she should mainly have arranged for in London was not a series of thrills for herself. She had a bad conscience, indeed almost a sense of immorality, in having to recognise that she was, as she said, carried away. . . . and the principle of her uneasiness was that Mrs. Lowder's life bristled for her with elements that she was really having to look at for the first time. They represented, she believed, the world, the world that, as a consequence of the cold shoulder turned to it by the Pilgrim Fathers, had never yet boldly crossed to Boston—it would surely have sunk the stoutest Cunarder—and she couldn't pretend that she faced the prospect simply because Milly had had a caprice. She was in the act of having one, directed precisely to their present spectacle. She could but seek strength in the thought that she had never had one—or had never yielded to one, which came to the same thing—before. The sustaining sense of it all, moreover, as literary material—that quite dropped from her. She must wait, at any rate, she should see: it struck her, so far as she had got, as vast, obscure, lurid. She reflected in the watches of the night that she was probably just going to love it for itself—that is for itself and

Milly. . . . It was a mercy, at all events, for the hour, that their fancies jumped together (pp. 188–189).

The Puritan conscience is at work in full force. Poor Susan, lying awake nights, trying to pacify her scruples, does an ingenious bit of rationalizing, the kind that a false conscience easily produces. The distrust of the works and pomps of the world is however only assuaged by her stronger feelings of loyalty to her friend. Milly loves it, and Susan can think of this fact without dread. The New York conscience rides easily in the London milieu.

The passage quoted above is the best instance of the contrast between Susan and Milly. It accounts also for Susan's breathless voyage in her little rocking boat behind the "leviathan" from New York. It is not that Milly Theale is so great in herself; but that for the little New England mind she is simply tremendous. To be in harmony with Milly's fancies is Susan's consolation and salvation, since in her extremity of introspection, the literary excuse fails her utterly.

To be able to get inside Mrs. Stringham's mind is the great advantage of making her one of several centers of consciousness. *The Wings of the Dove* is the outstanding example of this method, of which *The Portrait of a Lady* is a forerunner. Susan, however, is more thoroughly a "register" than Madame Merle or Henrietta Stackpole, although these two do have their scenes without Isabel Archer, in which James uses their points of view. But the analysis of their feelings and motives is less ample than that of Susan Stringham. This is no doubt owing to the plan which James describes in the Preface to *The Portrait*: to ". . . press least hard, in short, on the consciousness of your heroine's satellites, especially the male; make it an interest contributive only to the greater one."[5] In *The Wings of the Dove* the whole point of the novel is to "press hard" on the consciousness of the other characters:—Kate Croy, Merton Densher, and Susan Stringham all have "blocks" devoted to their view of Milly

Theale. Milly herself must be content with only one Book and part of two others; and one feels that this is a concession to completeness of treatment.

Although the subject of several "pictures," Susan as "center" appears only in one long dramatized scene and two short ones. In Book Third and Fourth she reflects on her romantic attachment to Milly and their success in London. From here on until Book Seventh, what we learn of Susan is refracted through the minds of Milly, whose amused opinion we have just observed, and Kate and Densher. The scene of confidential exchanges between Susan and Milly on their tour occurs in the evening at the inn on the Brünig Pass, high in the mountains. At this time Milly confides her doubt that she will have much of what she's got: " '. . . shall I have it for long?' " (p. 146). This note of alarm raises certain anxieties in the confidante's heart, but her inveterate romanticism soon interprets the girl's predicament as "the excess of the joy of life" (p. 148). It is a false security which the London triumph increases. One must remember that Milly's terror at seeing the portrait of the "dead" lady—her likeness—is not witnessed by Susan; so when Milly confesses her having consulted a doctor, Mrs. Stringham is not unduly shaken. She is of course sustained by her Byzantine propriety, which protects her against visible shock, "so that she only desired, the next thing, perfectly to possess the facts" (p. 312). Milly, whose point of view is operative in this picture, seeks to assuage any pain her confidante may feel, and stresses the fact that Sir Luke Strett wishes to "meet quite apart, some one interested in her. Who therefore so interested as her faithful Susan?" (p. 312). Milly places great trust in Susan's not asking her reasons for her earlier secrecy. And she is not disappointed. Milly herself is very spare in her confidences.

The evening scene of confidence in the inn is followed by other midnight conferences in London, when the two friends exchange their views of the Lancaster Gate group. Since Susan, acting as *ficelle*, has provided the connection with these people, it is on her that James first focuses in Chapter VII. The dinner at Lancaster Gate is, in Milly's eyes, "really romantic," and the girl views her quaint little friend in the imagery of a nursery book. Susie has only had to wave her

neat little wand for the fairy-tale to begin at once; in consequence of which Susie now glittered—for, with Mrs. Stringham's new sense of success, it came to that—in the character of a fairy godmother. Milly had almost insisted on dressing her, for the present occasion, as one; and it was no fault of the girl's if the good lady had not now appeared in a peaked hat, a short petticoat and diamond shoe-buckles, brandishing the magic crutch. The good lady, in truth, bore herself not less contentedly than if these insignia had marked her work . . . (pp. 161–162).

During the dinner she manages to exchange with Milly an understanding that approaches the intensity of their evening experience on the Swiss pass, when Milly had confessed to Susan "that what she wanted of Europe was 'people'. . . . She was all for scenery—yes; but she wanted it human and personal, and all she could say was that there would be in London—wouldn't there?—more of that kind than anywhere else" (p. 134). This dinner is the beginning of their real adventure, so both these romantic women feel, "as if, properly, they were in the position of having ventured on a small joke and found the answer out of proportion grave" (p. 162). How grave it will eventually be is mercifully concealed from their presently shining eyes.

Milly continues to confide in Susie; now however her confidences are drawn from her observations of the "wonderful" Kate, rather than from her own desires. Susan promptly classifies Kate as "the chosen daughter of the burgesses" deputed to wait upon her princess (p. 189). On her part, Susan is blissfully ignorant of the disdain with which Mrs. Lowder and her niece regard herself. Kate admits this attitude to Milly without bothering to extenuate. In Milly's eyes, this admission sheds much light on Kate and the world of Lancaster Gate, where exception can be taken to Susie. It is clearly a place of more dangers than New York or Boston ever dreamed of.

Not only does Susan bore the niece; but her quaintness amuses the aunt, who partially conceals her disdain, for the pragmatic sake of using her. When Milly, preferring to stay at the hotel, sends Susan out with Mrs. Lowder, to an evening party, Milly herself delights in it, especially this time, because the New England lady is wearing a gown cut lower than usual in the back. Aunt Maud, however, derives no pleasure from taking "out the new American girl's funny friend instead of the new American girl herself" (p. 287). She does it, nevertheless,

confessing even as much to poor Susie—because, frankly, she *was* good-natured. When Mrs. Stringham observed that her own light was too abjectly borrowed [from the princess] and that it was as a link alone, fortunately not missing, that she was valued, Aunt Maud concurred to the extent of the remark: "Well, my dear, you're better than nothing" (pp. 287–288).

By this time Mrs. Lowder has gained the ascendancy over Mrs. Stringham, having invited her to join her plan of uniting the two girls, Kate and Milly; and furthermore, having extracted pertinent information from her about Milly's knowing Merton Densher. Again Susan is acting as the *ficelle,* or useful string. It is important for Mrs. Lowder to know early of Milly's acquaintance with Densher, so that she may get her strategy in motion to lure him away from Kate. Susan's first act as Maud's blind accomplice is to tell Milly to say nothing to Kate about Densher. From this point it is only a step for Mrs. Lowder to ask Milly to spy on Kate. But Milly, as has already been pointed out, has more of the serpent's wisdom than her confidante.

The fact is that Susan is as impressed by Mrs. Lowder's material splendor as she is by Milly's wealth and prospects. Poor Susan is quite a materialist herself. Her redeeming features are, however, her undying devotion to Milly and her deep appreciation of her interior qualities. Susan's beautiful adaptability unites her closely to her confider, but it also entangles her with Mrs. Lowder. As she admits to Milly in one of their nocturnal colloquies:

> . . . Maud Manningham . . . did her worldliness with grand proper silences—if it mightn't better be put perhaps that she did her detachment with grand occasional pushes. However Susie put it, in truth, she was really, in justice to herself, thinking of the difference, as favourites of fortune, between her old friend and her new. Aunt Maud sat somehow in the midst of her money, founded on it and surrounded by it, even if with a clever high manner about it, her manner of looking, hard and bright, as if it weren't there. Milly, about hers, had no manner at all—which was possibly, from a point of view, a fault: she was at any rate far away on the edge of it. . . . It was clear, on the other hand, that Mrs. Lowder was keeping her wealth as for purposes, imaginations, ambitions, that would figure as large, as honourably unselfish, on the day they should take effect (p. 216).

Chapter IX presents two scenes between Susan and Milly, who discuss their impressions of Kate and her relatives. In the first one, Mrs. Stringham relates to Milly how she and Mrs. Lowder chanced on the topic of Merton Densher, and how Susan revealed Milly's connection with him. Her embarrassment she tries to cover up by adding that there was no secret about it, to which Milly concurs. But the reaction of Maud was not missed by Susan; there was in it a definite pulling up, as of reservations being instantly made. This detail is one of the numerous fine clues given by the author to the double conspiracy that is to surround his heroine. In perceiving it, though only superficially, Susan is acting again as his *ficelle*—the note of warning is sounded: it " 'may mean something,' " Susan concludes; but she fails to link it up with later clues (p. 205). For her the important thing is Maud's request not to mention Densher to Kate—not because there's something between them, but, she guesses, because Maud is "afraid of something." Susan's conclusion is accurate enough: " 'My dear child, we move in a labyrinth.' " At which Milly takes a childish pleasure: " 'Of course we do. That's just the fun of it! . . . I want abysses' " (pp. 205-206). Susan appears to doubt the sagacity of this reaction, but, like the good lady-in-waiting, she submits to "her highest law to be light when the girl was light. . . . 'Ah, then let us hope we shall sound the depths—I'm prepared for the worst—of sorrow and sin!' " (p. 206). In the light of future developments, this is a pathetically ironical statement. Susan, in her blind invocation of tragedy is poles apart from Maria Gostrey, who reads far into the future and tries to dodge catastrophe.

The second scene further serves expository purposes, by recording Milly's impressions of Mrs. Condrip, Kate's sister. Again Merton Densher was the subject of conversation, and again secrecy has been imposed. Susan notices Milly's exaltation as, like so many other Jamesian characters, the latter makes out the situation while reporting on it. The narrator comments: "That was the great thing with Milly—it was her characteristic poetry; or at least it was Susan Shepherd's" (p. 214). The beauty of insight in *The Wings of the Dove* is rarely accorded to the confidante; instead it is granted to the other three centers of consciousness. In this scene Susan's function is like Bob Assingham's, who, by means of simple questions, draws out the acute interpretations of his wife. Milly's explanations of what she has seen and heard come only upon probing from Susan. Once her questions provoke a look from Milly "as if she were almost venerably simple, but also as if this were what one loved her for" (p. 218). The love holding these two women together is symbolized by the image of the sea, an image to which James often recurs in his writing, when dealing with deep human relationships:

It dispelled, on the spot—something, to the elder woman's ear, in the sad, sweet sound of it—any ghost of any need of explaining. The sense was constant for her that their relation was as if afloat, like some island of the south, in a great warm sea that made, for every conceivable chance, a margin, an outer sphere of general emotion; and the effect of the occurrence of anything in particular was to make the sea submerge the island, the margin flood the text. The great wave now for a moment swept over. "I'll go anywhere else in the world you like" [says Susan] (p. 219).

Their exploring the abyss together unites them ever more closely. The scene with Mrs. Condrip has suggested to Milly that Kate does not love Densher, and she clings to this idea, for personal reasons: " 'I don't think Mrs. Condrip imagines *she's* in love' " (p. 222). Literal-minded Susan wants to know if Milly asked Mrs. Condrip directly; but this was something too close to Milly's own heart to be risked, and the girl shows considerable reserve in this matter even toward her confidante. The rest is left to the inference of the reader.

Book Fifth, written from Milly's point of view, opens at Matcham, Lord Mark's estate. It is here that Mrs. Lowder unctuously tells Milly that

"nothing for a long time has happened to me so good as that you and [Kate] should have become friends. It's beautiful; it's great; it's everything. What makes it perfect is that it should have come about through our dear delightful Susie, restored to me, after so many years, by such a miracle. No—that's more charming to me than even your hitting it off with Kate. God has been good to one— positively; for I couldn't at my age, have made a new friend—undertaken, I mean, out of whole cloth, the real thing. It's like changing one's bankers—after fifty; one doesn't do that. That's why Susie has been kept for me, as you seem to keep people in your wonderful country, in lavender and pink paper—coming back at last as straight as out of a fairy-tale and with you as an attendant fairy" (p. 236).

The falseness of Maud is symbolized by her reversing the roles which Milly and Susan have already appropriated to themselves —Milly is, by their mutual consent, the central character, and Susan only the attendant fairy godmother. Maud is visibly overdoing her flattery; this is so much more evident in its following directly upon her urging Milly to make her home among them, and to help her with Kate. This woman is such an accomplished schemer that her words impress Milly as sincere, while her momentary benevolence extends to everyone, even the servants. But Milly also feels the oppressiveness of her "protective mantle," and the sense of suffocating under it. She is reminded of Susan's characterization of Aunt Maud as "a natural force."

As Milly moves through the great house at the side of Lord Mark, meeting knowing eyes right and left, she asks herself "if Susie could, inconceivably, have been blatant about her" (p. 240); but instantly she dismisses the thought, because she had "elected" Susan Shepherd just for "her being precisely the person in the world least possibly a trumpeter" (p. 240). If nothing worse occurs than the staring of these people—! Milly feels a premonition of danger, but Susan remains unaware. Unfortunately for Milly's confidence in Susan, the reader learns from a conversation between Kate and Densher in Chapter XX that " 'Her fortune's absolutely huge; Aunt Maud has had all the facts, or enough of them, in the last confidence, from "Susie," and Susie speaks by book' " (p. 57).[6] It is only one of the several indiscretions committed by a devoted but fallible confidante.

If Aunt Maud knows how to manipulate Susan Stringham, her niece is no less adroit in doing the same. When Milly bursts in upon her friend with Kate and Densher in her wake, poor Susan, already dazed by the visit of the doctor, is indeed perplexed. Her bewilderment only increases when Kate promptly monopolizes her during and after the meal. Milly notices that suddenly Kate is no longer bored by Susie. The suggestion that she prefers honest Susan Shepherd to Merton Densher is taken by Milly to mean "everything." It is just what Milly wants to see and believe—that Kate does not return Densher's affection. Already knowing that Mrs. Lowder does not favor his suit, the girl proceeds now with more confidence in encouraging that gentleman's attentions to herself. And it is just what Kate has planned. Like her friend, Susan falls into the same trap.

The next time Mrs. Stringham appears is at another dinner at Lancaster Gate, Chapter XIX. In this scene Densher is the center of consciousness. Milly, owing to an indisposition, has absented herself, sending Susan alone to represent both of them. Susan's entry into the "drama" that has already begun is characteristic of a person accustomed to a subordinate role: ". . . Mrs. Stringham . . . rustled in a little breathless and full of compunction of having had to come alone" (p. 39). In this brilliant scene, James gives his little New England author full scope. She is confronted by the two separate plotters, Kate and her aunt, whose deep designs upon Milly are as yet concealed from the reader. Susan feels drawn to Densher, basically because of his acquaintance with Milly, though of course Milly herself has never admitted to a deeper interest. For a more profound reason, however, Mrs. Stringham is attracted to the young man, and this feeling will prompt her later on to seek him out. His being the center of consciousness deepens the impression of their tacit communion.

Mrs. Lowder has introduced Milly as the topic of a conversation which presently grows very lively. She challenges Densher with having "invented the wonderful creature—through having seen her first, caught her in her native jungle" (p. 40). Poor Densher winces, as Maud proceeds to enlarge on Milly's social success in London of which he obviously knows nothing. Mrs. Stringham cannot come to his rescue, being as Milly's representative,

rather confined to the function of inhaling the incense; so that Kate, who treated her beautifully, smiling at her, cheering and consoling her across the table, appeared benevolently both to speak and to interpret for her. Kate spoke as if she wouldn't perhaps understand *their* [Mrs. Lowder's and her friends'] way of appreciating Milly, but would let them none the less, in justice to their goodwill, express it in their coarser fashion (p. 41).

Densher is aware of "a certain broad brotherhood with Mrs. Stringham," and watches her to see how American nerves will respond to this stimulus (p. 41).

They quivered, clearly, they hummed and drummed, they leaped and bounded in Mrs. Stringham's typical organism—this lady striking him as before all things excited, as, in the native phrase, keyed-up, to a perception of more elements in the occasion than he was himself able to count. She was accessible to sides of it, he imagined, that were as yet obscure to him; for, though she unmistakably rejoiced and soared, he none the less saw her at moments as even more agitated than pleasure required. It was a state of emotion in her that could scarce represent simply an impatience to report at home. Her little dry New England brightness—he had "sampled" all the shades of the American complexity, if complexity it were—had its actual reason for finding relief most in silence . . . (p. 42).

But Mrs. Lowder is only warming up. Her baiting of Densher continues with her question "if it were true that their friend had really not made in her own country the mark she had chalked so large in London" (p. 42). It takes only a few of his bungling replies to produce

in Mrs. Stringham a final feverish sally. She announced that if the point of view for a proper admiration of her young friend *had* seemed to fail a little in New York, there was no manner of doubt of her having carried Boston by storm. It pointed the moral that Boston, for the finer taste, left New York nowhere . . . (p. 43).

Then she turns to Densher with a solemn reproach: " 'You know nothing, sir—but not the least little bit—about my friend' " (p. 43). His response that he does know of her kindness to a traveller, is followed quickly by his unpremeditated retort: " 'Remember, Mrs. Stringham, that you weren't then present' " (p. 44). The hilarity with which this remark is received and the manner of Mrs. Lowder's underscoring, " 'You weren't present *then,* dearest. . . . You don't know,' she continued with mellow gaiety, 'how far things may have gone' " (p. 44)—these factors make the little woman completely lose her head. The occasion provides, moreover, a moment of communion between Susan and Densher—both at this moment the butts of ridicule for the sake of Milly—and from this moment Mrs. Stringham becomes his ally.

It was even already a little the effect of this communion that Mrs. Stringham perceptibly faltered in her retort to Mrs. Lowder's joke. "Oh it's precisely my point that Mr. Densher *can't* have had vast opportunities." And then she smiled at him. "I wasn't away, you know, long."

It made everything, in the oddest way in the world, immediately right for him. "And I wasn't *there* long, either." He positively saw, with it, that nothing, for him, so far as she was concerned, would again be wrong (p. 45).

The unspoken alliance into which Susan and Densher have glided under the persistent hints of Mrs. Lowder is fed at the fount of devotion to Milly—Susan, already there, offers to Densher the refreshing draught of admiration. " 'She's beautiful,' " he adds, " 'but I don't say she's easy to know.' 'Ah, she's a thousand and one things!' replied the good lady, as if now to keep well with him" (p. 45).

The interesting thing about this scene is that all three women are anxious to bring Densher closer to Milly: Mrs. Lowder, to separate him from Kate; Mrs. Stringham, for Milly's sake; and Kate, for her own reasons, as yet *sub rosa*. It is at this moment that Kate enters the fray with an "interesting" discrimination as to why Milly is "not easy to know," which brings them back to the puzzlement over her social triumph. Before this spectacle Mrs. Stringham sits

as some spectator in an old-time circus might have watched the oddity of a Christian maiden, in the arena, mildly, caressingly, martyred. It was the nosing and fumbling not of lions and tigers but of domestic animals let loose as for the joke. Even the joke made Mrs. Stringham uneasy, and her mute communion with Densher, to which we have alluded, was more and more determined by it (p. 46).

It is another clue to danger, this time faintly sensed by the good lady. As Kate now takes over the conversation by condescendingly explaining Milly's success, Susan begins to bristle with resentment toward her.

The recurrence of animal imagery in respect to Mrs. Lowder's circle is effective, especially since the reader is already aware of Kate's view of her as the lioness. That Milly will be martyred by these friendly people, and that Susan is already mysteriously and unwittingly in league with them, is established in the image of the circus. And Densher is to feel that Susan holds

that all the Kate Croys in Christendom were but dust for the feet of her Milly. That, it was true, would be what she must reveal only when driven to her last entrenchments and well cornered in her passion—the rare passion of friendship, the sole passion of her little life save the one other, more imperturbably cerebral, that she entertained for the art of Guy de Maupassant (pp. 49–50).[7]

Devoted as she is in friendship, Susan cannot refrain from seeing life through the writer's eyes. The fascination of grist for their mills is something she and Densher have in common; but Susan with her romantic views is further removed from reality than the journalist. Susan has already placed the wonderful Kate in her romantic picture of Milly; the girl is now considered a fit subject for a book. Densher has, of course, felt the literary possibilities in the story of Milly's London success. But he sees first Kate, and then Milly, primarily as human beings, not glorious inhabitants of a dream kingdom. His realism is the basic obstacle upon which Mrs. Stringham's romantic sentiment founders, when she urges him later to compromise himself further in order to save the girl. By temperament, Susan is afraid of hard facts. But facing the hard fact of his betrayal is what redeems Densher. The mutually illuminating contrast of these two writers is both successful from the point of view of character and necessary for the plot.

Susan's function in playing a double role is evident from this big scene. Feeling herself called on to defend Milly both against Kate's condescension and Densher's free and easy manner, she still welcomes the attempts to maneuver the young man into Milly's company. Susan is clearly beyond her depth in this scene, and her confusion is emphasized by various details already noted. Like Miss Wenham, Susan is a nonplussed confidante. In all her simplicity, Susan is the complement to Milly, the dove, and the necessary, helpless witness of her fate. A clairvoyant Maria Gostrey would have made the two plots impossible. By the end of the scene, one feels that Susan as much as Milly, has been made sport of by the other two women. Her brotherhood with Densher is truly a comradeship in being exploited; for both of them are manipulated into a complicity that—if she saw clearly—would instantly repel poor Susan. They are indeed the victims of a "joke."

This dinner party in Book Sixth is the climax in the development of Mrs. Stringham's character and role. It marks, first, the high point of her avowal of friendship for Milly. Secondly, it unites her with Densher—over the heads of the schemers, and without the knowledge of Milly herself. In their public-private communion, the two writers participate in a kind of gnosticism. They alone recognize the American girl for her true value, because as artists they possess deeper insight. Densher will soon realize that friendship with Milly means a claim on himself by Susan. Susan's friendship implies possession—the gentle possession of the timid soul—which can be just as embarrassing as the rough demands of the aggressive type. Milly has sensed it from the beginning; her reticence on the subject of Densher furnishes ample proof. Densher too will realize it when Susan approaches him in Venice. From now on, Mrs. Stringham's dramatic importance, although disguised by her diffidence, increases.

Susan's involvement with Densher on one hand and Mrs. Lowder on the other, becomes more complicated in Book Seventh, the second book written partially from Susan's point of view. The first scene returns in time to the end of Book Fifth, after Kate and Densher have had luncheon with Milly and Susan. Left alone, the two women face together the topic of Sir Luke Strett. Although amazingly little is revealed of Susan's conversation with the doctor, the main import of the scene is to convey Susan's overwhelmed feelings. With a quavering voice, and a heroic grimace, she bravely tries to meet Milly on her superior level of self-control and contempt for pity. She gives her pledge to "see Milly through," but "Nothing in fact came to the proof between them but that they could thus cling together—except indeed that, as we have indicated, the pledge of protection and support was all the young woman's own" (p. 113). As usual, Mrs. Stringham plays the subordinate role, this time of the distressed person in need of the consolation of hearing that she can be of use. Milly's illness and death have often been compared by critics to the fate of Minnie Temple; but her contempt for her disease and rejection of all pity are much more like the jeering attitude of Alice James, during her years of illness.[8] Susan, on her part,

had risen by Milly's aid to a certain command of what was before them; the ten minutes of their talk had, in fact, made her more distinctly aware of the presence in her mind of a new idea. It was really perhaps an old idea with a new value; it had at all events begun during the last hour, though at first but feebly, to shine with a special light (pp. 116–117).

The "idea" is simply Susan's growing awareness of a relation between Milly and Densher. It had been fixed by Sir Luke Strett's visit as a "star" in her firmament, for suddenly her mission to "see Milly through" has been identified with helping Milly to get a husband. With this noble motive impelling her, Mrs. Stringham only too readily lends herself to Mrs. Lowder's efforts in the same direction.

The second scene in Book Seventh returns the story to the present, and shows Susan, weighed down beneath the sorrow of her recent discoveries, turning to Maud for consolation. It gives Maud her chance to clinch the subservience of the New England lady, in whom the Puritan conscience is again at work. In "Maud Manningham's own sanctum" Susan gives a conscientious account of herself. "She never spared herself in short a proper sharpness of conception of how she had behaved . . ." (p. 118). Self-examination is Susan's means of regaining emotional balance, although in this particular crisis she cannot perform the time-honored Puritan act in Milly's presence, since tears "with Milly in observation," would be out of the question. It is, therefore, her very grief over Milly that drives her into the arms of Milly's foe.

Maud lets her have her cry, "knocking off" a note or two while waiting. "She could resist the contagion of tears" (p. 119). But she does not resist when Susan piteously asks her to help *make* Milly happy. She does, however, hold off long enough to whet poor Susan's sense of urgency. What happiness was the physician talking about, and is he certain it will cure?

> "Well, I should think we might know!" Mrs. Stringham delicately declared.
> "Ah, but we haven't the complaint."
> "Have you never, dearest, been in love?" Susan Shepherd inquired.
> "Yes, my child; but not by the doctor's direction" (pp. 123–124).

With this and similar remarks, Maud Manningham Lowder keeps putting Susan Shepherd in her place. (One notices that James inclines to designate the latter lady by her maiden name in those situations which show her at a disadvantage.) Mrs. Lowder's realism offsets Susan's romanticism: " 'But Milly won't be [magnificent], you know, if she marries Merton Densher.' 'Oh it's always magnificent to marry the man one loves,' " opines Susan Shepherd (p. 125). She weakly reiterates her plea for Maud's help, with the question, " 'How can he ever care for her?' " " 'By being put in the way of it,' " is the massive response. " 'For God's sake then,' " wails Susan, " '*put* him in the way! You have him, one feels, in your hand' " (p. 125). By assuring Mrs. Lowder that she handles "everyone," Susan is conscious of pleasing that formidable woman, who however denies

handling Kate. And this at last opens Susan's eyes to the possibility of Kate's caring for Densher. At the same time she realizes "a certain impatience" in Mrs. Lowder for "keeping back,
very hard, an important truth, and wouldn't have liked to hear
that she had not concealed it cleverly. Susie nevertheless felt
herself passing as something of a fool with her for not having
thought of it" (p. 126). Then Mrs. Lowder commands:

"*You* don't know it—that must be your line. Or rather your line
must be that you deny it utterly."
    "Deny that she cares for him?"
    "Deny that she so much as thinks that she does. Positively and
absolutely. Deny that you've so much as heard of it."
    Susie faced this new duty. "To Milly, you mean—if she asks?"
    "To Milly, naturally. No one else *will* ask" (p. 127).

But Susan knows she will be spared that lie, because Milly will
never ask. " 'And luckily for *me*. I lie badly.' 'I lie well, thank
God,' Mrs. Lowder almost snorted . . ." (p. 127).
    Susan "dimly" descries that Maud has found a reason for
helping Susan and that is that Susan can help Maud, "for which
she now desired to profess herself ready even to lying" (p. 127).
Furthermore, "Mrs. Stringham saw herself recruited for the removal of Kate's delusion—by arts, however, in truth, that she as
yet quite failed to compass. Or was it perhaps to be only for the
removal of Mr. Densher's?—success in which indeed might en-
tail other successes. Before that job, unfortunately, her heart had
already failed" (p. 128).
    In any case, Susan's involvement with Aunt Maud's plan is
complete and irrevocable. From now on she is no longer purely
and simply Milly's confidante, but she has committed her friend
into the hands of another confidante of her own, whom the girl
does not trust. Mrs. Stringham is well on her way to unconscious
betrayal. And although Susan is desirous of suffering for her
young friend, still "an odd independence" is beginning between
them, "an independence positively of action and custom—on

the subject of Milly's future. They went their separate ways, with the girl's intense assent. . . . She fairly favoured the idea that Susie had or was to have other encounters—private, pointed, personal; she favoured every idea, but most of all the idea that she herself was to go on as if nothing were the matter" (pp. 135-136). This simulated freedom in their relations only throws Mrs. Stringham more into Mrs. Lowder's company.

In Susan Stringham James created the very antithesis to Maria Gostrey. The latter is the accomplished woman of the world, the clever and independent confidante, whose consistency matches her determination. Susan, on the other hand, is the inexperienced lady from the provinces, easily overawed and influenced by characters more forceful than herself. Consistent only in her good will, she is easily led, first by Milly, then by Milly's enemy. Where Maria cautiously withdraws, Susan trustingly blunders in. But in both cases, James uses the quality of character for his specific ends. While he must remove Maria from the scene temporarily, he employs Susan on the spot to further unwittingly the plot against his heroine. In Book Seventh, when Susan has fallen completely into Mrs. Lowder's clutches, James lets the inimical forces close in upon Milly Theale. So whether it is by leaving or by remaining on the scene, James uses both confidantes as *ficelles,* both to enhance lucidity and to further the plot.

Susan's two scenes with Merton Densher, in Books Eighth and Ninth, give her her last opportunity to act opposite the leading man. These scenes in Venice should be considered as a continuation of the scene at Mrs. Lowder's dinner, Book Sixth, when the middle-aged lady establishes a definite rapport with the young journalist. All three scenes are written from Densher's point of view. His awareness of Susan Shepherd's attempted influence on himself becomes gradually clearer. The "certain broad brotherhood" first felt with Mrs. Stringham at Lancaster Gate has grown into his foreordained position in her imagined Veronese picture—where he is " 'the grand young man who

surpasses the others and holds up his head and the wine-cup' "
(p. 226). For although the party in the Venetian palace was
planned by Milly in honor of Sir Luke Strett, one feels distinctly
Mrs. Stringham's hand in casting Densher in his present role.
This is what the "good lady" considers "working for Milly,"
and she certainly "works" Densher for all he is worth.

Densher finds himself at last caught between Mrs. Stringham
on one side, urging him to be faithful to them—to stay on in-
definitely in Venice, and Kate on the other, finally revealing her
plot for him to marry Milly " 'since she's to die' " so that " 'in the
natural course [he will] have money' " (p. 246). Besides Susan
and Kate, Mrs. Lowder is also exerting pressure on him in the
same direction. The poor man wonders whether "it mightn't
be best just to consent, luxuriously, to *be* the ass the whole thing
involved. Trying not to be and yet keeping in it was of the two
things the more asinine. He was glad there was no male witness;
it was a circle of petticoats; he shouldn't have liked a man to
see him" (p. 229). To be caught among three women, each
armed with reasons and appeals of her own, is too much for
Densher.

Still romanticizing, Mrs. Stringham resumes her pressure by
reminding him that for the sake of her princess she has given
up "all," and she wishes he could do the same. "The whole sacrifice" to be made for the princess is one's career of writing. And
although Densher in self-defense points out that Milly is not his
princess, the devoted lady returns to the charge with

"And yet she has wanted to be kind."
It made him feel on the spot like a brute. "Of course she has. No
one could be more charming. She has treated me as if *I* were somebody. Call her my hostess as I've never had nor imagined a hostess,
and I'm with you altogether. Of course," he added in the right
spirit for her, "I do see that it's quite court life."
She promptly showed that this was almost all she wanted of him.
"That's all I mean, if you understand it of such a court as never
was: one of the courts of heaven, the court of an angel. That will
do perfectly" (p. 230).[9]

Densher sees it is useless to take a realistic view when discussing Milly Theale with her confidante. To remind her that his commitment is not the same as hers makes him a brute in her eyes; but the moment he enters into her picture-book vision of the court life she is cheered. Yet when he renews his protestations by pointing out that court life does not pay, her rejoinder is as romantically simple as the others:

"Yes, one has read; but this is beyond any book. That's just the beauty here; it's why she's the great and only princess. With her, at her court," said Mrs. Stringham, "it does pay." Then as if she had quite settled it for him: "You'll see for yourself."

He waited a moment, but said nothing to discourage her. "I think you were right just now. One must do something first."

"Well, you've done something."

"No—I don't see that. I can do more."

Oh well, she seemed to say, if he would have it so! "You can do everything, you know" (pp. 230–231).

The "everything" that he can do for Milly is obviously to offer her a motive for living. Since Sir Luke Strett is so interested in her case, it will be wise of Merton Densher to present his eligibility to the doctor's acute gaze. Resisting at first this plan of action preconceived by others for him, Densher eventually compromises by showing the doctor around Venice, but refuses to disclose his sentiments toward Miss Theale.

The hopeful anxiety with which Susan Stringham has watched the progress of Densher's attentions to Milly reaches its climax after Lord Mark's revelation has made Milly "turn her face to the wall." Desperately she seeks out Densher, pleading that he will stay on in Venice for her own sake. Then she amends, " 'Well, anything you do for me—*is* for her too' " (p. 295). But since Milly refuses to mention him, Densher sees it is all over between them: " 'No more than if you were dead.' 'Well,' he answered after a moment, 'I *am* dead.' 'Then *I* am,' said Susan Shepherd with a drop of her arms on her waterproof" (p. 296). She could make no clearer statement of her identification with the young man. From their brotherhood first experienced at Lancaster Gate to his present acquiescence to her interests in Milly's behalf, there is a link which resembles Fanny Assingham's connection with Prince Amerigo. Both women accept their minor roles provided they can watch and acclaim the gallant ventures of their heroes. In both women there is a faint regret at not being the first lady in the man's life. In an unguarded moment Susan betrays her almost unconscious feelings toward the young man:

> "Oh, I mean if you'll stay for me."
> "I'll do anything for you. Isn't it for you alone now I can?"
> She thought of it, and he could see even more of the relief she was taking from him. His presence, his face, his voice, the old rooms themselves, so meagre yet so charged, where Kate had admirably been to him—these things counted for her, now she had them, as the help she had been wanting: so that she still only stood there taking them all in. With it, however, characteristically, popped up a throb of her conscience. What she thus tasted was almost a personal joy. It told Densher of the three days she on her side had spent (p. 295).

Her personal feelings towards Densher are so tender as to gloss over completely any reference to his double game with Milly:

> He saw, and it stirred him, that she hadn't come to judge him; had come rather, so far as she might dare, to pity. This showed him her own abasement—that, at any rate, of grief; and made him feel with a rush of friendliness that he liked to be with her. . . .
> "We shall at all events—if that's anything—be together" [she states] (p. 297).

Their alliance had been foreseen by Kate, when she told Densher "that Mrs. Stringham was a person who *wouldn't,* at a pinch, in a stretch of confidence, wince" (p. 298). Indeed, Susan Stringham does not wince at Densher's apparent duplicity. Pragmatic like her sister-confidantes, she has counted only on the final result of his subterfuge. Milly's cure is to be achieved at all costs, because Susan worships Milly, and believes this is the only possible way to save her. The "rare passion" of friendship causes her to wink at the questionable means of deception. Only in passing does her Puritan conscience intervene, when Densher suggests she at least has done Milly no harm.

> Mrs. Stringham looked about in her darkness. "I don't know. I come and talk of her here with you."
> It made him again hesitate. "Does she utterly hate me?"
> "I don't know. How *can* I? No one ever will" (p. 300).

But in spite of her pang of conscience, in a moment both she and Densher are admitting that Milly brings them together:

> "I can't talk to any one about her."
> "Except to *me*," his friend continued.
> "Except to you." The ghost of her smile, a gleam of significance, had waited on her words, and it kept him, for honesty, looking at her. For honesty too—that is for his own words—he had quickly coloured: he was sinking so, at a stroke, the burden of his discourse with Kate (pp. 305–306).

Susan does not realize how close she comes in this scene to replacing Kate in the role of conspirator against Milly: ". . . Kate's presence affected him suddenly as having swooned or trembled away. Susan Shepherd's, thus prolonged, had suffused it with some influence under which it had ceased to act" (p. 307). Aware, perhaps, of her increasing influence, Mrs. Stringham tries first to convince Densher of his love for Milly, and then to force him into a denial of his engagement to Kate. The first attempt he evades; the second he endeavors to escape in several ways, only to be caught up each time by her persistency. Finally, she confronts him with:

> "If Sir Luke himself asks it of you as something you can do for *him*, will you deny to Milly herself what she has been made so dreadfully to believe?"

Oh, how he knew he hung back! But at last he said: "You're absolutely certain then that she does believe it?"

"Certain?" She appealed to their whole situation. "Judge!"

He took his time again to judge. "Do *you* believe it?"

He was conscious that his own appeal pressed her hard; it eased him a little that her answer must be a pain to her discretion. She answered, none the less, and he was truly the harder pressed. "What I believe will inevitably depend more or less on your action. You can perfectly settle it—if you care. I promise to believe you down to the ground if, to save her life, you consent to a denial" (pp. 318–319).

In asking Densher so to expose himself, Mrs. Stringham is really exposing herself too. Her keen interest in his cause succeeds finally in laying the Puritan conscience to rest. No more scruples, no more doubts for Susan Shepherd. From later developments one concludes that she has suggested to Sir Luke that he can ask this favor of Densher; but the doctor, superior in every way to the little New England lady, does not force the issue. As far as she is concerned, Densher and Kate *may* be engaged; but in her simplistic view, as long as he denies it to Milly, all will be well. One wonders how Mrs. Stringham consoled herself when Densher failed to meet her request. At any rate, their secret correspondence after Milly's death gives him a sense of security. His "belief in her power, or in her delicate disposition, to protect" his game from publicity consoles him to the end (p. 425).

It is difficult to justify Mrs. Stringham's pragmatic stand at the end of the novel. Mr. Ernest Sandeen claims that "her motives are of the best. She believes that love—even if only a delusion—may help Milly to live, or at the very least, give her the sense of having lived if it cannot repair her health."[10] To acknowledge the goodness of her motives is to highlight the simplicity of Susan's character. Overflowing with sincere regard for her confider, she does not stop to consider the latter's possible feelings. It is to be feared that Susan's romantic imagination, Byzantine proprieties, awed subservience to Mrs.

Lowder, and feeling of close kinship with Densher precipitate her moral decision in urging Densher to keep up the fraud. Much as we would like to excuse Susan, it can be only on grounds of myopia in regard to Milly. She would prefer Milly to live, even if she might doubt Densher's honesty; she would prefer herself to live beside Milly in a lying attitude (as she has promised Mrs. Lowder) in order to keep Milly alive. Milly, with her proud independence, would not prefer such an existence. But Susan wishes it for her.

I believe James's purpose was to portray in Susan an example of beautiful devotion unconsciously limited by human weakness. James clearly likes Susan; but he also gently adds touches of pathetic irony to her character. To suffer such deception at the hands of Mrs. Lowder and Kate is pathetic; and to wish for Milly's happiness under circumstances that would only offend the girl is more pathetic still. In his original plan the author envisioned a confidante of greater dramatic importance: "We were to have revelled in Mrs. Stringham, my heroine's attendant friend, her fairly choral Bostonian, a subject for innumerable touches, and in an extended and above all an *animated* reflexion of Milly Theale's experience of English society."[11] But she had to be reduced to "one fond hour" of acting as a "reflector" in Book Second.[12] Brief as it is, Susan's "hour" sets the tone for all of Milly's appearances. Her worship even pervades the scenes where Milly is absent—at the second dinner party, and in Densher's Venetian rooms. Mrs. Stringham is the chief means used by James to paint the aura around his heroine. If Milly Theale lives in the reader's imagination, it is due to her confidante's influence as center of consciousness. In this respect Susan is a very unique *ficelle;* for although Fleda's consciousness interprets the people around her, none of them are seen as worthy of the worship given by Susan to Milly.

As center of consciousness, Mrs. Stringham is important in respect to the heroine; and as confidante her role ranks with those of the major confidantes. Like Mrs. Wix she tries to take a hand in the action; like Maria Gostrey and Fanny Assingham, she takes vicarious pleasure in watching others; and like Henrietta Stackpole, she is devoted to her friend. Like Fleda Vetch in being a center of consciousness, she is yet very unlike her in background, temperament, and outlook. In the moral choice which both women face, Fleda's decision favors frankness, while Susan's implies a deception. Both Fleda and Susan are confidantes of women, and in both pairs of friends there is a mother-daughter relationship. While the attitude of Fleda tends towards disenchantment, Susan's amounts to the adulation of a trusting child.

When Susan is observed by other "centers," particularly Milly and Densher, we learn of her lovable and pathetic sides, and her feminine inclination toward Densher. Her characteristics as center of consciousness are consistent with those observed by others; so that in both ways James has presented a fully rounded character. Her shortcomings, which James disguises with subtlety, in order to preserve her attractiveness, are what make her character sometimes humorous, and always genuinely human.

When outlining *The Wings of the Dove* in his *Notebooks* James sketched

> ... a confidant of the hero's *evolution*, his emotions. I seem to see a vivid figure, and perhaps, for the hero, *that* figure—i.e., the 'confidant'—in the dying girl's *homme d'affaires*. I seem to see her perhaps as an American and this personage, the *homme d'affaires,* as a good American comedy-type. His wife would be the elderly woman."[13]

Although first conceived as a member of the opposite sex, and cast in a different role, the confidante in *The Wings of the Dove* had comic dimensions from the very start, and they come through the final portrait in spite of the tragic background of the novel. Susan Stringham's comic characteristics are seen and judged, kindly by Milly, her friend, disdainfully by Mrs.

Lowder, her exploiter. But her comic character is made pathetic by the awkwardness of her position. As the story took shape in the author's mind, a confidant for the hero became less imperative than one for the heroine, who by nature of her illness and her riches is isolated. It is always the isolated character in James who needs a confidante. Another significant change in her role was to equalize her social status with that of her friend. One wonders how the *homme d'affaires* would have bridged the gap, unless it would have been in a manner similar to Mrs. Wix's. Although Mrs. Stringham lacks financial resources comparable to those of Milly Theale, her profession as author gives her, like Densher, social status acceptable in higher circles. The artists in James's work may be impecunious, but they qualify intellectually and culturally.

Chapter 8

THE GOLDEN BOWL

Ɪɴ *The Golden Bowl* (1904), more so than in *The Ambassadors,* the role of the confidante is determined by the structure of the book. The symmetry of Fanny Assingham's scenes resembles superficially that of Maria Gostrey's; but the regularity of her appearances originates in a different structural source.

The Golden Bowl is built up of two large blocks, each with a principal center of consciousness: Book First (Parts First to Third), The Prince; Book Second (Parts Fourth to Sixth), The Princess. The principal consciousness reflects the other characters in the novel. James holds that this technique is justified, and disposes rather summarily of a possible objection from the reader:

. . . I take a moment only to meet a possible objection—should any reader be so far solicitous or even attentive—to what I have just said. It may be noted, that is, that the Prince, in the volume over which he nominally presides, is represented as in comprehensive cognition only of those aspects as to which Mrs. Assingham doesn't functionally—perhaps all too officiously, as the reader may sometimes feel it—supersede him. This disparity in my plan is, however, but superficial; the thing abides rigidly by its law of showing Maggie

Verver at first through her suitor's and her husband's exhibitory vision of her, and of then showing the Prince, with at least an equal intensity, through his wife's; the advantage thus being that these attributions of experience display the sentient subjects themselves at the same time and by the same stroke with the nearest possible approach to a desirable vividness.[1]

Everyone, even Mrs. Assingham, is seen at first through the eyes of the Prince; and so, James goes on to say, the procedure is repeated in the second half, with Maggie as the center of observation.

Had James developed his remarks on *The Golden Bowl* beyond the scant space they now occupy in one-fifth of the Preface, he might have enlarged on the subject of Mrs. Assingham, since the possible objections to her role had already occurred to him. In default of such fuller statements, one must have recourse mainly to the novel itself, in an effort to estimate and justify Fanny's role.

The two divisions described by James are naturally the first structural units to be considered. They are, as the author points out, controlled by the observations of their respective leading character—the Prince and the Princess. Nevertheless, within these main divisions there are subdivisions allotted to none other than the subordinate observer, Mrs. Assingham. Although it is true that the Prince observes her, the reverse is likewise true; and what she sees of him—as well as of the other characters—she transmits faithfully in a running commentary to her husband. On a smaller scale, the same pattern occurs in Book Second. As temporary center of consciousness, Fanny resembles Susan Stringham, although more scope is allotted to Fanny. This colorful lady is the "center" in the big scenes with her husband: Book First, Chapters IV, XVI, and XXIII-XXIV; Book Second, Chapter XXXI; all of which give her great opportunity to dramatize herself. The symmetry of her appearances can only be intentional. In Book First she occupies the stage with the Prince in two scenes. In Book Second she and the Princess face each other in four scenes. Of the four scenes with her husband, the largest, covering two chapters in Book First, is located at the very center of the novel. These minor compositional blocks devoted to Mrs. Assingham are dramatized by her sharp insights and vivid speeches. Their purpose, as James indicates in the Preface, is to supplement the insights given the reader through the central intelligence.[2]

Mrs. Assingham is not the only confidante of an enamored couple. A predecessor occurs in the short story, "Miss Gunton of Poughkeepsie" (1900). Lady Champer, the widow of an English baronet, sensible, dry, and farsighted, receives the confidences of an American girl, Lily Gunton, and her fiancé, a Roman Prince. The similarity in the situation together with the differences in character are very interesting. The marriage never materializes, but the confidante has the satisfaction of predicting the breakup. As an Englishwoman, Lady Champer hovers above the indiosyncrasies of democratic American and aristocratic Italian mores. Fanny is also poised between the two, although her origin, education, appearance and role are far more complex than Lady Champer's.

This lady's role provided the author with a kind of finger exercise before he launched into the bigger task required by *The Golden Bowl*. In the short story the confidante's role places her continually center-stage, where exposition is given under the theatrical guise of confidential talks with her. In the novel, such a simple device could scarcely bear the burden of sustained action; neither would it be adequate to convey the substance of the counterplot of Charlotte's intrigue. James was obliged, therefore, to use other means of dramatization and narration to supplement the activities of the confidante, Mrs. Assingham; and these are evident especially in the chapters where she is absent.

Fanny's prominence in the life of the Prince antedates the beginning of the novel. Her image arising in his mind is our introduction to her:

. . . there rose before him after a little, definitely, the image of a friend whom he had often found ironic. . . . the image of Mrs. Assingham made him presently stop a hansom. *Her* youth, her beauty were things more or less of the past, but to find her at home, as he possibly might, would be "doing" what he still had time for, would put something of a reason into his restlessness and thereby probably soothe it. . . . Mrs. Assingham, precisely, represented, embodied his pledges [to the Ververs]—was, in her pleasant person, the force that had set them successively in motion. She had *made* his marriage. . . .[3]

The Prince reflects upon their friendship and her arranging his marriage. Her interest in *him* is unaccountable. "On what did that sentiment, unsolicited and unrecompensed, rest?" (p. 14). To him, it seems a mystery. "The state of mind of his new friends, including Mrs. Assingham herself, had resemblances to a great white curtain," like the misty curtain in *A. Gordon Pym* (p. 15). As character motivation, Fanny's interest in the Prince will later be revealed as a vicarious participation in his life; as a technical device, it is the spark used by James to start the chain reaction of the story. As already shown, both uses of the confidante had a preliminary testing in *The American*.

To Prince Amerigo, Fanny and the Ververs are shrouded in the mystery of what they expect him to be. In her naïveté Maggie had already confessed merrily to him that " 'You're a rarity, an object of beauty, an object of price' "—a part of her father's rare collection (p. 7). In Mrs. Assingham's estimation, however, the Prince ranks as something very different. A worldly woman of her order would scarcely simplify a man's identity, even in terms expressing admiration. The clue for the Prince in his relation with his confidante remains to be discovered.

He makes an attempt to encompass that relation by defining his need: " '. . . I've already told you often enough how I depend on you to see me through. . . . Say what you will I shall need you. I'm not, you know . . . going to give you up for anybody' " (pp. 18-19). Presently the reason for his need comes to the surface of their talk:

> . . . then she said: "I don't in the least want to lose sight of you. But even if I did I shouldn't think it right."
>
> "Thank you for that—it's what I needed of you. I'm sure, after all, that the more you're with me the more I shall understand. It's the only thing in the world I want. I'm excellent, I really think, all round—except that I'm stupid. I can do pretty well anything I *see*. But I've got to see it first. . . . I don't in the least mind its having to be shown to me—in fact I like that better. Therefore it is that I want, that I shall always want, your eyes. Through *them* I wish to look—even at any risk of their showing me what I mayn't like" (pp. 20–21).

An appeal to a confidante for guidance could not be more explicit. Amerigo's fearful sense of his mysterious married future prompts him to entrust himself to the clairvoyance of this woman, who has already played the part of a guardian of his fate. In his case, the need for guidance is even more emphasized than in Strether's. It is principally to the care of her moral sense that he is recommending himself for a timely warning when he may, "*without* knowing it," have gone wrong. To have gone wrong in the eyes of the Ververs is what he is anxious to avoid. Fanny, being American by birth, is to prevent such an error. " 'The moral, dear Mrs. Assingham. I mean, always, as you others consider it' "; and, " 'I shall always have you to come to,' " he concludes after analyzing the differences between the American and the Roman moral sense (p. 21). Amerigo's uneasiness proves contagious to Fanny, and although she pledges her assistance, her nervousness betrays itself. His premonition foreshadows the Prince's involvement with Charlotte Stant, whose recent arrival in London is already known to Fanny.

Her revelation of this fact begins the dramatized exposition. Charlotte has already called on Fanny and given her some in-

formation. This the latter now conveys to Amerigo's discon-
certed attention. Her promise however to "look after" Charlotte
calms his barely concealed agitation. With two pledges, therefore, Mrs. Assingham has ratified their year-old friendship and
her position as his guardian. The scene concludes with Mrs.
Assingham's view of the Prince as a distinguished figure:

> The Prince's dark blue eyes were of the finest, and, on occasion,
> precisely, resembled nothing so much as the high windows of a
> Roman palace, of an historic front by one of the great old designers,
> thrown open on a feast-day to the golden air. . . . The young man's
> expression became . . . something vivid and concrete—a beautiful
> personal presence, that of a prince in very truth, a ruler, warrior,
> patron, lighting up brave architecture and diffusing the sense of a
> function (p. 29).

It is a picture that blends with her own, as he sees it:

> Her richness of hue, her generous nose, her eyebrows marked like
> those of an actress—these things, with an added amplitude of per-
> son on which middle age had set its seal, seemed to present her
> insistently as a daughter of the South, or still more of the East, a crea-
> ture formed by hammocks and divans, fed upon sherbets and waited
> upon by slaves. . . . She wore yellow and purple because she thought
> it better, as she said, while one was about it, to look like the Queen
> of Sheba than like a *revendeuse;* she put pearls in her hair and crim-
> son and gold in her tea-gown for the same reason; it was her theory
> that nature itself had overdressed her and that her only course was
> to drown, as it was hopeless to try to chasten, the overdressing (p.
> 23).

The mental kinship and confidence between this man and
woman are enhanced by their equally striking appearance; the
one by birth, the other by accident, each is endowed with the
past's grand style and luxury. Both of them are so set apart in
time and in features from common mortals—the commonality
being all too plainly represented by Colonel Assingham—that

in contrast, their timelessness is emphasized by two details: the Prince is likened to "the ghost of some proudest ancestor" (p. 29); and Fanny appears "as if her most active effort might be to take up, as she lay back, her mandolin, or to share a sugared fruit with a pet gazelle" (p. 23). The past lives in him; and for her, there appears to be no flux of the present, but only the stasis of enjoyment. Both of them are made to rule; the imagery of royalty, architecture, and palatial furnishings supports them in their function. There can be little doubt that in this manner James was trying to raise his confidante to the level of the protagonist, to meet the equality necessary for confidence. Strether and Maria Gostrey are more equally matched. In the case of the Prince and Fanny the disparity in age and origin can never be quite dispelled, and her name, "Fanny," is a sign of the contradiction in her role. Like "Bob" it has a common ring (common in the nineteenth century); and it suits her relations with her husband far better than those with the Prince. Actually, the names "Fanny" and "Bob" fit their later comic designation of "Darby and Joan." The Assinghams' popular names are definitely a formal contrast with the distinctive names of Amerigo, Charlotte, and Adam. Fanny's position is even more ambivalent than her husband's, because of her American birth, European "discipline," and Oriental features.

This exterior of manner and appearance which Mrs. Assingham presents to the world serves another purpose: that of concealing her two frustrations—"her want of children" and "her want of wealth." A case might be made out for Fanny as an unhappy woman, whose compensation is sought in arranging other people's lives. ". . . she was a person for whom life was multitudinous detail, detail that left her, as it at any moment found her, unappalled and unwearied" (p. 24). As for the Prince, he is a man setting out anew on the voyage of life—to explore parts unknown to him; his interests are therefore doubly hers. The thrill for her in setting out beside him affords her a kind of fulfillment. " 'My first impulse is always to behave, about everything, as if I feared complications. But I don't fear them—I really like them. They're quite my element' " (p. 29). That she revels in complications is quite true; but that they disturb her peace of mind is likewise true, and is borne out by Colonel Assingham's frequent objections to her tormented state, as for example, the first remark made in their introductory scene together: " 'I don't quite see, my dear . . . I'm bound to say, why you take it [Charlotte's arrival], even at the worst, so ferociously hard. It isn't *your* fault, after all, is it? I'll be hanged, at any rate, if it's mine,' " he adds in his characteristically humorous vein (p. 44).

As confidante, Fanny perceives the secrets of the Prince—at first openly confessed, later solely by her own guesswork. Only late in the novel does she receive the confidences of Maggie, although the two women have long been friends. Consequently, there is no such intimate relation between Fanny and the protagonists as there is between Maria Gostrey and Strether, or between Susan Stringham and Milly Theale. Being outside the quartet, she in turn needs a confidant, to whom she can impart the fruits of her speculation, and whom she can enlist as attendant in her plots. This minor role is filled by her husband, Colonel Bob Assingham, a late representative of the comparatively rare Jamesian species of dull man, of whom Paul Beever and Owen Gereth are forerunners.

In arranging for a subordinate confidant for Fanny, James was amplifying what he had already tried in *The Wings of the Dove*. Mrs. Stringham, as we have seen, takes her confidences to Mrs. Lowder and to Merton Densher; Mrs. Assingham turns even more to her husband. Finding herself soon ousted from the circle of the two couples, she becomes increasingly isolated, and her role as confidante is suspended from Chapter III to Chapter XXX. During the intervening time she acts as an observer in her own right, and this is where Bob's appearance is required. The subconfidant is introduced from Chapter IV on, to facilitate the utterance of Fanny's analyses for the benefit of the reader. The comparative dullness of her husband is an added device which occasions the dramatic tension between speaker and listener in these long scenes, and provides contrast in character, as well as requiring the fullest possible explanations on Fanny's part. The reader may feel discountenanced at being identified with Bob's mentality; still the contrast it makes with the supersubtlety of the other five characters proves refreshing. The Colonel, through Fanny, is the only nexus between the refined intelligences depicted in *The Golden Bowl* and peripheral reality. Retired from a practical profession, with his homey pipe and cigar, he represents unpretentious *genus homo*. The familiar name, "Bob," by which he is most frequently designated, is an outward sign, along with his constant smoking, of his comradeship with the reader. He keeps the story on the ground. Also, his unlimited endurance of his somewhat forensic wife and his unappreciated humorous sallies reinforce the appeal of his character.

These two *ficelles,* Fanny and Bob, created for the benefit of the reader, are, compared with Maria Gostrey, certainly ill-disguised. This is the reason for Edith Wharton's disgust:

In "The Golden Bowl," still unsatisfied, still in pursuit of an impossible perfection, he felt he must introduce a sort of *co-ordinating consciousness* detached from, but including, the characters principally concerned. The same attempt to wrest dramatic forms to the uses of the novel that caused "The Awkward Age" to be written in dialogue seems to have suggested the creation of Colonel and Mrs. Assingham as a sort of Greek chorus to the tragedy of "The Golden Bowl." This insufferable and incredible couple spend their days in espionage and delation, and their evenings in exchanging the reports of their eaves'-dropping with a minuteness and precision worthy of Scotland Yard. The utter improbability of such conduct on the part of a dull-witted and frivolous couple in the rush of London society shows that the author created them for the sole purpose of revealing details which he could not otherwise communicate without lapsing into the character of the mid-Victorian novelist chatting with his readers. . . . The Assinghams [are] forced into [the current of the story] for the sole purpose of acting as spies and eaves'-droppers.[4]

Mrs. Wharton's claim that Mrs. Assingham's consciousness is detached from the principal characters is certainly true. Not only is she connected merely by the slim ties of a year-old friendship, when the novel begins, but her class is distinctly inferior to that of the Prince. Her other associates, of whom we hear anything, are simply the battered old warrior friends of her husband. The assertion, however, that both wife and husband are "dull-witted" is a rash statement; and the "improbability" of their watching the quartet is not so great when one considers that these people are doubtless the most interesting friends of the Assinghams. What *is* peculiar—and Mrs. Wharton omits mentioning this— is that such upper-class persons would confide in a woman of Fanny's social rank. The best explanation of the station and character of the Assinghams is the purpose of contrast, which they do effectively serve. In condescending to confide in Fanny, the Prince resembles Sir Claude, who amuses himself doing the same with Mrs. Wix. Any observations made by Fanny are inevitably colored by her own fertile imagination, and throw a different light than do the reflections of the Prince and Maggie, although all three resemble each other in their pragmatism. Furthermore, it seems harsh, as Mr. Cargill points out, to accuse James of ineptitude.[5] A writer of his versatility was hardly limited to one means of revealing details. Rather, the justification of Fanny Assingham lies mainly in the structure of the novel and in her character.

It lies also in the role her intelligence is made to play. In *The Golden Bowl* James was aiming at an art still more refined and attenuated than anything he had yet attempted, with perhaps the exception of *The Sacred Fount*. The further removed from objective reality a work of art becomes, the greater its risk of exceeding intelligibility. In *The Golden Bowl,* James employs the altogether common human motive of curiosity, and transmutes it into something rare and fine, namely the movement of one intelligence toward others in an effort at total comprehension. Consciousness, he learned from his father, is the zenith of existence, and knowledge its greatest contributor. Hence, he addressed himself throughout his career more and more to the problem of gaining fuller knowledge and insight. Both he and his father would have endorsed the current view of the infinite capacity of man's mind. To maintain the almost infinite acuteness of the four minds in this novel within the orbit of lesser minds, James anchored their external reflector, Fanny, in the earthy consciousness of Bob. In spite of general disregard among the critics, Bob Assingham fills the vacuum in which the story has been said to exist. Bob is "the reader's friend." In him curiosity keeps its mundane vesture, without aspiring to something more rarefied. Bob's values bind him to earth; and though humorously delineating him, James does not satirize the figure.

Fanny, therefore, depends on both sides, the quartet and her husband, for her very *raison d'être*. Her justification is determined by her influence in both directions; and in her case, James did what he avoided in Maria's: he made the *ficelle* an active agent in the plot. Even more than Madame Merle, because of an already accepted prominence when the novel begins, Fanny initiates the action by marrying the two leading characters. Upon this initial interference the strength of all her subsequent meddling depends. Feeling strongly her responsibility in making the first match, she watches aghast as the Prince's marriage approaches the rocks, while her conscience torments her more and more. To balance her hypersensitivity James makes Bob almost insensitive, yet curious as to the final issue.

The interesting relation between Fanny and her husband contrasts with the married relations of Mr. Verver and Charlotte, and the Prince and Princess. One is so used to thinking of *The Golden Bowl* in terms of the quartet, that the Assinghams have been unfortunately neglected. The main tension between the exotic wife and her grim, gaunt, military husband arises from Fanny's own flamboyant temperament. Living in a world of airy meditation and facile speculation, she disdains Bob's "flat common sense." Never does she miss a chance to remind him of his dullness, his forgetfulness, his coarseness, his cynicism. When not openly disdainful, she is at best condescending: "His wife looked at him, the good dry man, as if now at last he was merely vulgar" (p. 61).

It is noteworthy, however, that this unflattering picture of Bob Assingham is drawn by his wife, not by the narrator. In his own right the Colonel appears differently than he does in her estimation. His manliness enables him to assert his independence:

"And don't, my dear," she further answered, "think it necessary to be horrid or low about them [Charlotte and the Prince]. They're the last people, really, to make anything of that sort come in right."

"I'm surely never horrid or low," he returned, "about anyone but my extravagant wife. I can do with all our friends—as I see them myself; what I can't do with is the figures you make of them. And when you take to adding your figures up—!" But he exhaled it again in smoke.

"My additions don't matter when you've not to pay the bill." With which her meditation again bore her through the air (p. 196).

Bob Assingham's self-reliance in judging people helps him, though with impatience bordering sometimes on exasperation, to withstand Fanny's flights. "He disengaged, he would be damned if he didn't—they were both phrases he repeatedly used —his responsibility [from her game]. The simplest, the sanest, the most obliging of men, he habitually indulged in extravagant language" (p. 44). James's making a point of Bob's language is significant, for in creating a character that avoids the usual Jamesian diction, the author was reverting to early realistic types, the Millers and Christopher Newman. Bob's indulgence in strong language Fanny condescendingly terms "*his* box of toy soldiers, his military game. . . . [in which] no one was ever killed" (p. 45). But it is his defense against her extravagance of mind, as he watches her at her own favorite game.

He had again and again sat up late to discuss those situations in which her finer consciousness abounded, but he had never failed to deny that anything in life, anything of hers, could be a situation for himself. She might be in fifty at once if she liked—and it was what women did like, at their ease, after all; there always being, when they had too much of any, some man, as they were well aware, to get them out (p. 45).

Then follows the delicious description of his attitude toward her during their first scene together, "quite as if he had paid a shilling" to watch "the celebrated lady who, in a slight, though tight, bathing-suit, turned somersaults and did tricks in the tank of water" at the Aquarium (p. 45).

Bob's shrewdness, moreover, gives him insight into the contradictions concealed beneath his wife's exotic surface. In a thorough, but brief, analysis he exposes her prime motive:

"Nothing can ever make you think anything you don't want to," the Colonel, still in his chair, remarked over his pipe. "You've got a precious power of thinking whatever you do want. You want also, from moment to moment, to think such desperately different things. What happened," he went on, "was that you fell violently in love with the Prince yourself, and that as you couldn't get *me* out of the way you had to take some roundabout course. *You* couldn't marry him, any more than Charlotte could—that is not to yourself. But you could to somebody else—it was always the Prince, it was always marriage. You could to your little friend, to whom there were no objections" (p. 57).

When faced with his wife's idiosyncrasies, Bob's powers of analysis prove to be equal to her own. One smiles—and wonders which of his women friends James was paying back in these passages. Even Bob, the simplest male, can estimate what Charlotte and the Prince will make of their future: " 'They'll manage in their own way' " (p. 201). Eminently practical, Bob is never tempted to romanticize about the lovers.

Perhaps it is here, as they alight from their hired brougham on that fateful evening after the state reception that Fanny first glimpses the depths in her husband, and they remind her at once of Amerigo's double aspect:

Their hall was lighted, and as he stood in the aperture looking back at her, his tall lean figure outlined in darkness and with his crush-hat, according to his wont, worn cavalierly, rather diabolically, askew, he seemed to prolong the sinister emphasis of his meaning. . . . Wasn't it simply what had been written in the Prince's own face *beneath* what he was saying?—didn't it correspond with the mocking presence there that she had had her troubled glimpse of? Wasn't, in fine, the pledge that they would "manage in their own way" the thing he had been feeling for his chance to invite her to take from him? Her husband's tone somehow fitted Amerigo's look—the one that had, for her, so strangely, peeped, from behind, over the shoulder of the one in front. She had not then read it—but wasn't she reading it when she now saw in it his surmise that she was perhaps to be squared? (p. 201).

It is Bob's moment of superiority. His own direct insight has leaped ahead and overtaken hours of her devious and tortuous confidential analyses.

The effect on Fanny is overwhelming. Although promising herself that "she wasn't to be squared," and reminding herself that "she had decided she couldn't be frightened," she is gravely disturbed (p. 201). "Shakiness" in her beloved Prince was not to be thought of; yet here is knowledge beyond her worst surmises. The Prince *is* shaky. The whole grandeur of her game has toppled. The glory of the Roman scion, with whom she had secretly seen her own remarkable qualities allied, seems to have shrunk. And, worst of all, it was she, who having married the Prince to Maggie, had next urged Maggie to bring Charlotte into her own household, for the grandeur of it. In this way she kept her pledge to the Prince, to "look after" Charlotte! Her fear now reduces her to helplessness. And this reduction of the woman who had promised her husband to be "magnificent" is comic. In spite of her disdain for her husband, her need of him has become apparent: "He made her, when they were together, talk, but as if for some other person; who was in fact for the most part herself. Yet she addressed herself with him as she could never have done without him" (p. 195). Now her need of him is greatest. As he draws her forth from the brougham in her traumatic state, they crawl "up their steps quite mildly and unitedly together, like some old Darby and Joan who have had a disappointment. It almost resembled a return from a funeral —unless indeed it resembled more the hushed approach to a house of mourning. What indeed had she come home for but to bury, as decently as possible, her mistake?" (p. 202).

The comic frustration of Fanny's "finer consciousness" may be a detached satirization by James of his own art, which is a dramatization of consciousness. Perhaps—and more likely—it is an indirect statement that the "finer consciousness" is not to be simulated by lesser mortals. At any rate, the shrinking of Mrs. Assingham's stature through an evaporation of her pretentious insights is necessary to unite her with the realistic Colonel, and the essentially comic-pathetic element in her role comes out clearly in this little picture. In creating this "inimitable pair" James was adding two more types to his gallery of comic figures. The process of Fanny's reduction in scale will be completed at Matcham, where through her own folly, prompted by the desire to watch the Prince and Charlotte, she will venture beyond her depth. But before proceeding to this scene, it is necessary to retrace her relation with the Prince, after Charlotte's arrival in London.

That event marks a change in the relations between the Prince and his confidante. She shares no more scenes with him, until the state reception (Chapter XV), when their confrontation has all the qualities of offense and defense. Charlotte has not only supplanted Fanny, but she has called a showdown to prove her innocence to that suspicious lady, and has moreover worsted her in argument. This scene between the two women (Chapter XIV) forms an interesting counterpart to the later one between Charlotte and Maggie. In this one, Charlotte is easily victorious in her immunity; in the later one she wins merely a Pyrrhic victory, the reason being that Fanny's resilience to Charlotte's velvet-gloved blows proves inadequate compared to

Maggie's crafty weakness. " '. . . You can't upset me.' 'I'm sure, my dear Charlotte,' Fanny Assingham laughed, 'I don't want to upset you.' 'Indeed, love, you simply *couldn't* even if you thought it necessary—that's all I mean' " (pp. 179-180).

The fear that grips Fanny as she listens to Charlotte in her security annihilates her before the Prince's approach. Two points must not be overlooked: first, that Charlotte makes her marriage boomerang on Fanny—" '[Mr. Verver] did tell me that he wanted me just *because* I could be useful about [Maggie].' With which Charlotte broke into a wonderful smile. 'So you see I *am!*' " (p. 184). She means of course that she is keeping the Prince off Maggie's hands, which Fanny herself had to do before Charlotte's advent into the menage; but Fanny dares question no further into this, "conscious above all that she was in presence of still deeper things than she had yet dared to fear . . ." (p. 184). She rises abruptly from her seat in an attempt to withdraw in good order, but when Charlotte makes a selection it is always the "most effective possible." In a beautiful pose of forlornness, Charlotte appeals to Fanny not to "forsake her," for at this time she needs her loyalty more than ever. Mrs. Assingham is routed. Made secure by the other woman's superior cleverness and subtle play-acting, she regains her balance only sufficiently to meet the Prince, with whom she shares the next scene. Their lack of confidence in each other is the constant factor in this scene. Fanny's role has changed from confidante to would-be accuser. It is only the suavity and inscrutability of the Prince that restrain her. She, who could not deny to her husband her interest in the Prince, finds herself suddenly turning "for a moment's refuge to a corner of her general consciousness in which she could say to herself that she was glad *she* wasn't in love with such a man" (p. 188). This sloughing of the confidante meets the technical requirement of making room for the rival woman. In *The Golden Bowl,* the rival replaces not only the confidante, but temporarily also the wife. It marks a step beyond *The Ambassadors* in James's development of the rival's role. Poor Fanny, with her middle-age pomp, has no chance beside the sleek, handsome, and youthful Charlotte, with her cunning histrionics. The Prince of course grasps the situation, and treats Fanny with amused imperturbability. Her disillusioned observations provide the reader with more information about the Prince. The whole scene, indeed, is written from Mrs. Assingham's point of view; and together with the preceding and following chapters it forms one of the minor blocks in the structure of the novel which are dominated by the confidante.

Mrs. Assingham's brave attempt in this scene is to probe into the Prince's conscience; but—

As with Charlotte just before, she was embarrassed by the difference between what she took in and what she could say, what she felt and what she could show. "It only appears to me of great importance that—now that you all seem more settled here—Charlotte should be known, for any presentation, any further circulation or introduction, as, in particular, her husband's wife; known in the least possible degree as anything else" (p. 188).

At these words the Prince blandly acknowledges his great indebtedness to Mr. Verver, not only for his munificence, but also for bringing himself and Charlotte together: " 'Isn't it rather as if we had, Charlotte and I, for bringing us together, a benefactor in common? . . . I somehow feel, half the time, as if he were *her* father-in-law too. It's as if he had saved us both —which is a fact in our lives, or at any rate in our hearts, to make of itself a link' " (p. 189).

Fanny's feelings move from discouraged apprehension through frozen recognition to outright fear of his final thrust:

"To *you,* nevertheless, [he says] I may make just one remark; for you're not stupid—you always understand so blessedly what one means."

. . . [But Fanny], invited . . . to understand, . . . held her breath for fear of showing she did, and this for the excellent reason that she was at last fairly afraid to. It was sharp for her, at the same time, that she was certain, in advance, of his remark; that she heard it before it had sounded, that she already tasted, in fine, the bitterness it would have for her special sensibility (p. 191).

His question is why Mr. Verver " 'should have wished to marry at all,' " and Mrs. Assingham receives it as a "thump at her heart, as distressing to her" (pp. 191-192). Knowing, as he does, her affiliation with Mr. Verver's marriage, the Prince can only be seen as invidiously putting her on the spot.

Her face had betrayed her trouble, and with that she was lost. "I'm afraid, however," the Prince said, "that I, for some reason, distress you—for which I beg your pardon. We've always talked so well together—it has been, from the beginning, the greatest pull for me." Nothing so much as such a tone could have quickened her collapse; she felt he had her now at his mercy, and he showed, as he went on, that he knew it. "We shall talk again, all the same, better than ever— I depend on it too much" (p. 192).

And he reminds her of his erstwhile plea for her guidance as his "original sponsor," his "fairy godmother." " 'I beg you to believe,' he added, 'that I look to you yet' " (p. 192). Knowing full well that their confidential relation is ended, Fanny feebly attempts to disown him. But with almost the identical words of Charlotte he appeals to her not to forsake him. With an evasive answer she makes her escape; it is the first time she has turned away from him.

Amerigo's abysmal hypocrisy annihilates Fanny. Even her European "discipline" fails utterly to account for these Roman depths of cunning and suavity. Mrs. Assingham's position is extremely ironic, for with all her penetration, she finds herself just as helpless as Maggie and her father. If Charlotte routed her, the Prince has done much worse. For confidence, the dearest gift of friendship, has been cynically betrayed. Amerigo is the male counterpart of Madame Merle. He also represents the reversal of treacherousness. It is equally bitter, whether the confidante or the confider turns traitor. Fanny's fear of the

Prince is her conscious expression of this bitterness. As confidante, she is at a greater disadvantage than any of her predecessors in the role. Her confider has deliberately converted her into a tool, while pretending she is still a friend. It is the worst degeneracy of all.

Fanny senses which way he is leading her, and it makes her integrity revolt; for, with all her exaggerations, Fanny still has a basic decency and fear of offending against propriety. What will become of it at his hands, remains yet to be seen. The germ of her surrender is already in her last words, given in reply to his last petition: " 'You must receive me at least,' he said. 'Oh, please, not till I'm ready for you!' " (p. 193). When indeed she is ready for him, she will be ready for capitulation; and that event is narrated in retrospect through the Prince's consciousness at Matcham. Before going to Matcham, however, the Prince is sure of his tool, as he expresses it to Charlotte: " 'She would do anything for us' " (p. 218).

It is at the great house party at Matcham that two particular successes of the Prince come into focus: first, the full acceptance of Charlotte as his confidante, and second, the downfall and surrender of Fanny Assingham. The latter had already ventured too far in her prying into the Prince's plans. Her eagerness to pin him down has exposed her unpreparedness to give him a reason for her curiosity. He, sensing her groping for an excuse, had, "not without mercy . . . in his friendliness" provided her with one by asking if she and the Colonel were also going? Fanny is by this time so poorly in possession of her wits that her lie is only obvious to the Prince. Nonetheless—and one can imagine the preliminary scene between herself and the Colonel—they get themselves invited to a place where they turn up at the very bottom of the social ladder. This *faux-pas* is what completely unsettles Fanny, as she later confesses to Amerigo as being "the sole and single frump of the party" (p. 239). But in his aristocratic good breeding on the one hand, and his covert diplomatic foresight on the other, he binds her to himself irrevocably by being the only one to be "nice" to her.

Without diplomatising to do so, with no effort to square her, none to bribe her to an attitude for which he would have had no use in her if it were not sincere, he yet felt how he both held her and moved her by the felicity of his taking pity, all instinctively, on her just discernible depression. By just so much as he guessed that she felt herself, as the slang was, out of it, out of the crystal current and the expensive picture, by just so much had his friendship charmingly made up to her, from hour to hour, for the penalties, as they might have been grossly called, of her mistake. Her mistake had only been, after all, in her wanting to seem to him straight . . . (p. 239).

What Fanny conveys to the Prince is that she risked all this for his sake—to prove to him *not* her espionage on, but her detachment from, him and his "pursuit of pleasure." Beginning with her feeble lie, it is a piteous little deceit, exercised by a woman who feels herself outwitted. It takes no great perspicacity for the Prince to see through it. But Fanny now is blinded, not only by her folly, but also by his "niceness," which "brought tears into her eyes" (p. 240). Her abasement is apparent to all but herself. Charlotte says of her: " 'She doesn't understand us. And really, my dear . . . Fanny Assingham doesn't matter" (p. 218). As if in a belated reply, the Prince, after witnessing Fanny's abjection, tells Charlotte at Matcham:

" . . . she understands all she needs to understand. She has taken her time, but she has at last made it out for herself: she sees how all we can desire is to give them [Maggie and her father] the life they prefer, to surround them with the peace and quiet, and above all with the sense of security, most favourable to it. She can't of course very well put it to us that we have, so far as she is concerned, but to make the best of our circumstances; she can't say in so many words, 'Don't think of me, for I too must make the best of mine: arrange as you can, only, and live as you must.' I don't quite get *that* from her, any more than I ask for it. But her tone and her whole manner mean nothing at all unless they mean that she trusts us . . ." (p. 240).

The Prince continues basking in his sense of having secured Mrs. Assingham to his chariot; but Charlotte, forgetful of her early debt to her, and desirous of being rid of her, shows no sympathy. Her scorn for the superfluous woman finally releases the question:

"What in the world can she do against us? There's not a word that she can breathe. She's helpless; she can't speak; she would be herself the first to be dished by it.

"I'm speaking of how she took, in her way, each time, *their* lives in hand, and how, therefore, that ties her up to-day. She can't go to them and say, 'It's very awkward of course, you poor dear things, but I was frivolously mistaken' " (p. 242).

As James understands it so well, it takes a woman to estimate the depth of humiliation of another woman. Fanny can blame only herself for arranging both the marriages; and although the Prince still hesitates over her reliability, Charlotte quite coldly assures him that she is "fixed."

So far Charlotte has been analyzing the mere external fact. When, in a moment, she puts her finger on the spring of Fanny's action, then that poor creature is definitely wriggling on a pin: " 'She's condemned to consistency; she's doomed, poor thing, to a genial optimism. That, luckily for her, however, is very much the law of her nature. She was born to soothe and to smooth. Now then, therefore,' Mrs. Verver gently laughed, 'she has the chance of her life!' " (p. 243). One senses the contempt of the successful woman for the "meddlesome fool"; but for the Prince's benefit Charlotte disguises it with gentleness. In the reader's eyes the abandoned confidante stands now fully exposed, with a nature condemned to genial optimism in the face of blackest perfidy. As the next scene between Fanny and Bob will show, Charlotte's diagnosis has been correct to the letter.

The Assinghams' next nocturnal discussion occurs after their return from Matcham to London. This is the big scene of summary and forecast, filling Chapters XXIII and XXIV, at the center of the novel. It shows fully the technical importance of the confidante in *The Golden Bowl,* and highlights the peculiar counterpointing of her double role as successful technical device and frustrated woman character. Heretofore, as technical device, the confidante has been useful for dramatizing expository material with the Prince and with her husband, and for presaging danger by her worries (Chapters II and IV). In Chapters XIV and XV, her challenge serves the purpose of exposing the situation between the Prince and Charlotte. Now, with her function as confidante temporarily suspended, she proves useful to the author as an observer, summarizing her impressions formed since leaving Matcham, and predicting the future. This crucial scene is hers entirely.

As dramatized character, however, Fanny's role has run a different course. Beginning as a strange, exotic person allied with a handsome Roman Prince, on the eve of his great marital adventure, she has suffered a rude displacement by a rival, and a sudden fall from favor. Furthermore, and perhaps more disastrously, she has shrunk in the eyes of the reader through manipulation by the narrator and by Charlotte's comments. She has proved her willingness to compromise her integrity, simply because it was her nature "to soothe and to smooth"; for although she is aware of his duplicity, and glad she is not in love with him, her attachment to the Prince proves nonetheless too strong for repudiation. Seeing her therefore in this light, one is prepared for her lengthy attempts at rationalizing and justifying the "beauty" of the lovers' strategy. It is the aim of the present scene to dramatize all this.

By giving this central (and longest) scene to Fanny and the Colonel, James is emphasizing the importance of his secondary couple. For the time being, and as if suspended between the two books representing the two worlds of the Prince and the Princess, Fanny Assingham is poised as observer. Her insights are communicated, for the reader's enlightenment, independently to her own confidant. In this manner James facilitates the transition from Book First to Book Second.

In the meantime, Fanny has made an apparent rebound in "finer perceptions"; she arrives home at midnight, clad in an "amber train" and "lemon-coloured mantle," "there to sink, overburdened, on the landing outside the drawing-room, into a great gilded Venetian chair—of which at first, however, she but made, with her brooding face, a sort of throne of meditation. She would thus have recalled a little, with her so free orientalism of type, the immemorially speechless Sphinx about at last to become articulate" (p. 259). Fanny, once more restored to her own milieu, with only her husband for an audience—like "some old pilgrim of the desert camping at the foot of that monument" —can, superficially, resume her former grandeur (p. 259). Superficially only, for Mrs. Assingham, before returning that night to her home, has had another disagreeable revelation, and her nerves are strained to the utmost to scale the heights of infallibility, before she breaks down: " 'I know. . . . They're wonderful' " (p. 261).

"Wonderful." Applied to Charlotte and the Prince by a woman of cosmopolitan standards, this word so rich in Jamesian connotations means "impervious." The lovers will never make the mistake of alerting Maggie and her father. They will be "heroic." They will carefully coddle the two children in their blindness. Only—and this gives Fanny pause—Maggie is an uncertain quantity. Even now she is showing uneasiness. This is the critical obervation Mrs. Assingham has made that day. Maggie is suspicious only because her husband and Charlotte have not yet returned from Matcham. Once more Fanny is placed in the tight position where her admiration and her conscience awkwardly clash:

" . . . what I really don't a bit want," she declared, "is to abet them or to protect them."

Her companion turned this over. "What is there to protect them from?—if, by your now so settled faith, they've done nothing that justly exposes them."

And it in fact half pulled her up. "Well, from a sudden scare. From the alarm, I mean, of what Maggie *may* think" (p. 265).

Rejected by Charlotte and used by the Prince, Mrs. Assingham resents the responsibility to which both lovers have tied her.

Nevertheless, before long she will compromise herself still more to protect them. Temporarily, the weight of this responsibility breaks her. With "a wail of distress, imperfectly smothered" she confesses her grief to Bob, and her fear that they may not yet have returned: " 'Whatever they've done I shall never know. Never, never—because I don't want to, and because nothing will induce me. So they may do as they like. But I've worked for them *all!*' " (p. 268). The sense of her guilt gains the upper hand, and she collapses. The Colonel, however, meets her trouble with kindness and comfort; and the scene keeps its serious tenor by means of the imagery used. Instead of the Darby and Joan image of the earlier scene, the "mystic lake" of understanding unites the couple here.

And the beauty of what thus passed between them, passed with her cry of pain, with her burst of tears, with his wonderment and his kindness and his comfort, with the moments of their silence, above all, which might have represented their sinking together, hand in hand, for a time, into the mystic lake where he had begun, as we have hinted, by seeing her paddle alone—the beauty of it was that they now could really talk better than before, because the basis had at last, once for all, defined itself. What was the basis, which Fanny absolutely exacted, but that Charlotte and the Prince must be saved —so far as consistently speaking of them as still safe might save them? It did save them, somehow, for Fanny's troubled mind—for that was the nature of the mind of women. He conveyed to her now, at all events, by refusing her no gentleness, that he had sufficiently got the tip, and that the tip was all he had wanted (p. 269).

This beautiful passage, briefly transfiguring a rather earthy couple, marks the climax of the scene. The "mystic lake" ranks beside Maggie's mysterious porcelain-covered "pagoda" as a minor symbol. James recurs at various times in his career to water as the symbol of impenetrable mysteries. Its function in this sense pervades *The Ambassadors*. In this scene its meaning shifts from the inscrutability of the situation in general to the undefined extent of Maggie's comprehension. Emerging from this lake, the Assinghams share the conviction that the Prince and Charlotte (and consequently Fanny herself) will be saved by Maggie. The extended metaphor of the mystic lake illustrates the method James employs in these scenes of analysis. As the scene opens, the confidante never appears to possess full knowledge of the subject in hand. She, along with the listening character and the reader, seems to clarify for herself the situation step by step, arriving, with the other two, at full comprehension only at the end of the scene. The dramatic value of this procedure is self-evident. The anxious manner in which her listener attends to her soundings enhances the dramatic suspense created around a few simple facts which could otherwise be summarized in a paragraph. This method contributes to the artistry of the later phase, which exasperated Edith Wharton and provoked a cruel yet amusing parody from H. G. Wells.[6]

To believe in the lovers' safety amounts to what Fanny asks of her husband—"for that was the nature of the mind of women." Her personal interest in their safety naturally is great, for an exposure of their affair will not only destroy the happiness of Mr. Verver and his daughter; it will also reflect on Fanny as the destructive agent. Her salvation, as she proceeds to the next point in her elucidation, lies in Maggie, who, as Fanny predicts,

"won't do with it anything anyone else would. She'll take it all herself. . . . She'll see me somehow through!"

"See *you*—?"

"Yes, me. I'm the worst. For," said Fanny Assingham, now with a harder exaltation, "I did it all. I recognise that—I accept it. She won't cast it up at me—she won't cast up anything. So I throw myself upon her—she'll bear me up. . . . She'll carry the whole weight of us" (pp. 270-271).

And later:

"Ah no—don't pity her! . . . Now . . . she has begun to live. . . . The way it comes to me is that she *will* live. The way it comes to me is that she'll triumph" (p. 272).

The prognosis is complete. From this point on, the action and narration of the rest of the novel simply illuminate more clearly Maggie's triumph; and it will be achieved, as Fanny sees it, only by the opening of her sense to Evil, and becoming a mature woman. Furthermore, Maggie's duty will be " 'To keep her father from her own knowledge. *That* . . . will be work cut out!' " (p. 274).

After this bit of prophecy, which is later corroborated by events, Mrs. Assingham favors her inquiring husband with exposition of a matter too weighty and delicate to have been revealed heretofore. She is justified in having married Charlotte and Mr. Verver because thereby she saved him from a worse marriage, either first, to a vulgar woman, or second, to a woman whom the Prince " 'would *really* have cared for' " (p. 277). The revelation that he does *not* care for Charlotte strikes the reader as new, but it is later proved correct, and a backward glance at his exploitation of Mr. Verver and of Mrs. Assingham herself explains it. Ironically, Fanny approximates Charlotte's insight in judging the latter's case, for again, only a woman can know best when another woman is exploited. Later she adds, " 'I mean that men don't [really care], when it has all been too easy. That's how, in nine cases out of ten, a woman *is* treated who has risked her life' " (p. 283). Fanny knows whereof she speaks. The effect of Amerigo's rejection of Charlotte and his return to his wife is neither shocking nor edifying.

Reasserting her moral innocence, Fanny pins it on the originally good intentions of the Prince and Charlotte. " 'Otherwise . . . I should have been a wretch. And I've not been a wretch. I've only been a double-dyed donkey' " (p. 278). In short, the vicious circle was begun by Maggie, who started veering between her father and husband in vain efforts to "make up" to each for being deprived of her company. "Her feverish little sense of justice," as Fanny lucidly calls it, was her nearly-tragic irony (p. 281).

Several times the Colonel has made her continue, even though she had given signs of wishing to terminate the discussion. This little dramatic trick James employs once more with Bob's final question, " 'And how must Charlotte—if anything happens—take him?' " At which his wife, gripping his arm, protests, " 'Nothing—in spite of everything—*will* happen. Nothing *has* happened. Nothing *is* happening' " (p. 284). But here she errs. *Everything* will happen, because Maggie will turn out to be what no one suspected, able to think. But everything will take place in a "portentous intelligent stillness." And Charlotte will take it, as Fanny had to, as the inevitable. The parallel between the confidante and the rival in being used and abandoned contrasts with the dissimilarities between Maria Gostrey and Madame de Vionnet.

The last exchange of this peculiar couple in their remarkable midnight colloquy consists of a pact: " 'We know nothing on earth.' It was like the soldiers' watchword at night" (p. 284). They are to pretend the innocence of "absolute idiots." Facilitating them in this pose will be, first, the already firm conviction of both the Prince and Charlotte that the Assinghams *are* idiots; second, Mr. Verver's not really counting, although he does believe in their intelligence; and finally, the use Maggie can make of such a pretense, for Maggie does not want it known that *she* knows. With this, "a last wave of clearness" breaks for Mrs. Assingham. She realizes *how* she became aware this afternoon of Maggie's knowing—it was in the way the latter watched her father for a sign of *his* knowing, which never appeared. " 'She couldn't keep it from me—though she left her post on purpose: came home with me to throw dust in my eyes. I took it all—her dust; but it was what showed me.' With which supreme lucidity she reached the door of her room. 'Luckily it showed me also how she has succeeded. Nothing—from him—*has* come. . . . Nothing *will*' " (pp. 285-286). With this final prediction the great scene closes.

The sense of anticipation which the central scene provides is adequately satisfied in Book Second, where James undertakes

to dramatize directly, and portray by internal analysis, the fulfillment of Mrs. Assingham's clairvoyance. In the process of
her enlightenment Maggie turns to her for help. "Our young
woman's idea, in particular, was that her safety, her escape
from being herself suspected of suspicion, would proceed from
this friend's power to cover, to protect and, as might be, even
showily to represent her—represent, that is, her relation to the
form of the life they were all actually leading" (p. 360). Once
more Fanny resumes her role of confidante.

When Maggie approaches her with the first pointed question,
" 'What awfulness, in heaven's name, is there between them?
What do you believe, what do you *know?'* " Fanny is on her
guard (p. 365). Her allegiance to the Prince having been restored at Matcham, her subsequent pact with her husband to
"know nothing" easily holds out against the less experienced
woman and even turns the tables on her. Evading her questions
with another question, she bullies Maggie in order to protect her
safety: " 'What your idea imputes is a criminal intrigue carried
on, from day to day, amid perfect trust and sympathy, not only
under your eyes, but under your father's. That's an idea it's impossible for me for a moment to entertain' " (p. 373). And
Fanny substantiates this statement with a solemn denial.

One's judgment of Fanny's sincerity depends on the interpretation of her reply. A "criminal intrigue" is what Maggie would
call the affair if she knew all. But in Fanny's more sophisticated
view, their management of the affair has been "wonderful."
The intention of the lovers to protect the father and daughter in
their happy innocence so they in turn could profit by it is only
"beautiful" in Fanny's eyes. As long as the proprieties are maintained, she is full of admiration. For her, only flagrancy would
have been criminal. Although influenced by her surrender to the
Prince, her basic attitude has always been one of compromise.
This is Fanny's dilemma: as long as the forms are preserved, she
is concealing treachery. But in speaking she would create even
greater harm. And so her lying and silence turn to profit for the

Princess, who preserves the "positively portentous silence" in which we first observed the Prince and his confidante.

It is essential to James's moral sense that so many of his confidantes are placed in positions necessitating crucial moral choices. Most of them choose with clear-sightedness and determination. But Mrs. Grose and Fanny Assingham are compromisers by nature. Good fortune, rather than force of character, helps them out of their tight spots. In such a diversified exhibition of feminine portraits, these two timeservers have their rightful place, and bear witness to the author's insight into human weakness.

Meanwhile, the Assinghams continue to watch Maggie, admiring her success in manipulating everyone according to her increasing wisdom. And the confidante reminds her husband of their necessity to lie until they are "black in the face."

The tempo accelerates again in Chapter XXXIII, the great confrontation scene over the golden bowl. Summoned to Maggie's room, Mrs. Assingham knows before entering "that her feared crisis had popped up as at the touch of a spring, that her impossible hour was before her" (p. 396). The upshot is that the Princess faces the matchmaker with the whole truth as she has just learned it by purchasing the golden bowl. Amerigo and Charlotte were intimate before and during Maggie's engagement. The golden bowl "has turned witness."

It remains now for Fanny to explain, not only her position, but the possibility of saving Maggie's marriage. They were all so believing, and Fanny herself believed in Charlotte and the Prince, and still does, and she wanted to "help" Charlotte and everyone. Maggie, understandingly, puts most of the words into Fanny's mouth. Not only does Maggie believe, but, as Fanny had predicted, she takes it all on herself: " 'I've thought only too much [of my father]!' " (p. 412). With several strong hints Mrs. Assingham tries to "help" Maggie see her future way more clearly—to keep Mr. Verver in ignorance and to trust her husband, because, " 'There's only one knowledge that con-

cerns us—one fact with which we can have anything to do. . . .
The fact that your husband has. . . . Never been half so interested in you as now' " (p. 416). When Maggie denies this,
pointing out that Amerigo has dropped even his forms and has
kept away from her on account of the cup, Mrs. Assingham
seizes her cue to shatter the golden bowl. It is the last service of
the confidante, done to save the marriages she had arranged.
With the shattering of the bowl, the Prince re-enters his wife's
room, melodramatically, and symbolically.

After this momentous event Mrs. Assingham gains a renewed social ascendancy, forming with her husband a part of
the frequent company at Fawns, and glorying in her position
there as the "*revanche* . . . of her obscured lustre at Matcham"
(p. 437). As Maggie's friend she is now in full possession.
James, however, depends less on his *ficelle* in Book Second, and
her scenes now are shorter. More important is the change of her
status from confidante of the Prince to confidante of the Princess. She does not enlighten Maggie, but listens to her revelations; and with the passage of time she grows more intimate
with her. Her contribution is perhaps more disinterested. In the
second-last of their interviews, Maggie confides to Fanny her
observation that the Prince has never told Charlotte that his
wife knows. " '*Nothing* has passed between them—that's what
has happened. It explains . . . it explains!' " (p. 438). Her discovery recalls the similar one of Fanny's, that the Prince does
not care for Charlotte. Maggie thus conveys her sense of power
over Charlotte: " 'He'll *never* tell her now' " (p. 439).

It is Mrs. Assingham's turn to wonder and to elicit information. The scene proceeds by the dramatization of Maggie's new-
est realizations. She has let her husband see that she is not stupid
after all, which is a pleasant revelation for him. Secondly, Maggie confides to Fanny that the Prince is leaving Charlotte alone.
It seems quite obvious, too, that he has lied to her to protect his
wife's *knowing*. This information relieves Fanny immensely.
Maggie has measured up to Fanny's prediction; she is protect-

ing them all. The friendship between the two women now is soldered for life, and the rehabilitation of the confidante is complete. No longer will she need to fill the role of isolated observer, for in her restored dependent capacity she will receive the pearls of intelligence as the Princess lets them fall. With the reconstitution of the protagonist-confidante relation, the author's need for Colonel Assingham ceases, and Bob is seen only in such minor positions as taking Charlotte's place at the card table, when the latter sets upon Maggie in that climactic encounter on the terrace.

The last scene between the Princess and her confidante occurs in Chapter XL. Fanny, having borne much privation of intercourse, comes once more to Fawns for the latest information about Charlotte and the Prince. Since her last conversation with Maggie, Mr. Verver has announced his impending departure with his wife for America. All that remains for Maggie and Fanny is to gaze at the remnants of the splendid quartet. Charlotte has met bitter defeat; Maggie is sorry for her; and the Prince "decently" waits for a last private call from Charlotte which does not come. " 'She won't [come],' " says Maggie. " 'But he ought to [see her]' " (p. 518). Fanny, drawing on her own fund of experience with the Prince, advises Maggie to " 'trust him . . . to keep himself absent' " (p. 522). And the confidante, who has spent approximately six years watching the Prince and Maggie, sums them up with " 'You think, both of you, so abysmally and yet so quietly. But it's what will have saved you' " (p. 522). The satisfaction with which she says this implies her own security in being likewise "saved."

With all this lucidity, one final bit of information yet remains concealed. " 'Your father. He knows what *you* know? I mean,' Fanny faltered—'well, how much does he know?' Maggie's silence and Maggie's eyes had in fact arrested the push of the question. . . ." But as Fanny pursues the point, Maggie responds with another question: " 'Do you think he does?' " Which Mrs. Assingham evades with, " 'He's beyond me.' " " 'Then do you yourself know?' " Maggie pursues her in turn. But Fanny is too quick for her, and answers: " 'I've told you before that I know absolutely nothing.' " " 'Well—that's what *I* know,' " replies the Princess (pp. 523-524). Technically, Fanny has spoken truly by denying knowledge of the affair. But we know how deeply her sense of falsehood has pervaded her consciousness; and her complex reasons for adopting this course were strongly influenced by the Prince, when he saw her wavering in her loyalty.

The verbal fencing between the two women indicates the limits of their mutual confidence. Like Isabel Archer and Strether, Maggie has secrets which she withholds even from her confidante. Under no circumstances will she betray her father. The communications between father and daughter, whether spoken or only felt, have been too precious to debase in open discussion with someone else. The same holds for Maggie's relation with her husband. When Fanny tries prying into that secret, she is quietly repulsed: " 'Oh, I can't tell you that!' " (p. 525). So in the end Fanny Assingham is kept in her secondary place.

In *The Golden Bowl,* James makes the most complex use of the confidante. Pinning her importance to the structure of the novel, he causes her role to rise from the secondary capacity of listener and adviser to the eminence of observer in her own right, and then descend again to her secondary function. The two Books determine Mrs. Assingham's role as confidante, first of the Prince, then of his wife. Her brief period of independent observation is wedged in the center of the novel between the main action of both Books.

A further aspect of Fanny's complexity is the change in her character from exotic, successful friend of the Prince, through the Darby and Joan abjection to an assured friendship with the Princess. This fall and rise is counterpointed with her progress as technical device of confidante-observer-confidante.

James also added to the intricacy of her part by making her a receiver and bestower of confidence. Fanny's early estrangement from the Prince calls for a subconfidant for herself, to justify her remaining prominent in the novel. This subconfidant, the Colonel, is requisitioned to aid in her observations, especially at those times when her own role as confidante is lagging. Bob Assingham is one of the few men confidants in James's work; but he is a better foil for Fanny than a subsidiary female character would have been. His qualities indicate lower middle-class origins, and distinguish him from the other characters. By making him so utterly different from the Prince, James avoided repetition in juxtaposing Fanny to another man. Any objections to the improbability of their marriage are obviated by its early description as "bold and original."

The interesting double focus of confidante and observer who in turn confides in a third party, is the means by which James filters down the truth of observation. Fanny makes a better success of this experiment than Susan Stringham does. At the top are the fine intelligences of the Prince and the Princess. The rays of their insights are refracted through Fanny Assingham, and when mirrored by the Colonel, finally reach the reader. When the reader, on the other hand, receives his impressions directly from either the Prince or Maggie, they are not dramatized, or so enriched as when they are handed on with Fanny's commentary. In those scenes where Bob's naturalistic suggestions are added, the reader's experience is still further stimulated. This type of writing is what Conrad worked with in *Lord Jim,* in an attempt to turn as many mirrors as possible toward the central character and event. It is a type of highly sophisticated art, which in the case of *The Golden Bowl* is still connected with reality by the slender thread of Fanny's relation to Bob, much as Conrad keeps the reader in touch with the story through the personality of Marlow.[7]

Conclusion

As a favorite technique, James uses the confidante in a great number of novels and short stories. So important is it to his whole narrative method that the protagonists' mature friends outside this category are limited in number. Mrs. Penniman in *Washington Square,* Mrs. Beever in *The Other House,* Mrs. Brookenham in *The Awkward Age,* and Mrs. Brissenden in *The Sacred Fount* are the chief representatives; but there are a few minor ones, such as Mrs. Munden in "The Beldonald Holbein." As a rule, these women friends fulfill the simple function of lending an ear and giving information; but for various reasons they are not confidantes in the fullest sense, although their roles may in some respects parallel the type as already defined. Frequently too, their characters are less fully developed. That James created these women at various times in his career illustrates his versatility and independence of his own favorite devices.

Of these pseudo-confidantes, Mrs. Penniman in *Washington Square* (1880) is the first example in the Jamesian canon. Chronologically, her place falls between "Daisy Miller" and *The Portrait of a Lady.* In character, Mrs. Penniman resembles Mrs. Tristram, the primitive type of confidante and fruitless schemer, rather than Mrs. Costello or the two major confidantes who succeed her in *The Portrait.* There is, however, a resemb-

247

lance between Mrs. Penniman and the Countess Gemini. Both in temperament and in relative technical unimportance, this woman is a successor to Lavinia. The change in the trend from Mrs. Tristram through Mrs. Penniman to the Countess is perhaps significant: it shows the functional decline of the flighty meddler from chief confidante (among three in the same novel) through the pseudo-confidante to the minor character outside the circle of confidence. There is also a downward movement in moral stamina: Mrs. Tristram resorts only to a minor deception; Mrs. Penniman fairly ornaments her schemes with subterfuge; and the Countess is a person for whom truth and falsehood are interchangeable.

If Mrs. Penniman had had her way, she would have been the most officious confidante of all. But James held her in check, thwarting her aspirations, and capitalizing on the comic potentialities of her frustration. Her dreams of filling a central part in an elopement and in a final tableau of reconciliation are like Mrs. Stringham's projections, only more selfish and less sensible. Try as she might, Lavinia fails to be a confidante, although Morris Townsend does tell her his life story, hoping at first to enlist her aid effectively toward his private ends. But Catherine, the protagonist, not only mistrusts her aunt's sagacity, she also resents her interference. Furthermore, Mrs. Penniman lacks the intelligence of the genuine confidantes. She is easily deceived, because a romantic haze envelops her judgment; and she utterly lacks the powers of divination and prognostication.

As a technical device she also differs from the real confidantes. James uses her as a comic go-between whose services are neither solicited by the young couple nor needed by the author for expository purposes. Only once is she employed to give information, and she bungles it badly. Catherine's and Townsend's feelings are revealed through direct analyses by the omniscient author, and any information Mrs. Penniman can give them is superfluous.

Finally, the author's ironic attitude toward, and treatment of,

Mrs. Penniman segregates her from most of his confidante-characters. Dealing with her omnisciently, he can easily explore this woman's private thoughts, directly exposing her fatuousness. This is a right which he denies himself in the novels written from the restricted point of view. Mrs. Wix, of course, is treated ironically, but in a dramatic way—through her speeches and actions—not by direct commentary.

In view of these differences, the similarities of seeking vicarious pleasure in the lives of others, and of listening to and taking an active interest in a young man's affairs, do not suffice to qualify Mrs. Penniman as a real Jamesian confidante. In no way is her role designed to extend a limited consciousness, nor does she possess the moral qualifications most frequently associated by James with the role. By means of all these incongruities, James really turned her into a caricature of a confidante, an inversion, in many respects, of what he seriously essayed in other novels.

Closer to the maternal role of the genuine confidantes stands Mrs. Beever (*The Other House,* 1896). But this formidable lady is only a confidante in a general sense to the young people around her. Liberal with her advice, she listens to all of them alike. The dramatic mode which James adapted for this novel, as for *The Awkward Age* (1899), would in itself have made a confidante extremely useful; but in both novels James was able to dispense with the *ficelle*. Mrs. Brookenham herself is a mature woman, cast, however, by her degraded character as the rival of her own daughter for the affections of Vanderbank. Van's dependence on her thwarts his attraction for Nanda, and makes his position similar to Owen Gereth's subservience to Mona Brigstock. In a sense Mrs. Brook acts as Van's confidante, although their dramatic positions are reversed from the normal confidante-protagonist relation. Van is hardly the protagonist in a novel that pictures from all sides a social set which is dominated by the malignant Mrs. Brookenham.

Another deviation from James's usual practice is Mrs. Bris-

senden in *The Sacred Fount*. This lady, a friend of the first person narrator, is pressed by him to listen to his suppositions and
surmises about another person among their fellow-guests. She
appears to agree with him that Long, the gentleman in question,
has tapped the sacred fount of youthful energy of some uniden-
tified lady in their midst. The theory builds up nicely until as the
narrator thinks, she perceives the implications regarding her
own relations with her husband. Then she turns on the narrator
with a frank rejection of his finespun theories. The position of
Mrs. Brissenden is purely functional in this rare tour de force.
Consciousness is the sole medium by which the story unfolds.
The two voices of narrator and listener echo in a kind of vault
of imagination, with the barest indications of setting given to
make the transitions from private reverie to conversation hinge
together. There is no indication that the protagonist is intimately
befriended by Mrs. Brissenden, or that he intends to show her
any marks of close friendship. Their own acquaintance, in fact,
turns out to be an example of vampirism, as Mrs. Briss succeeds
in draining the narrator of his intellectual energy.[1] The revelations made by the narrator are not personal. They are esoteric
rather than confidential. In this novel James was not concerned
with his ideal of friendship and its moral significance. Although
the theme of vampirism in *The Sacred Fount* suggests a related-
ness to the theme of betrayal in other novels, it does not make
the acquaintance between Mrs. Brissenden and the narrator
a confidante-"center" relation.

When he deviated from the use of the confidante, James ex-
perimented with other female roles, choosing either the minor
comic figure, or the major schemer. All the women friends discussed here show certain features of the confidante's role. But
these four deviations show a lack of "the wisdom, as James conceived it, of suffering and understanding,"[2] qualities which are
outstanding in many of his authentic confidantes.

Seeing that the confidante's role figures so prominently in
technical uses and character portrayal, one also recognizes that

its place in James's moral sense is no less considerable. From his earliest novels, the author concerned himself increasingly with moral problems, which, as Mr. Bowden has indicated, are much broader than the mere ethical choices between right and wrong. The moral interest, as Mr. Bowden views it in four of James's novels, "is essentially a thoughtful and serious interest in the obligations and opportunities of the soul in this human life."[3] Naturally, the total moral sense of Henry James is difficult to encompass. The vision of a man of such wide reading, keen observation, and diversified experience, who thought and felt profoundly, eludes the narrow compass of a single critical view. To approach that vision even from afar is to participate somehow in the experience of life; and a readiness for such an experience is perhaps the best attitude to take. In his vision of life James gives prominence to the relation of friendship between man and woman. And within the terms of that friendship he frequently cast the woman in the role of the confidante. Consequently, an assessment of the implications of his use of the confidante for his total moral sense necessarily involves a consideration of the Jamesian ethos of friendship.

Although James left his impress on the world before the modern philosophies of the person became popular, his ideas on friendship have a strikingly modern cast. By dramatization, the novelist recreates the exigencies of friendship. A real encounter between two friends requires both self-awareness and openness to the friend. In the encounter with the other person (dialogic union) lies the actualization of one's own person. But real encounter means listening to the other, rather than to oneself. It is a challenge to stand "unprotected" before the friend, with all one's armor laid aside, with all one's masks down. Once the encounter is established, the friend becomes a link between the self and all the values of the world. The discovery of beauty in the world is enriched by such a friendship, and is nourished by conversation. That James himself experienced elements of the ideal friendship is evident from his life and letters. That he envisioned friendship in an artistic and moral frame is clear from his treatment of the confidante-"center" relation and its analogues. His awareness too of the impermanence of friendship without faith and fidelity is represented in the numerous instances of betrayal and abandonment in his fiction.

Betrayal is, in fact, one of James's constant themes. The more intimate and satisfying the friendship, the more terrible is the betrayal. It is closely associated with the discovery of the self, which constitutes another major Jamesian theme, for this discovery progresses usually through friendship and matures in the realization of betrayal and abandonment. The confidantes who are most deeply committed suffer rejection and alienation at the hands of their confiders. James saw friendship as an attempt of the individual to move out from isolation into a dialogic union, a union which requires reverence and commitment from both friends. In order to enter such a relation, the person must know and choose freely.

Influenced by their father, both William and Henry James were absorbed in the subject of consciousness. As Mr. Matthiessen and Mr. Anderson have pointed out, the novelist was intent on making consciousness the supreme subject of his art.[4] Speculation, an activity of human consciousness, and knowledge, its fruit, became the distinguishing features of his major characters. Knowledge must precede friendship; and understanding, a more refined form of knowledge, solders it. Most of the Jamesian friendships between men and women are intellectual in this sense. Endowed with extraordinary intelligence and refined sensibilities, his major characters engage in lengthy discussions of personal matters, which bear on their own relation. Their self-awareness and deep insight form a bond, prescribing its own code of behavior, which opens the way to the choice required of each friend. This choice is existential: freely made, it involves commitment and fidelity, or exploitation and betrayal, with far-reaching consequences affecting the destiny of both friends. According to this view, human dignity is based primarily on individual consciousness. The ability to know more and more deeply—both one's own mind and that of others—is the first achievement of the human being.

The second achievement is to make the existential choice. As knowledge leads to choice, so the freedom to choose leads to experience, which is the discovery of the self. Isabel Archer's choice is freely made; it is impossible to have chosen more freely; and she rightly expects the fullness of experience. As Strether likewise insists, this choice calls for seeing, feeling, *living;* and "it's a mistake not to" make it. For this reason, Milly Theale seeks human company in preference to the silent splendor of nature; and Maggie Verver suddenly awakens to the sense of loss in her empty marriage. Maggie alone succeeds in establishing a living relation, while Isabel, Strether, and Milly are foiled in making theirs permanent.

The confidante-"center" relation is essentially one of friendship, for at least one of each couple is potentially a selfless friend. Hence, the relation implies the three main concepts in James's moral view of friendship: consciousness, existential choice, and the virtues of commitment and fidelity. Usually, it is the confidante who is ready to offer these virtues to her friend and confider. Both Fleda Vetch and Maria Gostrey attempt to break through their isolation and that of their confidential friends. Their choice is existential—it involves risk; and an error in judgment—a mark of the fallible consciousness—invariably leads to disaster. Fleda makes the error of trusting her confiders too far, and Maria overestimates Strether's devotion to herself. The failure to make or sustain a dialogic union spells frustration and desolation for the individual person. This is what happens to the confidential friendships of Isabel Archer, Fleda Vetch, and Maria Gostrey. In the first relation, the confidantes, Madame Merle and (in a different way) Henrietta Stackpole, are found wanting; in the other two, the confiders fall short of the relations which they themselves began. Neither the Gereths nor Lambert Strether are capable of the unselfish commitment which their confidantes are ready to offer and expect to receive in return.

Such a failure is due to a moral retardation. It is quite usual for Jamesian characters to be defective in the principal virtues of commitment and fidelity. Hence the obverse vices, exploitation and betrayal, come to the foreground in many of James's works. The foregoing chapters indicate how closely the relations between confidante and protagonist are linked with these virtues and vices. The confidantes are intelligent women facing an existential choice. Their choice inevitably falls on a virtue or an evil deed. If they are good women, they choose, as Henrietta Stackpole and Maria Gostery do, the virtues of commitment and fidelity. If they are simply weak in judgment or in will, they muddle through as best they can, as do Mrs. Wix, Mrs. Grose, and Mrs. Assingham. The evil woman, Madame Merle, chooses exploitation and betrayal.

Fidelity is James's cardinal virtue. All others hinge upon it, and in his own life the author prized it highly.[5] Fidelity is rooted in commitment, or the gift of oneself to the other. If a person can effect a dialogic union with a friend, then fidelity to that friend is begun. But it does not necessarily continue. The friendship can be terminated by a failure of one or the other party to measure up to the exigencies of the relation. The friendship of May Bartram for John Marcher is very nearly perfect in her openness and transparency toward him; Maria Gostrey comes close to it in her friendship with Strether; and before her involvement in London Mrs. Stringham's love for Milly Theale is respectfully open. In the case of Maria and Susan, the confidante provides the bridge for her confider to the deeper appreciation of beauty in the world. The turning point in these two friendships occurs when circumstances necessitate an assumption of masks. With her new knowledge of the situation, Maria feels she can no longer face Strether honestly, so she departs. By leaving him she loses him. Susan's openness is compromised by her promise to Mrs. Lowder, and a shadow falls on her relation with Milly, which her "passion of friendship" cannot disperse. According to James, therefore, friendship requires openness and real encounter; it demands reverence, receptiveness, and trust; it enriches the discovery of beauty in art. Betrayal occurs when the personal element declines, and one of the parties uses the friend as a thing. As the role of the confidante gains in prominence in James's fiction, so it also becomes more intricately and variously related to the themes of fidelity and betrayal.

1. The Minor Confidantes

In *Roderick Hudson* the confidante-"center" relation is still outside the theme of betrayal, which is sustained by the involvement of Roderick with Christina Light. Rowland Mallet, looking on, as an interested, yet uncommitted observer, preserves himself from betrayal. Cecilia, his confidante, is still less concerned with the theme, for in her ancillary role she remains on the periphery of the action.

But as the confidante-"center" relation moves closer to the foreground of the action, it begins to share the burden of the theme of betrayal. In *The American* there is as yet only a touch of betrayal in the relation between Christopher Newman and Mrs. Tristram, his confidante. This touch is indicated when belatedly she admits her selfish motive of curiosity in furthering Newman's suit. In concealing her doubts of his success, and keeping up his false hopes, she was working subtly against him.

More subtly still, in "Daisy Miller" Mrs. Costello's influence on her nephew Winterbourne amounts to an inducement for him to betray his better instincts. Caught as he is in the heart-versus-head conflict over Daisy Miller, he finally succumbs to apparently righteous forces, which, however, his better self finally disavows. James's moral sense is more refined in this story than in *The American*. The blatant evil of the Bellegardes and the curiosity of the meddlesome confidante are replaced by Mrs. Costello's quiet snobbery and cruel prejudice. Regardless of whether Daisy is innocent or guilty, James makes Mrs. Costello's attitude reprehensible in its sweeping censure. By making Winterbourne arrive at a more balanced view of the girl the author indicates his own attitude toward her. His protagonist is indeed misled in a treacherous way, but he can still right himself. His own moral sense—although no longer spontaneous—finally regains the control of his judgment. At the end, James wisely allows Mrs. Costello no words of self-defense. In her own eyes, her position is unassailable and in the narrator's it is hopeless. For such an odd mixture of American prudishness and European conventionality, a sudden conversion would be unthinkable. And against the background of her impregnable code, Winterbourne's final statement defending Daisy rings more convincing. In the conflict of his own mind he forms his final judgment, and in the face of his aunt's silent opposition he proposes to maintain it. In this manner his revised opinion of Daisy is a moral accomplishment for the young man. Yet it falls below what he might have achieved for Daisy had he possessed the stamina for moral commitment. Winterbourne illustrates the dilemma of a person caught between conflicting moral allegiances; and his greatest problem is discernment. Appearance and reality intermingle in a most perplexing way, and the odds are in favor of appearance, with Mrs. Costello's and the expatriates' denunciations weighting the scales against Daisy. No defense is made for her to equal the barrage of accusations against her. From the start one senses the inequality of the struggle. No one is committed in Daisy's favor, not even her immediate family. Giovanelli, who comes forward at the end with his important evidence, could not in character do so any earlier.

"Daisy Miller" is outstanding for its singular treament of the theme of betrayal. The source of betrayal, lodged in Mrs. Costello's prejudice, gives rise to a primary force, but it emanates from a secondary character. As in the other works of the early and middle periods (except for *The Portrait*) this confidante is excluded from the confider's intimate life. Hence the betrayal does not arise immediately from their intersubjectivity, nor does it separate them. It does, however, demonstrate the principle in James's moral sense that fidelity to another person springs from fidelity to one's own instinctive sense of right and wrong. If Winterbourne's instinct had not become stifled by his aunt's prejudice and by European taboos, he would have been loyal to Daisy in her primal—if reckless—innocence. Moral spontaneity, which James extolled in Minny Temple, would have inspired Winterbourne with the esteem which Daisy so justly desired. The confusion resulting in his mind was caused by his mistaken attempt to apply an alien moral code to a given case. Nevertheless, the fact that he could still recover his balanced judgment shows a vestige of the native moral sense in the perplexed young man.

In the next work, *The Princess Casamassima,* James moves fully into the realm of society with its moral standards. Christina Light, appearing now at the height of her powers, offends not only against propriety, but also against the Jamesian virtues of commitment and fidelity. Her judge, Madame Grandoni, being a member of the same society, can criticize her actions in the same framework of their inception. Madame Grandoni judges less by instinct than by accepted norms, but her judgments are nonetheless accurate. In her minor role of confidante, she tries to prevent the betrayal of Hyacinth Robinson. Although still on the periphery of the moral tensions in the novel, as witness and judge, this confidante acts as the vehicle of the narrator's moral sense. Her important function becomes clear as one by one, her prognostications are verified by events; and the atmosphere of the latter part of the novel becomes suffused with pity for Hyacinth, the emotion both felt and expressed by the old lady. The comic-seriousness of her part does not lessen the usefulness of her figure as moral commentator.

James's moral sense discloses itself in another way in "The Aspern Papers." Here the protagonist narrowly escapes performing a traitorous act against his confidante, Miss Tina; but their relation is not a friendship, because openness is lacking. No real encounter is possible. The delusion under which the poor woman labors is a study of the fallible consciousness, which reads mistaken meanings into a relation differing greatly from what is supposed. It is a more painful deception than the mere trickery with which the protagonist gets into the house. The morality of the "publishing scoundrel's" single purpose would be a nice problem for ethical analysis. The editor, however, feels no need to justify his greed; and he bypasses the conclusion of the protagonist in "The Real Right Thing" (1900) that the secrets of dead authors are best left undisturbed.

Fortunately, however, for the moral appeal of his character, the editor draws back from the greatest deception of all, a promise to marry Tina in return for the prized papers. In horror over the false impression he has created, he pities the woman, whom his editorial rapacity has inconsiderately victimized. James's talent for placing women in pathetically ironical positions is clearly operative here, even though Miss Tina's suffering is not induced by a deliberate betrayal. A victim of her sense of duty to her aunt as well as her own false hopes, she represents the moral problem of being a dupe. In this unenviable position she claims distant kinship with the later confidantes whose friendship is rewarded with deliberate betrayal by inconsiderate or selfish men.

Similarly, the relation between Laura Wing and Lady Davenant in "A London Life" is hardly a real friendship since the older woman seeks to impose her will on the girl in a fashion that precipitates only a rupture. Lady Davenant's good intentions make her err against the ethos of personal friendship and the reverence it implies. But while her meddling is reprehensible in Laura's eyes, it is excusable from the technical point of view. Perhaps it makes "A London Life" an example of technique versus character, where an otherwise prudent woman imprudently forces a crisis.

Most of the minor confidantes of the 1890's and later possess characteristics of James's mature moral sense. Self-denial and unlimited devotedness to the confider are the dominant traits of Mrs. Alsager in "Nona Vincent," as well as of the confidantes in the ghostly tales, and of Cornelia Rasch in "Crapy Cornelia." In the author's total vision of friendship, these minor confidantes are the satellites around the greater luminaries, Fleda Vetch, Maria Gostrey, and Susan Stringham. James expresses his respect for these women in the serious treatment he accords to each.

In a class by itself, Mrs. Grose's ethical position in "The Turn of the Screw" is at best ambiguous. Her desire to do what is right by the children is confused by her fear of her betters, and her unwillingness to make a stand. The theme of betrayal gives way before the general onslaught of the nameless evil at Bly, which absorbs the attention of both confider and confidante alike, leaving little room for a moral clash between them. The moral limitations of Mrs. Grose are also required to give free rein to the terrible events. This helpless woman's disapproval is scarcely a deterrent to the will of either the governess or the ghosts. She suspends judgment, and so does the author; and so, in perplexity, must the reader. Wrapped in the mystery of this creation, James is content to bypass the usual treatment of betrayal in the confidante-"center" relation.

Mrs. Grose's vacillating attitude is very different from the commitment of the confidantes in "The Beast in the Jungle" and "The Jolly Corner." By the time he wrote these stories, James had already created his major confidantes, and the moral position of the confidante was firmly established in his mind. By now the confidante-"center" relation has been intimately linked with the theme of exploitation and betrayal. From "The Altar of the Dead" (1895) and *The Spoils of Poynton* (1896) on, the confidante is the object of betrayal. Except for Mrs.

Grose, and Mrs. Stringham, the confidante is betrayed by her confider, who, excepting Mrs. Gereth, is in every case a man. The men are morally inferior to the women, both in commitment and in constancy. James never much favored heroism in his male characters; but in his later period he certainly did not grant an inch of it to his protagonists. George Stransom, John Marcher, Spencer Brydon and White-Mason are rather pitiable specimens of manhood, as are Owen Gereth and Sir Claude. The others, Lambert Strether, Merton Densher and Prince Amerigo, are gentlemen whose refinement includes either a cultivated selfishness, or a weakness, none the less destructive for all its charm. Prefigured by the consummate and cruel selfishness of Gilbert Osmond, the later male characters are perhaps more starkly drawn in the short stories than in the novels. The economy of the former genre restricts portraiture to the bare essentials, and emphasizes the selfish isolation and pitiable need of Stransom, Marcher, Brydon, and White-Mason.

The atmosphere of the later work is heavily charged with frustration, blighted lives, base ingratitude. And most of the confidante-"center" relations of this later work are marred by these negations. The isolation so strongly emphasized in *The Portrait* extends now into a void of alienation which constricts the heart and consumes the spirit in silent suffering. George Stransom's nameless friend, already inured to suffering by her faithless lover, accepts Stransom's refusal without a struggle. It means a break in their friendship, an end to their confidences. But her action is perfectly consistent with the image of woman which James projects in these last short stories. It is an image of total, unquestioning acceptance—first of devotedness, then of rejection. May Bartram portrays the image even more fully. The sweetness of her acceptance is almost miraculous for flesh and blood, and yet it never cloys, never repels. It is an unbelievable generosity that dies to give itself, and gives even in dying: " 'It's never too late.' "

When compared with Miss Tina's exalted delusion of being

loved, May Bartram's luster in the purity of her offer is com-
plemented. Both portraits reveal the heights of expectation of a
confidante and would-be lover. And a miserable disenchantment awaits both women. It matters little that the editor of "The
Aspern Papers" and John Marcher withhold their affections for
very different reasons. The constant factor apparent in both
cases is the main principle of James's moral sense: the obligation to commitment in an existential choice. The editor refrains
from making the choice for sound reasons; but his rationality
offers poor Tina no consolation. Marcher also fails to make
the choice of commitment; he uses May as a thing until her
death, and that is his supreme loss. All his conversations with
May are monologues, not dialogues. The woman is used as a
listener; her own ideas are unwanted. Again, Gilbert Osmond
prefigures the selfish male confider in his bold utterance: " 'She
[Isabel] has only one fault. . . . Too many ideas.' " Marcher, like
Osmond, never appreciates the beauty of the woman's commitment, for he himself is incapable of offering the same. Selfishness having blinded his inner eye, Marcher is an example of
arrested consciousness. His thoughts run in the narrow groove
of self-absorption. Both he and Spencer Brydon are mono-
maniacs and paranoiacs. According to James's moral sense,
these men are incapable of the existential choice because they
lack the awareness of "the other." The ego and the alter ego are
the objects of their worshipful attention. It is the tragedy of the
two women, May and Alice, that they should love hopeless
cases. Their fate can be none other than exploitation.

As in "The Beast in the Jungle," so in "The Altar of the
Dead" and "The Jolly Corner," the committed woman is
morally superior to the selfish man. James's ideal of woman
comes out strongly and strangely in these three ghostly tales. It
is as if he were making a final effort to exalt the woman as a
vessel purified of all dross, an almost ethereal being endowed
with divine goodness and forgiveness. The elderly James is
sublimating his own friendships, and perhaps castigating him-

self for his own withdrawn and introspective manner. The author's moral sense has taken wings and borne him into a realm of romantic fancy, where, in default of any other reward, unselfishness is its own compensation.

2. *The Major Confidantes*

Between these three minor confidantes and the major confidantes there are several close parallels. The theme of exploitation and betrayal is matured in the novels beginning with *The Portrait of a Lady,* so that it closely involves the confidante-"center" relation. In *The Portrait,* the confidante, Madame Merle, betrays her confider, Isabel Archer, while in *The Spoils of Poynton, The Ambassadors,* and *The Golden Bowl,* the confidante herself suffers betrayal of one kind or another. In *What Maisie Knew* and *The Wings of the Dove* the confidantes are placed in exceptional positions which bewilder them and test their resourcefulness to the utmost. Mrs. Wix fights what she considers betrayal at the hands of Sir Claude, whereas Mrs. Stringham contributes unwittingly to the betrayal of her confider.

The degree to which the major confidantes can commit themselves in friendship determines their moral worth. Madame Merle, impelled as she is by mother-love to use Isabel as a tool, eventually regrets her betrayal. Having suffered a similar fate, her woman's heart softens toward her fellow victim. This compassion is Madame Merle's redeeming feature. Fleda Vetch, generously if imprudently, gives herself to conflicting parties and is caught between them. Maria Gostrey devotes herself to Strether to the point of self-effacement; but this commitment does not impair her cleverness and prudence. Mrs. Wix and Fanny Assingham make a gift of themselves that is tainted with self-love and a thirst for thrills. The moral limitations of Mrs. Tristram survive in them. Mrs. Stringham, the idealist, is consumed with devotion to Milly Theale. Her great grief is that in the engagement with superior forces she cannot save her.

James's essentially tragic view of life pervades these novels. The betrayal which the major confidantes experience is all the more grievous on account of their own self-dedication in their friendships. Not one of the confidante-"center" relations in these works finds fulfillment. Rather, they terminate in disappointment, frustration, and isolation. The confidantes, whose role is both maternal and lover-like (Fleda and Maria) are perhaps the most unfortunate of all, because theirs is a double rejection. The insurmountable inequalities separating the confidantes from their confiders seem to indicate a belief on the author's part in a fate which divides and conquers. There are few happy unions anywhere in James's work; and only two among the twenty-three confidantes. It also seems that this fate of the confidante is somehow fitted to the nature of her role. Irrespective of age, she is a maternal woman, someone to be leaned on, to be followed. She dispenses advice and encouragement as a mother does food and drink. Her function as mother marks her for use, even for exploitation, and for final abandonment. James goes back to the primeval, and terrible, law of nature that the offspring leave the mother; and while civilization has sought to ameliorate this law by enjoining respect and familial care for the parents, the modern trend in Western culture seems to be returning, fundamentally at least, to the practice of separating the used-up mothers and fathers from the young adults. Fleda Vetch, Mrs. Wix, Maria Gostrey, and Fanny Assingham all serve in a maternal manner the needs of their confiders, before being abandoned.

Consciousness, existential choice, and the virtues of commitment and fidelity—the main concepts in James's moral order—receive their first full embodiment in the confidante-"center" relation in *The Portrait of a Lady*. The unusual awareness of Isabel, the young heroine, to which we are first introduced, soon shrinks beside the keener and deeper perceptiveness of

Madame Merle, her confidante. This lady, "the cleverest woman in the world," is able to plumb the depths of other persons' consciousness and divine their secrets. She executes her plot with farsighted awareness, and as long as she acts according to her intelligence she is safe. It is only her mother's passion that causes her to betray herself. Because of her exceptional awareness, it must be conceded to Madame Merle that she chooses freely. Her choice to make Isabel first an interesting friend, then a useful tool, is thoroughly self-centered. Like Maud Manningham Lowder, Madame Merle is always looking for profitable returns from her friendships. These two women are utterly incapable of a dialogic union, because they are by nature exploiters. Other people are objects for them, or in Sartre's language, they constitute the hell for other people. A grim satisfaction results for the exploiters; but inner isolation is nonetheless their fate.

With Madame Merle on one side, James might have provided a different Henrietta Stackpole on the other, with whom Isabel could have formed a truly confidential friendship. But such a balance would have righted the wrong of exploitation and betrayal in which Madame Merle is to succeed so well. The novel's theme is to be betrayal, not fidelity; hence the latter, although present, must be muted. Consequently, both Henrietta and Isabel are deficient in ability to communicate with each other. The former is too pushing; the latter too reticent. Each obeys an inner norm of behavior which conflicts with the other's. It is ironical that both women love freedom so passionately and so much at cross purposes. It is also ironical that both are destined for the supreme choice of giving up their country by marriage. The gift of themselves for love entails their whole heritage. But they cannot give themselves to each other. The closest they come to it is after Isabel's confession; but sorrow has already begun to seal her heart, and Henrietta's response is diagnostic rather than remedial. Thus, although faithfully committed, Henrietta is foiled by the limitations of personality.

In assessing the weight of James's moral sense in this novel one must consider the complexity of the characters involved. Madame Merle, the dramatic villainess, is still an abandoned lover and frustrated mother. These aspects of her role cannot fail to evoke sympathy. Henrietta, for all her good will, is slightly obnoxious and ridiculous in her forwardness. Isabel, who fails to commit herself to her true admirers, trusts the man and woman who betray her. The man who loves her most dies, the other two are thwarted by her own resistance. In this respect the novel is a maze of errors in judgment and wasted affection.

But the sadness of Isabel's fate is largely the result of her own character. Her stubborn idealism blinds her and makes her a ready victim of the Osmond-Merle deception. When contrasted with her first confidante's propitious prospects of marriage, Isabel's fatal choice of a husband seems to imply that the idealist fails where the opportunist succeeds. But success, for James, is at best only a crude thing. In his moral sense, it is much more refined to suffer—to be like Sisyphus. This conviction is evident in the suffering of all of James's fine characters. The world, in this view, is compounded of base elements, and has little sympathy for refined and sensitive persons. The tragedy of Isabel is repeated in the fate of Hyacinth Robinson, Morgan Moreen, Fleda Vetch, and Milly Theale. James would have us believe that for these people suffering is inescapable, and that it is the consequence, as well as the agent, of moral refinement.

But that suffering refines Isabel is not beyond question. True, her growth in awareness throughout the novel leads her ever more deeply into it; and her patience and fortitude are remarkable. But isolation, in humanistic terms, is a destructive force. It paralyzes the personality by closing off its channels for communication; and life under such circumstances is a living death. James's imagery evokes death conspicuously. In her future married life Isabel—now without confidantes—has nothing to look forward to except what consolation she may derive from helping Pansy. To condemn oneself to such an existence is contrary to reason, but James sets his approval on Isabel's fidelity. In her circumstances, therefore, living death is nobler than a free life. Of the many choices made in her career, the last one crowns them all in renunciation. There is a good deal of stoicism and some affinity to modern existentialism in the view of life expounded in *The Portrait*. Isabel's commitment, although unreasonable from the point of view of her own right to life, is shown as noble simply because it is a commitment and a free choice.

For this reason it is dramatically necessary to make Isabel tower above her confidantes and would-be advisers. Her fidelity to her promises counterpoints Madame Merle's betrayal and the wrongheaded counsels of Henrietta and the Countess. Like *The Wings of the Dove*, this novel is a singular study in female portraits. In *The Portrait*, the confidantes make a morally poor showing; for even Henrietta, in spite of her kindliness, is a comic figure and lacks the moral depth requisite for the role of confidante. Although James compares her functionally to Maria Gostrey, he overlooks the glaring differences in their characters. The moral diminution of the confidantes in *The Portrait* is of course necessary for the exaltation of the heroine's moral grandeur. It is a useful device in a novel where the two roles of confidante and center of consciousness are separate. But in the next novel, the separation gives way to fusion, and James resorts to other means to portray moral refinement.

The means employed in *The Spoils of Poynton* radiate from the inner conflict in the protagonist's mind and heart. Fleda is generous to a fault; she enters into the aims and ambitions of her friends, the Gereths, with a touching simplicity and uprightness. She is the perfect listener, so easily won by arguments that her inner turmoil begins at a very early stage. A keen awareness, instead of aiding, as it does for Madame Merle, only uncovers further aspects of her dilemma. Her sympathetic heart exposes her to the uninhibited and immature greediness of her confiders. From inside and out, the girl is exposed and delivered

up to be used and exploited. No private life is possible to her;
she is invaded and all her secrets are wrung from her. Not only
is the furniture the spoils, but far worse, this human heart likewise becomes the spoils of war.

Under such conditions it is exceedingly difficult for Fleda to
rise above the other characters. In some way their faults infect
her moral beauty. She feels besmirched in the struggle, and
takes flight to save herself. Commitment seems to militate directly against autonomy, the more so as the confiders are child-
ishly demanding. Yet James held for the freedom of the person
to be himself, even in dedication to others. Human dignity is unthinkable without freedom, and for Fleda the struggle finally resolves itself into a struggle to save her inner liberty. No other
major confidante is so harassed as Fleda, and none is so tied
down. The others have an advantage in age and in position.
Mrs. Wix can suitably fight, and Miss Gostrey can withdraw
with propriety, while Mrs. Assingham conveniently possesses
a husband to fall back on in time of rejection. But the young girl
Fleda has only a makeshift refuge with her relatives.

In depicting the position of his heroine, James drew on his
moral sense in a way which contrasts with the scheme followed
in *The Portrait*. Most obviously, the union of confidante and
"center" in one person is the first distinction. This anomaly
calls secondly for a reversed intersubjectivity between herself
and the confiders. Point of view shifts onto the secondary characters, because they are the confiders. Their importance increases
in proportion as they succeed in impressing the confidante
and "center." Although not morally superior to the confidantes in *The Portrait,* the confiders in *Poynton* claim more
attention not only by their vociferousness, but also by their pre-
eminent position as confiders, which requires that they do most
of the talking. Consequently, their ideas and passions color the
atmosphere of the novel and set its moral tone. The low family
squabble which provided James with his "germ," is carried over
into the novel to debase the high ideals of aestheticism set up

beside it. The debasing process is clearly seen in the deterioration of Mrs. Gereth, who declines from fanaticism to senility, and in the moral servitude in which Owen by nature must live, irrespective of who dominates him.

Consciousness, vibrating in the confidante and "center," reflects the family upheaval. Fleda probes weaknesses in the Gereth character, but balks at essaying a remedy in an existential choice. Her inability to choose prolongs the tension. When finally she does choose, it is her moral choice that leads to material disaster—the loss of Owen and destruction of the spoils. But James makes it clear that Fleda's choice arises from her very being—"to keep faith" is the ideal with which she lives and she cannot accept a man who falls below it. Just as the "things" look ugly after their misappropriation, so she shrinks from snatching at another girl's expectations of happiness. Again, James appears to favor his protagonist's views. Like Isabel, Fleda is an idealist, and has a refined consciousness doomed to suffering in a world which is divided between Brigstock vulgarity and Gereth tyranny.

By making his heroine insist on keeping faith, James plainly gives fidelity pre-eminence in this novel. The betrayal which Mrs. Gereth inflicts by meddling in Fleda's affairs is in itself a minor thing, but in its repercussions it achieves major proportions. It indicates the degree of possessiveness with which Mrs. Gereth tries to manipulate Fleda's life, and approximates the selfishness of John Marcher. Owen, on his part, is too immature to effect a dialogic union with the girl he comes to love. What he loves in her is the tender maternal desire to shelter him; the child in him craves a mother-substitute. When she tries to put him on his own feet, he fails her, being morally only an infant. Both his mother and he leave Fleda in an isolation more bitter than the state in which they found her. But since they are not endowed with sensitive awareness, they completely overlook this fact.

Caught between the neurotic mother and her immature son,

extent with Madame Merle—of prevenient knowledge. Unlike Strether, she does not mistake European beauty for moral goodness. Experience has taught her—as it later teaches him—that "evil is an attribute of beauty."[6] She has also learned to live with both, without letting them impede her personality. The eminently personal life which Maria leads distinguishes her in a brilliant group of women. Her capacity for encounter and solidarity are rooted in her personal approach to life—in her eyes everything has meaning and value.

The little globe-trotter's saving independence sets her aside as one who can ultimately dispense with sympathy, although in a generous measure she gives it to her confider. Knowledge, in Maria's use, leads to understanding and forgiveness, because it is the basis of the existential commitment to another. As her knowledge encompasses the whole scene, so her compassion embraces all the persons present: Strether, of course, first and foremost; but also in no mean measure, the rival woman; and, by extension, Chad as well. Her prediction of Chad's forsaking Madame de Vionnet is simple realism, without any trace of meanness. At the end, when it seems doubtful that even she will reap any benefits from Strether, she still tries to help Madame to do so. " 'Poor dear thing!' " is her expression of compassion for the woman who has gained and lost so much. Such feeling contrasts with Strether's coolness and self-centeredness. But it is also the expression of her own loss, which clothes itself in pity for the other member of her sex. It may be an unconscious subterfuge, but in her consciousness it is sincere enough.

The will to act, which James finds lacking in his "poor sensitive gentlemen," predominates in both Henrietta Stackpole and Maria Gostrey; but the later confidante has mastered the balance between activity and passivity, which her predecessor had not done. Maria's power of choice, therefore, is both expansive and restrictive. She can diminish and withdraw her influence in order to obtain a remoter goal. By departing from Paris she avoids telling Strether the truth about Chad's affair. This act has been termed a deception that prevents Strether's "spiritual decay";[7] in other words, an evil that obtains a good result. But to call her evasion a deception, even "in effect," is rather strong; particularly since her declaration to Strether that she will not receive Madame de Vionnet, followed by her departure, should normally have aroused his suspicion rather than lulled him into false security. To leave Strether is, really, the only way to dodge deceiving him, as Madame de Vionnet would have held her to a false representation of the facts. Under the circumstances, Maria's withdrawal is not only sensible but also morally defensible. Rather than a deception, it could be taken as a warning by anyone alert enough to do so. Madame de Vionnet's sly remarks about it also point up the fact that something remiss has caused her flight. Strether's obtuseness does not alter the nature of her action.

The withdrawal of Maria Gostrey reflects the passivity which is basic to the role of the confidante. Even after her return, it continues, in as much as she is "so out of it." Essentially, she is a listener. When a substitute is found she can be dispensed with. Hers is therefore primarily, not a role of action—nor of active influence—but rather, one of passion—of endurance, and silent suffering. The useableness of the confidante corresponds to one of the most outstanding features in woman's makeup, which renders her inferior to man. Nature uses her; man uses her; and the harsh law of both is that when used up, she may be cast aside. With all his fine, sensitive soul James realized the basic passivity of woman, and made it an integral part of her multiple roles in his work. The role of the confidante as victim is consequently inevitable in his moral sense, because it is attendant upon woman's natural function.

Consequently, Maria's restraint when offering Strether her home is much more suitable than Mrs. Wix's coarse insinuations. Never does Miss Gostrey lose sight of the limits and the demands of her role. Her ability to rise to every occasion implies a strong sense of duty, a pure fidelity, and a deep self-effacement. These virtues are common to the other confidantes whom James proposes as morally mature—Fleda Vetch, May Bartram, and Susan Stringham.

An even more perplexing choice confronts the last named of these women. Susan Stringham lacks the perspicacity and insight of her immediate predecessor, but she shares her devotedness in commitment to her confider. Besides, Susan has the technical advantage over Maria in being, for a time at least, "center," which makes her admiration more emphatic. The whole ethic of Mrs. Stringham's relation with the New York heiress revolves upon her own sense of duty. Milly in some way seems helpless and in need of patronage. This the confidante sets out to procure, from the first letter to Mrs. Lowder, announcing their impending arrival in England, to the last interview with Densher in Venice. With purest intentions Susan blunders further and further beyond her depth. Without realizing, she exposes her friend and herself to forces, both intellectual and moral, beyond her reckoning. With Susan, James is testing the feasibility of commitment without keen judgment. Sagacity, he implies in *The Ambassadors,* is the virtue or strength of self-dedication. But in *The Wings of the Dove,* the serpent's wisdom is peculiarly cast in opposition to both confidante and confider. Mrs. Stringham lacks the first important asset in the Jamesian moral scheme: insight. Her consciousness —ironically—may be sensitive, but only to the kindly aspects of life. In other words, her comprehension of persons and events is limited by her own benevolence. She sees good in everyone's motives, even Lord Mark's. It is a case of one moral asset contravening the other. Hence Susan lacks the proportion and balance of Maria Gostrey. Consequently, also, she is easily intimidated; and her experiences with Milly and the London set contribute continually to her discomposure.

Two factors determine Susan's existential choice. In committing herself so utterly to Milly she is swayed first by love, then by fear. Love predominates. It fires her hopes for the social success of her "princess." But fear for Milly's health soon makes her doubt and hesitate. It takes the powerful injunctions of Mrs. Lowder to keep her on the course already adopted. Fear of making a mistake, of her own inadequacy, is constantly tormenting this timid lady. Susan is a visionary. Envisioning life as a large canvas, she places her friends in it as an artist would, guided by a sense for style and glamor, but thereby losing her foothold in reality. Milly's Venetian party lifts Susan quite off the ground. And at that precise moment she becomes morally vulnerable. It is only a matter of time until she requests Densher to keep up the deception to save Milly. Love certainly contributes to this decision, and fear may be an extenuating factor in her moral responsibility, but her blindness to the consequences remains to be faced. According to James, blindness is a limitation with moral implications, because it predisposes the subject to erroneous choices. If the consciousness of Isabel Archer and of Strether is refined through trial and error, it will never be compromised thereafter. But for Susan Stringham, who never exceeds the limitations of her early awareness, error remains a continued menace, and error in the existential choice of commitment involves morality. To choose wrongly is to violate in some degree the freedom of the other. This Susan does —still blindly—by hoping to prolong Milly's life at the expense of her right to knowledge.

There is even a suggestion that Susan deliberately remains blind: " 'I promise to believe you down to the ground if, to save her life, you consent to a denial.' " The basis of her petition to Densher is therefore the rescue of Milly, not the question of his moral uprightness. Naturally, his affairs are not her concern; but her commitment to Milly would lead one to expect her to share the girl's feelings about a possible deception. Susan's choice in this matter indicates that her judgment is swayed more by love than by wisdom.

Milly's silence to Susan about Densher has something to do with her surrender to death. It marks a severing of the bond of confidence, and is probably the hardest thing Susan has to bear. For although her blindness excuses her from culpability, she shares somehow in the silent rebuke of the dying girl. It constitutes the pathos of this little confidante, with her Byzantine imagination and her touching devotion; for fate punishes her with this alienation. Unable to change, Mrs. Stringham, upon the loss of Milly's confidence, transfers her solicitude to Densher. His sense of the protection with which her silence covers his deed is the source of his consolation. It is another indication from James that Mrs. Stringham indeed *knew*. No confidante tries harder than Susan in her commitment and intended fidelity. And a woman of her sincerity cuts a very pathetic figure as a confidante unwittingly accessory to the betrayal of her confider. In her case, fidelity is awkwardly inverted. James's attitude toward her is one of kindly sympathy, reflected through the consciousness of Merton Densher. Susan's new relation with Densher gives the conclusion a new stability: for if both of them have failed Milly more or less involuntarily, at least they have the security of understanding each other's moral dilemma.

In this manner James ends the role of his one confidante who is closely involved in a tragedy—more closely than Mrs. Costello, or even Stransom's lady. Mrs. Stringham's ordeal is diametrically opposed to Mrs. Wix's sordid comedy; and her mild passivity contrasts further with the latter's loud vocife. tions. In both women James has shown the interaction of manners and morals upon choice and patterns of behavior.

In *The Golden Bowl,* Mrs. Assingham combines with her husband to complete the gallery of confidantes, and their positions in James's moral universe is none the less important for their eccentricities and comic dimension. Experimenting technically with this interesting couple, the author plumbed with them anew the depths of his moral sense, which involves friendship, betrayal, and the discovery of the self. In Fanny he left us a portrait of a woman baffled, like Susan Stringham, by superior cunning; but, like Maria Gostrey, resourceful enough to devise her own strategy. Fanny's exterior exoticism seems to be a blind covering the moral flaw of slick opportunism and an increasing sense of guilt. Bob, her earthy husband, represents in James's scheme the incarnation of the slow, plodding intellect. But his common sense and practicality anchor him in reality, from whence he tries to pin down the extravagant imagination of his wife.

Consciousness in the Prince, Charlotte, and Fanny is exceedingly refined, but it does not necessarily imply moral rectitude. Fanny Assingham is really cast in the same mold as Charlotte Stant; she withdraws from the scene only under compulsion, not, like Miss Gostrey, from moral distaste. When Maria returns upon the scene, it is only to remain "out of it"; but from beyond the pale Fanny casts longing and admiring eyes upon the couple that have excluded her. As Bob says, she lives vicariously in the Prince's marriage; and she lives all the more dangerously in his successful affair with Charlotte.

Mrs. Assingham's refined consciousness enables her to comprehend swiftly and accurately the nature of the Prince's affair and the tactics which the lovers intend to pursue. This knowledge of Fanny's in turn leads her to make her choice of action: to lie and to have her husband lie to protect the Prince and Charlotte from suspicion. Her commitment to Amerigo, her erstwhile confider, determines this course of action. In itself the devotedness behind her decision is just as selfless a that of honest Susan, were it not for Fanny's own inescapable complicity in the affair. Consequently, to lie becomes doubly imperative, to safeguard her own reputation and the two marriages she has made. In Fanny, James made a perceptive study of a woman caught in a trap of her own devising. The pathos of her position is deepened by the inversion of the virtues of commitment and fidelity. Without freedom, these virtues degenerate to a mockery of friendship. Fanny, held tightly by her fear of exposure more than by her love for the Prince, must remain faithful to him and the rival woman in spite of their rejection of herself. Amerigo's friendship with Mrs. Assingham demands subservience and betrayal of her other friend, his wife. It is consequently a dehumanizing relation between confidante and confider. Fortunately for Fanny's mental balance this schizophrenic position is met by her own opportunistic moral code. After a brief emotional collapse, she pulls herself together and falls back on her "utilitarian and merely social conception of morality."[8] She resolves thenceforth to enter into the deception being played on Maggie; and in order to rationalize her position, she claims to do this to protect the Ververs' happy ignorance. It does not enter Fanny's head that Maggie will initiate action and succeed where she herself has been restrained. One senses a veiled condescension in the older woman's attitude toward the younger. All the greater is her wonder when she perceives Maggie's diplomacy taking shape.

Maggie' success, to which more deceit must contribute, is a fine example of James's belief in the moral value of consciousness. Maggie's growing awareness of evil is a moral victory in itself. For Mrs. Assingham, on the other hand, knowledge does not lead to redemption. Rather, it confirms her subservience and loss of dignity. The shrinking of her influence in Book Second is indicative of her loss of moral integrity. It is not the lying until she and Bob are "black in the face" that causes this decline; but her bondage to the Prince. Fanny is no longer a free agent. Not only does she refuse to advise Maggie, but she lacks the moral backbone to dispense spiritual nourishment. Fanny can never fill the role of maternal friend that suits Maria Gostrey so well. She always remains an object of curiosity, an exotic import from the East. Hence Maggie makes her own decisions, and no relation of committed friendship exists between the two women. Maggie's confidences are used by James merely to further the development of the action; and she reserves her deepest secrets. Fanny's position is, among the major confidantes, the most purely technical.

Fanny's position is also the most ironical, since she can help the Princess only by abetting the deception of the adulterers. This holding off provides the heroine with the chance to mature by acting on her own initiative. But as Mr. Ward points out, this deceit is worse than the adultery itself.[9] Wishing to preserve Maggie's marriage, Mrs. Assingham is forced to deny its imperilled state. But in shattering the golden bowl she comes closest to an admission of the flaw in her friends' affairs. This she does only when it is quite safe to approximate such an admission.

Fanny's failing to aid Maggie in the desperate struggle to win back her husband is a commentary on her own failure as a wife. Her selfish, scornful use of Bob as listener and support continues only because of his selfless understanding of her limitations. In spite of his acknowledged slowness, the Colonel's analyses of his wife indicate sufficient awareness to qualify him for appearance in a Jamesian novel; and his patience with her recommends him as a confidant endowed with the Jamesian virtues, to a moderate degree, at least.

Not the Colonel, but Mrs. Assingham cuts the pathetic figure. She errs in her calculations before the marriage of Mr. Verver; she fails in her attempt to free herself from commitment to the Prince and Charlotte, and she fails to render guidance to Maggie. Both women see through her—first Charlotte, in despising her helplessness—then Maggie, in refusing to communicate her deepest secrets. Still, Fanny's case is one of moral inadequacy rather than of culpability. As with Madame Merle, James is more interested in portraying weakness than criminality. As confidante, Fanny is a victim comparable to the minor confidantes of the later ghostly tales, May Bartram and Alice Staverton, who are exploited by their confiders. But in Fanny's case there is more personal responsibility for her being in this position, because she undertook to make both marriages. In arranging the second one her shortsightedness was singular, and one can truly say of her, she reaped what she sowed.

Fanny's moral flaw adds to the irony of her position; for her career began as the Prince's moral adviser. The American moral sense which "sends you up like a rocket" is what frightens Amerigo on the eve of his marriage. In her pledge to help him measure up to it she sadly fails. In moral stature, therefore, Fanny falls far below Miss Gostrey, who preserves a healthy moral independence. In her moral distinctions Fanny shows more cleverness than Mrs. Stringham, but in selfless love she lags far behind the little New Englander.

The freedom which James postulates as a basis for the existential choice arises from the full knowledge provided by the refined consciousness; and the choice in turn devolves upon the virtues of commitment and fidelity, or the vices of exploitation and betrayal. It is Fanny's mistake to forfeit this freedom by making two conflicting commitments, the issue of which she is not astute enough to foresee. In realizing her big mistake, Fanny discovers her vulnerability, and it humbles her to the level of Darby and Joan. Poor Fanny never really establishes a dialogic union with either confider after the Prince's marriage; and her relation with her husband is only unilateral. The loneliness of this woman may not equal Fleda's, or Madame Merle's; but it suffices to wring from her the cry, " 'I've worked for them *all!*' "

One is inclined to lay the blame on Fanny's own moral obliqueness. For the moral strength of Maria or Susan is lacking in her character; and her refined consciousness is adrift, unanchored by basic rectitude. The Prince proves to have a deeper rectitude and generosity in his final response to his wife; but neither Maggie before her awakening, nor Fanny, could call forth his hidden strength. Since Amerigo is a person of deep emotion, his failure in the confidential relation indicates a previous lack in the confidante's response. All her attraction seems to be exterior, without depth of sympathy or kindness. Added to this lack, the biggest irony is that with her perspicacity she should be guilty of the initial mistake. When all is considered, finally, this confidante is truly frustrated, both within and without.

The treatment of the confidante in *The Golden Bowl* marks the end of James's important work in this respect. Since the writing of *Roderick Hudson,* the evolution of this fictive character is constant and varied. It manifests the versatility and depth of the author's talent, and the breadth of his vision of life. As a secondary character, the confidante assumes increasing technical importance and richer moral value with each succeeding period of James's creativity. In the later period, she attains the fullness of her development, represented in the short stories by the second consciousness, and in the novels by the most perfect *ficelle,* Maria Gostrey. It is in these works that the confidential relation becomes more of an interaction between mind and mind, and that the theme of friendship is most fully explored. In James's ideas on friendship lies the total meaningfulness of the confidante-"center" relation.

James's constant preoccupation with the deeper moral issues involved in friendship is related to his wider concern with the isolation of the individual in society, with the confrontation of the American with Europe, and with the choice between art and convention. If it is possible to cull a generalization from that all-pervading moral sense, it would present primarily the terrible isolation of the human being who by his natural endowments is refined for the suffering which overtakes him. The finer the intelligence and the sensibility of James's characters, the more exposed they are to the suffering of betrayal and abandonment.

But James is not a pessimist. His faith in the sublimity of the refined consciousness and will power declares itself in the purifying effect of suffering on his heroines and confidantes. In his fictive society of the middle and later periods *noblesse oblige* holds in the existential sense: to be an aristocrat of sensitivity one must undergo purgation. Those who are spared are persons of only minor moral stature. Friendship—the confidential relation—is a precious thing in James's estimation. That he should record its brevity so many times places him very near to the modern thinkers and writers whose contemplation of man's isolation and anxiety has made them encounter the anguish of the human heart with compassion, fear, and trembling.

The modernity of Henry James is clearly seen, not only in his exploration of the meaning of friendship, but also in his selection and perfection of a new novelistic technique, the limited point of view. That selection most probably was prompted by an inner need to express his own experience of life in a personal and untried manner, particularly his experiences of friendship, in which he was continually feeling for new contacts and new awareness. The author as observer transformed himself gradually into the character as observer, or the fictive center of consciousness. " 'I'm an inveterate, almost a professional observer,' " declares the male "center" in "The Patagonia." And as the timid, sensitive author in life leaned on his mature women friends, so the sensitive protagonists lean on their confidantes. In consequence, the evolution and moral value of the Jamesian confidante arise naturally from the author's person—his temperament, ideas, inclinations—and from his artistic need to extend the limited point of view. The art of telling a story about the conscious life is very close to the art of living itself. James was an artist both of the recorded consciousness and of the lived life. As a profound student of the moral-psychological problems of human existence as well as a creator of an historically significant technique—the confidante-"center" relation—Henry James manifests the modernity of his achievement.

The first reference in the notes to a work by James gives the edition used. Every subsequent page reference in the text to that same work is to the same edition. Dates of works, unless otherwise specified, indicate first book publication. For brevity the following abbreviations are used:

Blackmur - *The Art of the Novel: Critical Prefaces by Henry James* with an Introduction by Richard P. Blackmur (New York: Charles Scribner's Sons, 1934).

Letters - *The Letters of Henry James,* 2 vols., Selected and edited by Percy Lubbock (New York: Charles Scribner's Sons, 1920)

Notebooks - *The Notebooks of Henry James,* ed. F. O. Matthiessen and Kenneth B. Murdock (New York: George Braziller, Inc., 1955) Copyright 1947 by Oxford University Press, Inc.

N Y Edn. *The Novels and Tales of Henry James,* New York Edition, 24 vols. (New York: Charles Scribner's Sons, 1907-1909).

Notes to Introduction
Pages xi–xxx

1. Charles G. Hoffmann, in *The Short Novels of Henry James* (New York: Bookman Associates, 1957) does not make any distinction between the friend who receives confidences in a narrative poem *(Troilus and Criseyde)* or a novel written from the omiscient point of view *(Washington Square)*, and the function of the confidante in a novel written from the limited point of view *(What Maisie Knew).* That there is a great technical difference between Mrs. Penniman and Mrs. Wix I hope

to show in the proper place. Hoffmann surprisingly denies that Horatio is a confidant, but he does point out that Mrs. Wix is used "as a supplement to the observations of the central intelligence, Maisie . . ." (pp. 32-33).

Another observation on the technical role of the confidante in fiction is made by Marvin Mudrick, who points out in *Jane Austen: Irony as Defense and Discovery* (Princeton, N. J.: Princeton University Press, 1952), p. 40, that the confidante of the Gothic novel is a "relic of the epistolary novel."

2. *Henry James: The Middle Years, 1882–1895* (Philadelphia: J. B. Lippincott Company, 1962), pp. 38, 36.

3. See his description of Vernon Lee, *ibid.*, p. 211; also his caricatures, Mrs. Penniman and the Countess Gemini.

4. *The Madonna of the Future, A Bundle of Letters, The Diary of a Man of Fifty, Eugene Pickering* (London: Macmillan and Co., 1883), p. 26.

5. July 28, 1883. *Letters*, I, pp. 100–101.

6. July 23, 1887. *Letters*, I, p. 128.

7. Christmas Day, 1897. *Letters*, I, p. 269.

8. March 5, 1907. *Letters*, II, p. 69.

9. June 8, 1879. *Letters*, I, p. 70.

10. "Frances Anne Kemble," in *Essays in London and Elsewhere* (New York: Harper & Brothers, 1893), p. 85.

11. December 13, 1909. *Letters*, II, p. 143.

12. February 8, 1910. *Letters*, II, p. 156.

13. November 9, 1911. *Letters*, II, p. 208.

14. F. W. Dupee, *Henry James*. The American Men of Letters Series. (New York: William Sloane Associates, 1951), p. 207.

15. *Henry James: The Conquest of London, 1870–1881* (Philadelphia: J. B. Lippincott Company, 1962), pp. 356–357.

16. Letter to Alice James, cited in Dupee, p. 145.

17. "Mrs. Humphrey Ward," in *Essays in London and Elsewhere*, pp. 254–255. In this same essay James praises the ability of his friend, Mrs. Ward, "to represent with an authority widely recognized the multitudinous, much-entangled human scene" (p. 258). Later he made a sweeping disavowal of all that essay contained. (See *Henry James: The Middle Years*, p. 207.)

18. "Miss Alcott's 'Moods,' " in *Notes and Reviews* (Cambridge, Mass.: Dunster House, 1921), pp. 49–58. This review was first published in *The North American Review*, July 1865. Edith Wharton, *A Backward Glance* (New York: D. Appleton Century Company, 1936), pp. 169–196.

19. "Miss Woolson," in *Henry James: The American Essays*, ed. Leon Edel (New York: Vintage Books, 1956), p. 164. This essay first appeared in *Harper's Weekly*, February 12, 1887.

20. Albert Cook, in *The Meaning of Fiction* (Detroit: Wayne State University Press, 1960), states that "all [James's] characters are *ficelles* by virtue of his consciousness of them as fictive appearances, and none are *ficelles* by virtue of their reality. This paradox is true of any fiction. Only in James is the paradox between the artifice and the reality of the characters in a plot made to reflect—veritably to coruscate with—the theme of the novel" (p. 136).

21. Joseph Warren Beach describes the role of the confidantes: "These persons do not tend to confuse the point of view. They serve rather to strengthen the light thrown upon the situation from the mind of the chief observer. They are his confederates, acting and above all making observations in his interest. They give information and suggestion without which he could hardly arrive at a proper understanding of the case. They set him right when he goes astray. Above all, as sympathetic and intelligent listeners, they encourage him to express in words his view of the case he is observing and of his own position in relation to it. They are thus serving him and the author at the same time." *The Method of Henry James* (Philadelphia: Albert Saifer, 1954), p. 71. Another observation was made by Frederick J. Hoffman in *The Modern Novel in America, 1900–1950* (Chicago: Henry Regnery Company, 1951): "In many instances he was to supplement points of view by introducing the confidant or confidants, who have a varying but always minor importance in the novel. . . . But the use had its risks; the confidant was too often irritatingly drawn in because a central consciousness could not give a completely satisfactory view either to the reader or to himself" (pp. 6-7).

22. *Notebooks*, p. 174. I think this account of the transformation is more accurate than to say that the confidant originally planned turned into Eugenio. Eugenio, it is true, is Milly's *homme d'affaires* in Venice; but he is far from being Densher's friend. The main factor in the first conception of such a figure was his role as confidant. This role, in all its importance, was reassigned to a woman, and its benefits were bestowed mainly on the heroine.

23. *The Ghostly Tales of Henry James*, ed. Leon Edel (New Brunswick: Rutgers University Press, 1948), p. 668.

24. "The Siege of London" (1883) describes the daring conquest of London society made by an erstwhile American adventuress. During her campaign Mrs. Headway bestows unsolicited confidences on Rupert Waterville in a manner most distressing to himself. They are all in character, however, and invite speculation as to James's reasons for reversing the sexes in this confidential relation. Is it only a woman "with a past" who would even think of confiding in a male friend?—There are also two apparent exceptions: Daisy Miller depends on the courier Eugenio in a manner derisively termed "intimate" by Mrs. Costello in "Daisy Miller"; and Milly Theale 'has confidential relations with her

expert major-domo, likewise named Eugenio, in *The Wings of the Dove*. But these relationships are of minor importance in their respective works; and in the novel the role of the servant is never overlooked. Furthermore, the two Eugenios are not needed to extend the point of view.

Notes to Chapter 1
Pages 3–27

1. *N Y Edn.*, I, 7–8.
2. *N Y Edn.*, II, 35.
3. Mrs. Tristram's awkward attempts at matchmaking are only a prelude to the skillful machination of Madame Merle in *The Portrait of a Lady*. In one respect, the difference is due to the four-year development between the two novels; in another, it is the result of diversity of character.
4. The note of cynicism is already a feature of the confidante's character. It will appear more plainly in Mrs. Costello and Madame Merle.
5. "Daisy Miller," in *Henry James: Selected Fiction*, ed. Leon Edel (New York: E. P. Dutton & Co., Inc., 1953), p. 16.
6. *N Y Edn.*, VI, 393.
7. "The Aspern Papers," in *Henry James: Selected Fiction*, p. 292.
8. These tendencies are discussed by William Bysshe Stein in *"The Aspern Papers:* A comedy of Masks," *Nineteenth-Century Fiction* (September 1959), pp. 172–178.
9. See *The Bostonians*, "The Patagonia," "Brooksmith," "The Pupil," and "The Coxon Fund." Some of these women are particularly stupid; most of them are minor characters.
10. Mr. Edel suggests plausible parallels between the relation of the editor and Miss Tina and that of James and Miss Woolson, *Henry James: The Middle Years*, pp. 224–227.
11. *Notebooks*, p. 78.
12. *A London Life* (New York: Grove Press, Inc., 1957), p. 107.
13. *Notebooks*, p. 79.
14. Blackmur, p. 130.

Notes to Chapter 2
Pages 28–63

1. 'Nona Vincent" in *The Real Thing and Other Tales* (London: Macmillan and Co., 1893), p. 131.
2. "The Death of the Lion" in *Terminations* (New York: Harper & Brothers, 1895), p. 30.
3. "Flickerbridge" in *The Better Sort* (London: Methuen & Co., 1903), p. 111.

4. *The Ambassadors,* first mentioned in the *Notebooks,* October 31, 1895, was completed in 1901. "Flickerbridge," first conceived February 19, 1899, appeared in *Scribner's Magazine,* February 1902.

5. The fate awaiting Miss Wenham occurs to Mrs. Brash in "The Beldonald Holbein" (1903).

6. "The Turn of the Screw" in *A Casebook on Henry James's "The Turn of the Screw,"* ed. Gerald Willen (New York: Thomas Y. Crowell Company, 1960), p. 49.

7. Oscar Cargill, "Henry James as a Freudian Pioneer," in *A Casebook,* p. 228.

8. Harold C. Goddard, "A Pre-Freudian Reading of *The Turn of the Screw,*" in *A Casebook,* p. 258.

9. Blackmur, p. 175.

10. *Ibid.,* p. 176.

11. "The Altar of the Dead" in *Terminations,* p. 203.

12. *Notebooks,* p. 311.

13. "The Beast in the Jungle" in *The Better Sort,* p. 142.

14. "The Jolly Corner" in *Henry James: Selected Fiction,* p. 548.

15. "Crapy Cornelia" in *The Finer Grain* (London: Methuen & Co. Ltd., 1910), pp. 188–189.

Notes to Chapter 3
Pages 67–96

1. Blackmur, p. 54. The following five references are to the Preface in this edition.

2. The parallels between Henrietta and Susan Stringham as confidantes have been pointed out by Ernest Sandeen, *"The Wings of the Dove* and *The Portrait of a Lady:* A Study of Henry James's Later Phase," *PMLA,* LXIX (December 1954), 1060–1075. The author notes that Henrietta is a caricature.

3. *The Portrait of a Lady,* ed. Leon Edel (Boston: Houghton Mifflin Company, 1956), p. 79.

4. Her first appearance as "center" is in the scene with Mrs. Touchett (Chapter 20).

5. James's satire in this treatment of the emancipated woman was later made more explicit in *The Bostonians.*

6. James's early reflections on this point attribute a different motive to Madame Merle: ". . . Isabel . . . hesitates. Then Madame Merle, who wishes her to make a *coup de tête,* to leave Osmond, so that she may be away from Pansy, reveals to her her belief that it was Ralph who induced her [sic] father to leave her the £70,000. Isabel, then, violently affected and overcome, starts directly for England." (*Notebooks,* p. 17). In the novel, however, Isabel has already made arrangements to "go to

England tonight." And Madame Merle recovers herself when she realizes that Isabel's motive is only Ralph's illness (p. 451). This would seem to justify my view that Madame Merle's intention is to glory in her superior knowledge, little else indeed being left her to glory in, although there still may be a latent desire to get rid of Isabel.

Notes to Chapter 4
Pages 97–126

1. Melvin Friedman states that *The Spoils of Poynton* is "The first novel to be written with this consistent point of view retained throughout. . . . It is clear that James shows a decided favoritism for Fleda Vetch, he favors her simply by making *hers* the interpreting consciousness. . . . More important is that Fleda Vetch is the first of James's characters to be analyzed completely from the inside." *Stream of Consciousness: A Study in Literary Method* (New Haven: Yale University Press, 1955), p. 43.

2. Blackmur, pp. 127–129. The next three references are to this Preface.

3. *The Spoils of Poynton* (Boston and New York: Houghton Mifflin and Company, 1897), p. 9.

4. F. O. Matthiessen declares that "In *The Spoils of Poynton* . . . [James] attributed an absolute worth to the accumulated property itself, to what he called in his preface 'the felt beauty and value of the . . . Things, always the splendid Things.' " *American Renaissance* (London: Oxford University Press, 1941), p. 363. A closer reading of *Poynton,* however, discloses a very different attitude on the part of the author, as I shall try to establish in this chapter.

5. In the New York Edition James added this sentence: " 'Don't you know a little more, you absurd affected thing, what men *are*, the brutes?' " (X, 141).

6. This theme of vampirism James later developed more fully in *The Sacred Fount.* Already evident in Osmond's treatment of his wife in *The Portrait,* it is a theme which interested James all his life. Was not the famous dream of the Galerie d'Apollon a sign of the need he felt to defend the inviolability of the person?

7. Blackmur, pp. 129–130. The editors of the *Notebooks* comment on Fleda thus: "Those who object that Fleda's passivity in yielding Owen is abnormal and neurotic should at least ponder James's full awareness of what he was trying for. He wanted to present Fleda as the quintessence of 'the free spirit,' possessing taste, of which Mona should have no glimmering, and possessing tenderness and moral imagination beyond Mrs. Gereth's scope." *Notebooks,* p. 254.

Notes to Chapter 5
Pages 127–149

1. *What Maisie Knew* (Garden City, N. Y.: Doubleday and Company, Inc., n.d.), p. 34.

2. Sir Claude accepts Mrs. Wix in spite of her inferior social status in the free and easy manner of Christopher Newman. It is due perhaps more to kindness than a flair for democracy.

3. *The Complex Fate* (London: Chatto and Windus, 1952), p. 100. F. R. Leavis, in his "Disagreement," refutes these imputations against Mrs. Wix and defends her respectability, asserting that "it should surely be plain enough (even if we hadn't James's note to that effect) that Mrs. Wix's and Maisie's 'adorations' are of the same order. . . . Sir Claude, in short, is the *beau idéal* of her romantic day dreams, and her feeling about him is as much, and as little, 'erotic' as Maisie's, if more positively a matter of comedy—since, after all, a childish 'adoration' in her is less in place than in a child. I concede to Mr. Bewley, without embarrassment, that perhaps Maisie as well as Mrs. Wix is jealous of Mrs. Beale." (In Bewley, pp. 128–129). James's "note" cited by Leavis is in the *Notebooks*, p. 257. It reads: "Mrs. Wix is there—Mrs. Wix must explain things to the child. She adores—they BOTH adore—Sir Claude. He must be very nice, very charming to Maisie, but he must get a little tired of her." On p. 259, the author continues: "He [Sir Claude] resents her [Ida's] neglect of her child and makes up for it to the little girl: comes up to the nursery or schoolroom, rather, to see her, charms Mrs. Wix more and more (she's in love with him). . . ." Further on James adds: "The small touching oddity (with her secret passion for him) of her offering *herself* as a rescue from the temptation, the impropriety of Mrs. Beale" (p. 262). These last two passages, which Leavis ignores, qualify the first one considerably. From later evidence in the novel which I shall adduce it seems truer that Mrs. Wix's attachment to Sir Claude is far from childish. James W. Gargano, however, holds that "Maisie is motivated by the ideal of loyalty to Sir Claude—an ideal that Mrs. Wix cannot sustain." —"*What Maisie Knew:* the Evolution of a 'Moral Sense,' " *Nineteenth Century Fiction*, XVI (June 1961).

4. Harris W. Wilson, "What *Did* Maisie Know?" *College English*, XVII (February 1956), 279–282; Edward Wasiolek, "Maisie: Pure or Corrupt?" *College English*, XXII (December 1960), 167–172. Leavis and Gargano hold for her moral consistency although conceding the comic effect of her role.

5. This position of Mrs. Wix is the technical difference between her and Mrs. Penniman in *Washington Square*. Mrs. Wix extends the range of consciousness of Maisie, the "center," whereas Mrs. Penniman acts as any other minor character in her novel; she comes and goes under the observation of the omniscient author.

6. The point of Mrs. Wix's delight in the fast living of Ida and Sir Claude is completely overlooked by Gargano. He sees Mrs. Wix only as assessing "human action by doctrinal requirements," although he does reject the interpretation of other critics who would make her "the moral norm of the novel, forgetting that she is often actuated by materialistic considerations" (Gargano, 40, 42).

7. Bewley, p. 100.

8. See Gargano, 42.

9. Wilson believes that Maisie is prepared to offer her virginity to Sir Claude. Leavis disputes the allusions to Maisie's sexual attraction to Sir Claude: ". . . though her attitude towards Sir Claude is feminine right enough, she remains to the end uninterested in, and uncognizant of, sex." (In Bewley, p. 130).

10. Bewley, p. 101.

11. Bewley supports this view in his "Rejoinder" to Leavis, p. 141.

Notes to Chapter 6
Pages 150–180

1. Blackmur, p. 322. The next three citations are to this work. *The Ambassadors* was already outlined by September 1, 1900, almost a year before *The Wings of the Dove* was begun; its publication was delayed until 1903. Its priority in date of composition determines its place in this study.

2. *The Ambassadors,* ed. Leon Edel (Boston: Houghton Mifflin Company, 1960), p. 19.

3. Blackmur, p. 323. Matthiessen stresses James's difficulty and failure to justify her presence, in *Henry James: The Major Phase* (New York: Oxford University Press, 1944), p. 38: "But his device of having her fall in love with Strether and hope wistfully to marry him does not achieve such reality." This seems a rather sweeping statement which I hope to refute.

4. Blackmur, p. 323.

5. "The Literary Convictions of Henry James," *Modern Fiction Studies,* III (Spring 1957), 3–10.

6. *Notebooks,* p. 378.

7. Mary Freeman, "The Marginal Sex," *Commonweal,* LXXV (February 2, 1962), 483–486. Among other thought-provoking statements the author writes: "Culture-wise each woman is on her own and must reconcile her needs and necessities privately for herself—a feat calling for no mean psychological strength" (485)

8. *Notebooks,* p. 378.

9. Oscar Cargill, in *The Novels of Henry James* (New York: Macmillan, 1961), p. 322, implies that Maria escapes, leaving little Bilham to

tell the lie. This is inaccurate, since he has already done so before her departure (Book Fourth, II).

10. Cargill (p. 324) asserts that Strether refuses Maria because he loves Madame de Vionnet, and that he gives the reason that will best save Maria's pride. This theory seems sound, since everything else in Maria's offer does actually attract him.

11. In his *Project* James wrote: "He *can't* accept or assent. He won't. He doesn't. It's too late. It mightn't have been sooner—but it is, yes, distinctly, now. He has come so far through his total experience that he has come out on the other side—on the other side, even, of a union with Miss Gostrey. He must go back as he came—or rather, really, so quite other that, in comparison, marrying Miss Gostrey would be almost of the old order. Yes, he goes back other—to other things. We see him on the eve of departure, with whatever awaits him *là-bas*, and their lingering, ripe separation is the last note." *Notebooks,* p. 415.

Notes to Chapter 7
Pages 181–213

1. Blackmur, p. 291.

2. *The Wings of the Dove* (New York: The Modern Library, n.d.), p. 117. This is the same as the 1902 edition.

3. James may be poking fun at the New England local colorists. Of Miss Mary Wilkins he wrote in the English magazine, *Literature,* July 9, 1898: "Miss Wilkins, in *Silence*—a collection of six short tales— has 'gone in' for the romantic with visible relish. . . . The actual, the immediate, the whole sound and sense of the dry realities of rustic New England are what, for comedy and elegy, she has touched with the firmest hand. In her new book, however, she invokes in a manner the muse of history, summons to her aid with much earnestness the predominant picturesqueness . . . of the past. I cannot help thinking that, in spite of her good will, the past withholds from her that natural note which she extracts so happily from the present. The natural note is the touching, the stirring one; and thus it befalls that she really plays the trick, the trick the romancer tries for, much more effectually with the common objects about her than with the objects preserved, and sufficiently faded and dusty, in the cracked glass case of the rococo."—In *Henry James: The American Essays,* p. 257.

4. Cargill wonders that no critic has pointed out the comparative absence of "comic relief" in this novel. In spite of the truth of his observation there are comic traits in Susan Stringham's character. Her simplicity, romantic enthusiasm, and flustered timidity amuse in turn her confider and her exploiters in London. Also, James seems to mock gently at her literary efforts, and her Puritan fling. *Novels,* p. 382.

5. Blackmur, p. 51.

6. From here on, the citations are from the second volume, which in the Modern Library edition is indicated only by renewed pagination.

7. At first glance, Maupassant seems incongruous in Susan's hall of fame, for his scorn for romantic writers is well known. Still, it is his "art" which the New England critic admires. This art is marked by its creation of atmosphere, by means of the objective technique; what appears to the senses only is valid in his estimation. Mrs. Stringham herself is captivated by what appears to the senses.

8. "Alice met all attempts at sympathy with jeers and laughter, having her own brave philosophy, which was to keep her attention turned to things outside her sick-room and away from herself." *Alice James: Her Brothers—Her Journal,* ed. Anna Robeson Burr (New York, 1934), p. 79. Matthiessen observes that ". . . the only world in which she could deploy her force was the inner world of HJ's typical heroines." *The James Family* (New York: Alfred A. Knopf, 1947), p. 273.

9. The second-last sentence of this quotation was recast in an exaggerated style for the New York Edition: ". . . the court of a reigning seraph, a sort of a vice-queen of an angel" (XX, 211). The change underscores my point that James intended Susan to be a romantic visionary.

10. Sandeen, 1066.

11. Blackmur, p. 299.

12. *Ibid.,* p. 301.

13. *Notebooks,* p. 174.

Notes to Chapter 8
Pages 214–246

1. Blackmur, p. 330.

2. A complete survey of these blocks is as follows: BOOK FIRST: Chapter II—scene with the Prince. Chapter IV—scene with Bob. Chapters XIV-XVI—state reception (encounters with Charlotte and the Prince) and drive home with Bob. Chapters XXIII-XXIV—big scene with Bob. BOOK SECOND: Chapter XXX—scene with Maggie. Chapter XXXI—scene with Bob. Chapter XXXIII—scene with Maggie (golden bowl). Chapter XXXV—scene with Maggie. Chapter XL—scene with Maggie.

3. *The Golden Bowl* (New York: Grove Press, Inc., n. d.), p. 13.

4. *The Writing of Fiction* (New York: Charles Scribner's Sons, 1925), pp. 90-92.

5. *Novels,* pp. 423–424. The author presents a sympathetic and perceptive defense of the role of the Assinghams.

6. H. G. Wells, *Boon, The Mind of the Race, The Asses of the Devil, and The Last Trump* (New York: George H. Doran Company, 1915), pp. 86–130. Wells singles out *The Golden Bowl* for special mention.

7. Edith Wharton's question to James, "What was your idea in suspending the four principal characters in 'The Golden Bowl' in the void?" received no explanation from the unhappily surprised author other than, "My dear—I didn't know I had!" His reply suggests that his intention had supplied one which she missed. *A Backward Glance,* p. 191.

Notes to Conclusion
Pages 247–283

1. See Norma Phillips, *"The Sacred Fount:* The Narrator and the Vampires," *PMLA,* LXXVI (September 1961), 407–412.
2. Dupee, p. 149.
3. Edwin T. Bowden, *The Themes of Henry James* (New Haven: Yale University Press, 1956), p. 53.
4. F. O. Matthiessen, *The James Family,* pp. 587–592, and Quentin Anderson, *The American Henry James* (New Brunswick: Rutgers University Press, 1957), pp. xi, xii, 9–10.
5. His voluminous correspondence reflects his devotedness to many friends. The rupture with H. G. Wells after a fifteen-year friendship caused the sensitive James great suffering, but his reaction was both gentlemanly and forgiving.
6. J. A. Ward, *The Imagination of Disaster* (Lincoln: University of Nebraska Press, 1961), p. 116.
7. *Ibid.,* p. 123.
8. *Ibid.,* p. 141.
9. *Ibid.,* p. 147.

Index

A

Addie (in "Flickerbridge"), 39
Aeschylus, xii
Alcott, Louisa May, *Moods,* xxi, 285
Alsager, Mrs. (in "Nona Vincent"), 29-32, 259
  and May Bartram, 59
  and Maria Gostrey, 29, 59
  and Miss Hurter, 32, 40
  and Alice Staverton, 59
  and Susan Stringham, 59
  and Fleda Vetch, 59
  and Miss Wenham, 40
Amerigo, Prince (in *The Golden Bowl*), xviii, xxv, xxvi, 26, 208, 214-221, 223-237, 239-246, 260, 278-281, 293
  and Bob Assingham, 227
  and Sir Claude, 223
  and Mrs. Gereth, 112
  and Frank Granger, 39
  and Madame Merle, 231
  and Strether, 218, 220, 221
Anderson, Quentin, 252; *The American Henry James,* 294
Archer, Isabel, Mrs. Osmond (in *The Portrait of a Lady*), 68-76, 78-96, 189, 253, 261, 262, 263-266, 276, 288-289
  and Maria Gostrey, 173, 253, 272
  and Morgan Moreen, 265
  and Hyacinth Robinson, 265

Archer, Isabel, Mrs. Osmond—*Cont.*
  and Susan Stringham, 276
  and Milly Theale, 265
  and Maggie Verver, 245
  and Fleda Vetch, 98, 253, 265, 268
Ash, Susan (in *What Maisie Knew*), 137
Assingham, Colonel Bob (in *The Golden Bowl*), xxiv, xxv, 219, 221-228, 232, 234-240, 242, 244, 246, 277-280, 293
  and Prince Amerigo, 227
  and Paul Beever, 221
  and Owen Gereth, 221
  and Maria Gostrey, 222
  and Mrs. Grose, 42
  and Christopher Newman, 225
  and Susan Stringham, 194
Assingham, Fanny (in *The Golden Bowl*), xxii, xxiv, xxv, xxvii, 26, 39, 214-246, 277-281, 293
  and May Bartram, 280
  and Lady Davenant, 27
  and Maria Gostrey, 180, 214, 220, 221, 222, 224, 263, 277, 278, 279, 281
  and Mrs. Grose, 242, 254
  and lady in "The Altar of the Dead," 48
  and Madame Merle, 90, 224, 280, 281
  and Lady Sandgate, 62
  and Charlotte Stant, 240, 278

295

Assingham, Fanny—*Cont.*
   and Alice Staverton, 280
   and Susan Stringham, 187, 208,
      212, 215, 221, 246, 277, 278,
      281
   and Fleda Vetch, 98, 263, 267, 281
   and Mrs. Wix, 131, 134, 136, 254,
      262, 263

B

Bantling, Mr. (in *The Portrait of a
   Lady*), 68, 72, 87, 96
Barrace, Miss (in *The Ambassadors*),
   158, 160
Bartram, May (in "The Beast in the
   Jungle"), xxii, xxvi, xxvii, 51-56,
   57, 254, 261
   and Mrs. Alsager, 59
   and Fanny Assingham, 280
   and Miss Tina Bordereau, 21, 24,
      260-261
   and Maria Gostrey, 51, 53, 59, 155,
      162, 170, 180, 271, 275
   and lady in "The Altar of the
      Dead," 48, 52
   and Alice Staverton, 57, 59, 261
   and Susan Stringham, 59, 275
   and Fleda Vetch, 59, 113, 275
Bassanio, xii
Beach, Joseph Warren, *The Method
   of Henry James*, 286
Beale, Mrs. *see* Farange, Mrs. Beale
Beever, Mrs. (in *The Other House*),
   247, 249
Beever, Paul (in *The Other House*),
   and Bob Assingham, 221
Bellegardes (in *The American*), 7, 8,
   9, 255
Bewley, Marius, 129-130, 134, 147,
   291; *The Complex Fate,* 290;
   "Rejoinder," 291
Bilham (in *The Ambassadors*), 160-
   164, 166, 291
Blackmur, Richard P. (ed.), *The Art
   of the Novel,* 284, 287, 288, 289,
   291, 292, 293
Bordereau, Miss Juliana (in "The
   Aspern Papers"), 18
Bordereau, Miss Tina (in "The As-
   pern Papers"), xxii, 14-15, 19-
   24, 67, 258, 261, 287

Bordereau, Miss Tina—*Cont.*
   and May Bartram 21, 24, 260-261
   and Cecilia, 15
   and Lady Davenant, 27
   and Maria Gostrey, 15, 21
   and lady in "The Altar of the
      Dead," 40
   and Mrs. Prest, 14, 19, 67
   and Mrs. Tristram, 15
   and Miss Wenham, 37
Bowden, Edwin T., 251, *The Themes
   of Henry James,* 294
Boyne, Martin (in *The Children*),
   xxix
Brash, Mrs. (in "The Beldonald Holbein"), 288
Bread, Mrs. (in *The American*), 8-9
   and Mrs. Wix, 148
Brigstock, Mona (in *The Spoils of
   Poynton*), 100-101, 104-108,
   112, 113-114, 115, 117, 118-119,
   121-124, 126, 249, 268, 289
Brigstock, Mrs. (in *The Spoils of
   Poynton*), 120, 122
Brissenden, Mrs. (in *The Sacred
   Fount*), 247, 249-250
Bronson, Mrs. Katherine, xvi
Bronte, Emily, *Wuthering Heights,*
   xii
Brookenham, Mrs. (in *The Awk-
   ward Age*), 247, 249
Brydon, Spencer (in "The Jolly Cor-
   ner"), xviii, xxix, 57-59, 107, 260
   and Mrs. Gereth, 112
   and John Marcher, 261
   and White-Mason, 60
Burr, Anna Robeson (ed.), *Alice
   James: Her Brothers—Her Jour-
   nal,* 293

C

Cardew, Mary (in "Crapy Corne-
   lia"), 61
Cargill, Oscar, 223; "Henry James as
   a Freudian Pioneer," 288; *The
   Novels of Henry James,* 291,
   292, 293
Casamassima, Prince (in *The Prin-
   cess Casamassima*), 16-17
Casamassima, Princess, *see* Light,
   Christina

Catherine (in *Washington Square*), 248
Cecilia (in *Roderick Hudson*), xxvii, 3, 4-5, 14, 255
and Miss Tina Bordereau, 15
and Miss Hurter, 35
and Mrs. Tristram, 14
Champer, Lady (in "Miss Gunton of Poughkeepsie"), 216
Cintré, Madame Claire de (in *The American*), 6-9, 96
Claude, Sir (in *What Maisie Knew*), 26, 127, 129-149, 260, 262, 269-271, 290, 291
and Prince Amerigo, 223
and Christopher Newman, 290
and Laura Wing, 26
Condrip, Mrs. (in *The Wings of the Dove*), 194-195
Conrad, Joseph, xxix; *Lord Jim*, 246
Cook, Albert, *The Meaning of Fiction*, 286
Costello, Mrs. (in "Daisy Miller"), xxvii, 3, 4, 9-14, 255-256, 286, 287
and Lady Davenant, 24, 27
and Marie Gostrey, 180
and Miss Hurter, 35
and Madame Merle, 12, 83
and Mrs. Penniman, 247
and Susan Stringham, 277
and Mrs. Tristram, 10, 14
Coventry, Mrs. (in "The Madonna of the Future"), 4
Croy, Kate (in *The Wings of the Dove*), 187, 189, 190, 191-197, 199-201, 204, 206, 208, 209, 210, 211

D

Davenant, Lady (in "A London Life"), xvi, 14, 24-27, 258-259
and Fanny Assingham, 27
and Miss Tina Bordereau, 27
and Mrs. Costello, 24, 27
and Mrs. Gereth, 27
and Mrs. Grose, 27
and Madame Merle, 27, 83
and Mrs. Tristram, 26
and Mrs. Wix, 26
Daudet, xv

Dean, Nelly (in *Wuthering Heights*), xii
Densher, Merton (in *The Wings of the Dove*), xxv, 184, 185, 189, 190, 192-213 221, 260, 275-277, 286
Don Quixote, 103
Draper, Mrs. (in "Madame de Mauves"), 4
Dupee, F. W., xviii, 294; *Henry James*, 285

E

Earnshaw, Catherine (in *Wuthering Heights*), xii
Edel, Leon, xiii, xviii, xix, xxvi, 152, 285
(ed.) *The Ambassadors*, 291
(ed.) *The Ghostly Tales of Henry James*, 29, 286
Henry James: The Conquest of London, 285
Henry James: The Middle Years, 285, 287
(ed.) *Henry James: Selected Fiction*, 287, 288
"The Literary Convictions of Henry James," 291
(ed.) *The Portrait of a Lady*, 288
Emerson, 185, 186
Eugenio (in "Daisy Miller"), 286
Eugenio (in *The Wings of the Dove*), 286, 287
Euripides, xii

F

Farange, Beale (in *What Maisie Knew*), 142
Farange, Mrs. Beale, Miss Overmore (in *What Maisie Knew*), 128, 130, 132-135, 137-139, 142-148, 269-270, 290
Farange, Mrs. Ida (in *What Maisie Knew*), 132, 137, 138, 291
Flaubert, 152
Freeman, Mary, "The Marginal Sex," 291
Friedman, Melvin, *Stream of Consciousness . . . .*, 289
Froude, 185, 186

G

Gardner, Mrs. Isabella, xvi
Gargano, James W., *"What Maisie Knew . . ."*, 290, 291
Gemini, Countess Amy (in *The Portrait of a Lady*), 68, 76, 80, 86, 87, 96, 248, 266, 285
  and Mrs. Penniman, 248
  and Henrietta Stackpole, 86
  and Mrs. Tristram, 248
Gereth, Mrs. Adela (in *The Spoils of Poynton*), 98, 99-113, 115-120, 122-126, 253, 260, 266, 268-269, 289
  and Prince Amerigo, 112
  and Spencer Brydon, 112
  and Lady Davenant, 27
  and John Marcher, 112, 268
  and Susan Stringham, 106
Gereth, Owen (in *The Spoils of Poynton*), xviii, xxiv, 98, 100-125, 253, 260, 266, 268-269, 289
  and Bob Assingham, 221
  and Vanderbank, 249
Gibbon, 185, 186
Giovanelli (in "Daisy Miller"), 12, 13, 256
Gloriani (in *The Ambassadors*), 159, 163
Goddard, Harold C., 41; "A Pre-Freudian Reading of *The Turn of the Screw*," 288
Goethe, *Iphigenie auf Tauris,* xii
Goodwood, Caspar (in *The Portrait of a Lady*), 81, 86-87, 95, 96
Gostrey, Maria (in *The Ambassadors*), xxii, xxiv, xxvii, 39, 150-180, 254, 259, 262, 271-275, 282, 291, 292
  and Mrs. Alsager, 29, 59
  and Isabel Archer, 173, 253, 272
  and Bob Assingham, 222
  and Fanny Assingham, 180, 214, 220, 221, 222, 224, 263, 277, 278, 279, 281
  and May Bartram, 51, 53, 59, 155, 162, 170, 180, 271, 275
  and Miss Tina Bordereau, 15, 21
  and Mrs. Costello, 180
  and Madame Grandoni, 180

Gostrey, Maria—*Cont.*
  and lady in "The Altar of the Dead," 48
  and Madame Merle, 152, 155, 170, 180, 273
  and Mrs. Newsome, 152, 154-155, 159
  and Mrs. Prest, 180
  and Lady Sandgate, 62
  and Henrietta Stackpole, 67-68, 180, 254, 266, 273
  and Alice Staverton, 59
  and Susan Stringham, 59, 180, 181, 187, 194, 201, 205, 212, 254, 271, 275
  and Milly Theale, 272
  and Mrs. Tristram 6, 180
  and Maggie Verver, 272
  and Fleda Vetch, 59, 107, 126, 253, 263, 267, 275
  and Madame de Vionnet, 161, 165-168, 172, 173-175, 177-178, 180, 240, 273-274
  and Miss Wenham, 162
  and Mrs. Wix, 134, 180, 263, 274
governess (in "The Turn of the Screw"), 41-46, 127
Grandoni, Madame (in *The Princess Casamassima*), xxi, xxiv, xxvi, 14-17, 257
  and Maria Gostrey, 180
  and Mrs. Prest, 17, 18
Granger, Frank (in "Flickerbridge"), 36-39
  and Prince Amerigo, 39
  and Miss Hurter, 36
  and Strether, 39
Gregorovius, 185, 186
Grey, Violet (in "Nona Vincent"), 30-32
Grose, Mrs. (in "The Turn of the Screw"), xxi, 40, 41-46, 127, 259, 260
  and Bob Assingham, 42
  and Fanny Assingham, 242, 254
  and Lady Davenant, 27
  and Miss Hurter, 42
  and Mrs. Wix, 42, 254
Gunton, Lily (in "Miss Gunton of Poughkeepsie"), 216

H

Hague, Acton (in "The Altar of the Dead"), 48-49, 51
Harpers (publishers), 154
Harper's Weekly, 285
Headway, Mrs. (in "The Siege of London"), 286
Heathcliff (in *Wuthering Heights*), xii
Henning, Millicent (in *The Princess Casamassima*), 140
Hoffman, Frederick J., *The Modern Novel in America*, 286
Hoffmann, Charles G., *The Short Novels of Henry James*, 284-285
Horatio, xii, 285
Hudson, Roderick (in *Roderick Hudson*), 5, 255
Hurter, Fanny (in "The Death of the Lion"), 32-36
  and Mrs. Alsager, 32, 40
  and Cecilia, 35
  and Mrs. Costello, 35
  and Frank Granger, 36
  and Mrs. Grose, 42
  and Mrs. Prest, 35
  and Lady Sandgate, 62
  and Henrietta Stackpole, 36, 95
  and Fleda Vetch, 35
  and Miss Wenham, 40

I

Iago, xii

J

James, Alice (sister), xiii, 202, 285, 293
James, Henry, writings of:
  "Altar of the Dead, The," 3, 40, 46-51, 259, 261, 288; Preface to, xvii
  Ambassadors, The, xviii, xxii, 38, 62, 125, 150-180, 262, 271-275, 288, 291; and *The Golden Bowl*, 214, 229; and *The Portrait of a Lady*, 271; *Project* of, xxvii, 51, 126, 154, 292;

James, Henry, writings of—*Cont.*
  Ambassadors, The—*Cont.*
  and *The Wings of the Dove*, 275
  American, The, xxii, xxv, xxvi, 3, 4, 6-9, 15, 26, 63, 217, 255
  American Essays, The, 285, 292
  "Aspern Papers, The," xxii, 14-15, 17-24, 27, 258, 287; Preface to, 46; and *The Wings of the Dove*, 23
  "Author of Beltraffio, The," xxii
  Awkward Age, The, 160, 222, 247, 249; and *What Maisie Knew*, 270-271
  "Beast in the Jungle, The," xviii, xxii, xxix, 3, 40, 51-57, 62, 259, 261, 288
  "Beldonald Holbein, The," 247, 288
  Better Sort, The, 287, 288
  Bostonians, The, xxvi, 287, 288
  "Brooksmith," 287
  "Coxon Fund, The," 287
  "Crapy Cornelia," 60-62, 288
  "Daisy Miller," xxvii, 3, 4, 9-14, 247, 255-257, 286, 287
  "Death of the Lion, The," xviii, 28, 29, 32-36, 287
  "Diary of a Man of Fifty, The," xxix
  Essays in London and Elsewhere, 285
  "Eugene Pickering," xxv
  "Europe," xxii
  Finer Grain, The, 288
  "Flickerbridge," 29, 36-40, 287, 288
  "Frances Anne Kemble," 285
  Golden Bowl, The, xviii, xxii, 214-246, 262, 277-282, 293, 294; and *The Ambassadors*, 214, 229
  "Jolly Corner, The," xviii, xxii, 3, 40, 53, 57-59, 62, 259, 261, 288
  "Lesson of the Master, The," xviii
  Letters, 284, 285
  "London Life, A," 14, 23, 24-27, 258-259, 287
  "Louisa Pallant," xxii

James, Henry, writings of—*Cont.*
"Madame de Mauves," 4
"Madonna of the Future, The," xiv, xxv, 4, 285
"Miss Alcott's 'Moods,' " xxi, 285
"Miss Gunton of Poughkeepsie," 216
"Miss Woolson," 285
"Mrs. Humphrey Ward," 285
New York Edition, 284, 287, 289, 293
"Nona Vincent," xviii, 28, 29-32, 259, 287
Notebooks, xxv, xxvii, xxviii, 25, 38, 51, 152, 212, 284, 286, 287, 288, 289, 290, 291, 292, 293
Notes and Reviews, 285
Other House, The, 247, 249
Outcry, The, xviii, xxiv, xxx, 62-63
"Pandora," xxii
"Patagonia, The," xxii, 283, 287
Portrait of a Lady, The, xxi, xxii, xxvii, xxviii, 14, 15, 19, 27, 67-96, 247, 257, 260, 262, 263-266, 287, 288, 289; Preface to, 189; and *The Spoils of Poynton,* 267, 269; and *The Wings of the Dove,* 189, 266
Prefaces, *see* Blackmur
Princess Casamassima, The, xxi, xxvi, 14-17, 27, 257
"Private Life, The," xxiv
"Pupil, The," 287
"Real Right Thing, The," 258
Real Thing and Other Tales, The, 287
Roderick Hudson, xxii, xxiv, xxvii, 3, 4-6, 15, 62, 63, 255, 280
Sacred Fount, The, xxiv, 223, 247, 250, 289
"Siege of London, The," 286
Spoils of Poynton, The, xviii, xxiv, xxvi, 97-126, 259, 262, 266-269, 289; and *The Portrait of a Lady,* 267, 269; Preface to, 26, 27
Terminations, 287, 288
"Tree of Knowledge, The," xxii
"Turn of the Screw, The," xxi, xxvii, 40, 41-46, 52, 146, 259, 288

James, Henry, writings of—*Cont.*
Washington Square, xxiii, 247, 284, 290
What Maisie Knew, xxi, 127-149, 262, 269-271, 284, 290; and *The Awkward Age,* 270-271
Wings of the Dove, The, xx, xxi, xxv, 23, 181-213, 262, 275-277, 287, 288, 291, 292; and *The Ambassadors,* 275; and "The Aspern Papers," 23; and *The Portrait of a Lady,* 189, 266
James, William (brother), xx, 252
James's father, xiii, 252
James's mother, xiii
Jessel, Miss (in "The Turn of the Screw"), 42, 43, 45
Jonson, xii

K

Kemble, Mrs. Fanny, xv, xvi, xix

L

lady (in "The Altar of the Dead"), 40, 46-51
and Fanny Assingham, 48
and May Bartram, 48, 52
and Miss Tina Bordereau, 40
and Maria Gostrey, 48
and Alice Staverton, 48
and Susan Stringham, 277
and Fleda Vetch, 48
Leavis, F. R., 148; "Disagreement," 290, 291
Lee, Vernon, 285
Light, Christina (in *Roderick Hudson* and *The Princess Casamassima*), 15-16, 255, 257
Literature, 292
Lockwood, Mr. (in *Wuthering Heights*), xii
Long (in *The Sacred Fount*), 250
Longdon, Mr. (in *The Awkward Age*), 271
Longfellow, 186
Loring, Miss, xix
Lowder, Mrs. Maud Manningham (in *The Wings of the Dove*),

Lowder, Mrs. Maud Manningham—
Cont.
183, 187-188, 191-193, 195-206,
211, 213, 221, 254, 275-276
and Madame Merle 264
Lubbock, see James, Henry, Letters

M

Maeterlinck, 185, 186
Maisie (in What Maisie Knew), 127-
149, 269-271, 285, 290
Mallet, Rowland (in Roderick Hud-
son), 4-5, 15, 255
Marbot, 185, 186
Marcher, John (in "The Beast in the
Jungle"), xviii, xxix, 52-57, 170,
254, 260, 261
and Spencer Brydon, 261
and editor in "The Aspern Papers,"
261
and Mrs. Gereth, 112, 268
and Gilbert Osmond, 261
and George Stransom, 55
and Strether, 51
and White-Mason, 60
Mark, Lord (in The Wings of the
Dove), 195-196, 207, 275
Marlow, 246
Matthiessen, F. O., 252; American
Renaissance, 289; Henry James:
The Major Phase, 291; The
James Family, 293, 294
Maupassant, Guy de, 200, 293
Merle, Madame (in The Portrait of
a Lady), xxii, xxvi, xxvii, 67-69,
72, 73-96, 253, 254, 262, 264-
266, 287, 288-289
and Prince Amerigo, 231
and Fanny Assingham, 90, 224,
280, 281
and Mrs. Costello, 12, 83
and Lady Davenant, 27, 83
and Maria Gostrey, 152, 155, 170,
180, 273
and Mrs. Lowder, 264
and Henrietta Stackpole, 67-69,
72, 74-75, 76, 77-78, 80-82,
88, 94-96
and Susan Stringham, 181, 189
and Mrs. Tristram, 83, 90, 96

Merle, Madame—Cont.
and Fleda Vetch, 97-98, 126, 266
and Mrs. Wix, 270
Miles and Flora (children in "The
Turn of the Screw"), 43-46, 52
Miller, Daisy (in "Daisy Miller"),
10-13, 255-257, 286
Millers, 225
Montaigne, xiv
Moreen, Morgan, 265
Mudrick, Marvin, Jane Austen . . .
285
Munden, Mrs. (in "The Beldonald
Holbein"), 247

N

Nanda (in The Awkward Age), 249
narrator, editor or protagonist (in
"The Aspern Papers"), 17-23,
258, 261, 287
and John Marcher, 261
narrator (in "The Death of the
Lion"), 32-35
narrator (in The Sacred Fount), 250
Nerissa, xii
Newman, Christopher (in The
American), xxvi, 6-9, 26, 255,
290
and Bob Assingham, 225
and Sir Claude, 290
and White-Mason, 60
Newsome, Chad (in The Ambassadors), 153, 156, 157, 158, 160-
167, 169, 171, 173-175, 179, 272,
273
Newsome, Mrs. (in The Ambassadors), 175, 178, 180
and Maria Gostrey, 152, 154-155,
159
North American Review, The, 285
Norton, Grace, xiv-xvi
Novalis, 185
Nurse, xii

O

Osmond, Gilbert (in The Portrait of
a Lady), 78-82, 85-87, 89-91,
96, 170, 260, 261, 265, 288
and John Marcher, 261

P

Pansy (in *The Portrait of a Lady*), 79, 83, 84, 85-86, 92, 93, 95, 265, 288
Paraday, Neil (in "The Death of the Lion"), 29, 32-35, 40
Pater, 185, 186
Penniman, Mrs. Lavinia (in *Washington Square*), 247-249, 285
and Mrs. Costello, 247
and Countess Gemini, 248
and Susan Stringham, 248
and Mrs. Tristram, 247-248
and Mrs. Wix, 249, 284, 290
Phillips, Norma, "The Sacred Fount . . .", 294
Pocock, Mamie (in *The Ambassadors*), 173
Pocock, Sarah (in *The Ambassadors*), 168, 169, 171, 173, 180
Pococks, 272
Prest, Mrs. (in "The Aspern Papers"), xvi, 14, 17-19, 67
and Miss Tina Bordereau, 14, 19, 67
and Maria Gostrey, 180
and Madame Grandoni, 17, 18
and Miss Hurter, 35
Procter, Mrs. Anne Benson, xvi, xvii
Pylades, xii
Pym, A. Gordon, 217
Pynsent, Miss (in *The Princess Casamassima*), 16

Q

Quint, Peter (in "The Turn of the Screw"), 42, 43, 45-46

R

Rasch, Cornelia (in "Crapy Cornelia"), 28, 60-62, 259
Robinson, Hyacinth (in *The Princess Casamassima*), 14-17, 257
and Isabel Archer, 265
and Morgan Moreen, 265
and Strether, 16
and Milly Theale, 265
and Fleda Vetch, 265

Rosier, Mr. (in *The Portrait of a Lady*), 83, 84, 85

S

Saint-Simon, 185, 186
Sandeen, Ernest, 210, 293; "The Wings of the Dove . . .", 288
Sandgate, Lady (in *The Outcry*), xxx, 28, 62-63
and Fanny Assingham, 62
and Maria Gostrey, 62
and Miss Hurter, 62
Sartre, 264
Scribner's Magazine, 288
Selina (in "A London Life"), 25
Sellars, Rose (in *The Children*), xxix
Shakespeare, xii
Sisyphus, 265
Stackpole, Henrietta (in *The Portrait of a Lady*), xxi, xxiv, xxvi, 67-76, 83, 86-88, 253, 264-266
and Countess Gemini, 86
and Maria Gostrey, 67-68, 180, 254, 266, 273
and Miss Hurter, 36, 95
and Madame Merle, 67-69, 72, 74-75, 76, 77-78, 80-82, 88, 94-96
and Susan Stringham, 181, 189, 212, 288
and Mrs. Tristram, 71
and Mrs. Wix, 136, 270
Stant, Charlotte (in *The Golden Bowl*) 216, 218-219, 220, 221, 224, 225, 226-240, 242, 243, 244, 278, 280, 293
and Fanny Assingham, 240, 278
Staverton, Alice (in "The Jolly Corner"), xxii, 57-59
and Mrs. Alsager, 59
and Fanny Assingham, 280
and May Bartram, 57, 59, 261
and Maria Gostrey, 59
and lady in "The Altar of the Dead," 48
and Susan Stringham, 59
and Fleda Vetch, 59, 107, 113
Stein, William Bysshe, "The Aspern Papers . . .", 287
Stewart, Mrs. Duncan, xvi, xvii

Stransom, George (in "The Altar of the Dead") xxix, 46-51, 260
and John Marcher, 55
Strether, Lambert (in *The Ambassadors*), xvii, xxvii, xxix, 96, 107, 150-180, 253, 254, 260, 262, 271-274, 276, 291, 292
and Prince Amerigo, 218, 220, 221
and Frank Granger, 39
and John Marcher, 51
and Hyacinth Robinson, 16
and Susan Stringham, 188, 276
and Maggie Verver, 245
and Fleda Vetch, 98
Strett, Sir Luke (in *The Wings of the Dove*), 190, 201-202, 206, 207, 209, 210
Stringham, Susan (in *The Wings of the Dove*), xx, xxi, xxv, 181-213, 254, 259, 260, 262-263, 275-277, 292, 293
and Mrs. Alsager, 59
and Isabel Archer, 276
and Bob Assingham, 194
and Fanny Assingham, 187, 208, 212, 215, 221, 246, 277, 278, 281
and May Bartram, 59, 275
and Mrs. Costello, 277
and Mrs. Gereth, 106
and Maria Gostrey, 59, 180, 181, 187, 194, 201, 205, 212, 254, 271, 275
and lady in "The Altar of the Dead," 277
and Madame Merle, 181, 189
and Mrs. Penniman, 248
and Henrietta Stackpole, 181, 189, 212, 288
and Alice Staverton, 59
and Strether, 188, 276
and Fleda Vetch, 59, 98, 99, 126, 181, 211, 212, 275
and Miss Wenham, 36, 201
and Mrs. Wix, 187, 211, 277

T

Temple, Minnie, xiii, 202, 257
Theale, Milly (in *The Wings of the*

Theale, Milly—*Cont.*
Dove), xxix, 146, 182-213, 221, 253, 254, 255, 271, 275-277, 286
and Isabel Archer, 265
and Maria Gostrey, 272
and Morgan Moreen, 265
and Hyacinth Robinson, 265
and Maggie Verver, 272
and Fleda Vetch, 265
Theign, Lord (in *The Outcry*), xviii, 62, 63
Touchett, Mr. (in *The Portrait of a Lady*), 96
Touchett, Mrs. (in *The Portrait of a Lady*), 68, 70, 74, 78, 86, 90, 93, 288
Touchett, Ralph (in *The Portrait of a Lady*), 69-70, 71, 72, 78, 79, 83, 86, 96, 98, 288-289
Tourneur, xii
Townsend, Morris (in *Washington Square*), 248
Tristram, Mrs. (in *The American*), 3, 4, 6-9, 26, 248, 255, 262, 287
and Miss Tina Bordereau, 15
and Cecilia, 14
and Mrs. Costello, 10, 14
and Lady Davenant, 26
and Countess Gemini, 248
and Maria Gostrey, 6, 180
and Madame Merle, 83, 90, 96
and Mrs. Penniman, 247-248
and Henrietta Stackpole, 71
and Mrs. Wix, 6, 131, 134
Tristram, Tom (in *The American*), xxv, 7
Troilus and Criseyde, 284

V

Valentin (in *The American*), xxv, 8-9
Vanderbank (in *The Awkward Age*), 249
and Owen Gereth, 249
Verver, Adam (in *The Golden Bowl*), 224, 230, 231, 238, 239, 240, 242, 280
Verver, Maggie, the Princess (in *The Golden Bowl*), 214-217, 221, 223, 224, 227, 228-229, 233, 237-246, 253, 279, 280, 281, 293

Verver, Maggie, the Princess—*Cont.*
   and Isabel Archer, 245
   and Maria Gostrey, 272
   and Strether, 245
   and Milly Theale, 272
Ververs, 217, 218, 279
Vetch, Fleda (in *The Spoils of Poyn-ton*), xxv, xxvi, 97-126, 259, 262, 266-269, 289
   and Mrs. Alsager, 59
   and Isabel Archer, 98, 253, 265, 268
   and Fanny Assingham, 98, 263, 267, 281
   and May Bartram, 59, 113, 275
   and Maria Gostrey, 59, 107, 126, 253, 263, 267, 275
   and Miss Hurter, 35
   and lady in "The Altar of the Dead," 48
   and Madame Merle, 97-98, 126, 266
   and Morgan Moreen, 265
   and Hyacinth Robinson, 265
   and Alice Staverton, 59, 107, 113
   and Strether, 98
   and Susan Stringham, 59, 98, 99, 126, 181, 211, 212, 275
   and Milly Theale, 265
   and Laura Wing, 27
   and Mrs. Wix, 263, 267
Vionnet, Countess Marie de (in *The Ambassadors*), 158, 162, 164, 169, 171, 272, 273, 292
   and Maria Gostrey, 161, 165-168, 172, 173-175, 177-178, 180, 240, 273-274

W

Walker, Mrs. (in "Daisy Miller"), 13
Warburton, Lord (in *The Portrait of a Lady*), 71, 75, 85-86, 91, 94
Ward, Mrs. Humphrey, xvi, xx, 285
Ward, J. A., 280; *The Imagination of Disaster*, 294
Wasiolek, Edward, "Maisie: Pure or Corrupt?", 290
Waterville, Rupert (in "The Siege of London"), 286
Waymarsh (in *The Ambassadors*),

Waymarsh—*Cont.*
   xxvii, 151, 152, 153, 157, 159, 161, 167, 169, 180
Wayworth, Allan (in "Nona Vincent"), xviii, 29-32
Wells, H. G., 238, 294; *Boon . . .,* 293
Wendover (in "A London Life"), 25-26
Wenham, Miss (in "Flickerbridge"), 36-40, 288
   and Mrs. Alsager, 40
   and Miss Tina Bordereau, 37
   and Maria Gostrey, 162
   and Miss Hurter, 40
   and Susan Stringham, 36, 201
Wharton, Mrs. Edith, xvi-xviii, xxi, 222-223, 238; *A Backward Glance,* xviii, 285, 294; *The Children,* xxix; *The Writing of Fiction,* 293
White-Mason (in "Crapy Cornelia"), 60-62, 260
   and Spencer Brydon, 60
   and John Marcher, 60
   and Christopher Newman, 60
Wilkins, Mary, *Silence,* 292
Willen, Gerald (ed.), *A Casebook . . .,* 288
Wilson, Harris W., "What *Did* Maisie Know?", 290, 291
Wimbush, Mrs. (in "The Death of the Lion"), 34
Wing, Laura (in "A London Life"), 24-27, 258
   and Sir Claude, 26
   and Fleda Vetch, 27
Winterbourne (in "Daisy Miller"), 10-13, 255-257
Wister, Mrs. Sarah Butler, xvi
Wix, Mrs. (in *What Maisie Knew*), xxi, xxvi, 26, 127-149, 213, 223, 262, 269-271, 285, 290, 291
   and Fanny Assingham, 131, 134, 136, 254, 262, 263
   and Mrs. Bread, 148
   and Lady Davenant, 26
   and Maria Gostrey, 134, 180, 263, **274**
   and Mrs. Grose, 42, 254

Wix, Mrs.—*Cont.*
  and Millicent Henning, 140
  and Madame Merle, 270
  and Mrs. Penniman, 249, 284, 290
  and Henrietta Stackpole, 136, 270
  and Susan Stringham, 187, 211,
    277

Wix, Mrs.—*Cont.*
  and Mrs. Tristram, 6, 131, 134
  and Fleda Vetch, 263, 267
Woolson, Miss, xix, xxi, 287
Worthingham, Mrs. (in "Crapy Cornelia"), 60-61

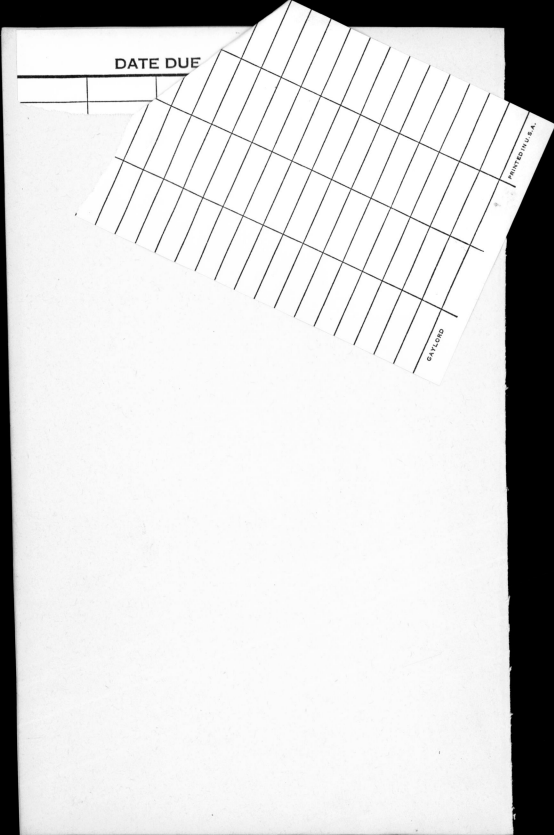

THE CONFIDANTE IN

THE CONFIDANTE IN Henry James